Your book is just what I was looking for to help me in my quest to obtain a quality education and a high GPA. . . . The "for adults only" sections let me know that you are very aware of the particular problems that older students have to deal with while trying to better their opportunities in life.

—Pam, AZ

I just purchased *College Rules!* and I just wish I would have read it earlier. Wow, if I could turn back time! I just wanted to thank you. I am determined to follow your "forty-hour rule" in order to do my best as a student. I feel like I'm totally prepared to attack college now!

—Kristina, GA

Thank you for writing *College Rules!*. . . . I read it a year before I decided to go back to school at the age of twenty. . . . It served as a key tool in my academic success. I didn't have great grades in high school . . . and now have a 3.0 GPA.

—Sarah, IA

On behalf of my students and the many others you've helped, I want to thank you for your book, *College Rules!*. . . . I'm pleased to say that in the two years I've used your book, [my students] have done increasingly well. I must have read a hundred books looking for one that could bring the strategies I wanted to teach to the students in an interesting way. You did it!

—Claudia, IN

I read the book a week before my classes started and it was amazing! I am now receiving As and will be sending a copy of this book to my little sister who is graduating high school in three months. Thank you for your wonderful work.

—Erin, IL

College Rules!

College Rules!

How to Study, Survive,
and Succeed in College

2nd Edition

SHERRIE NIST-OLEJNIK, PH.D., and
JODI PATRICK HOLSCHUH, PH.D.

TEN SPEED PRESS
Berkeley | Toronto

Ten Speed Press
PO Box 7123
Berkeley, California 94707
www.tenspeed.com

Distributed in Australia by Simon and Schuster Australia, in Canada by Ten Speed Press Canada, in New Zealand by Southern Publishers Group, in South Africa by Real Books, and in the United Kingdom and Europe by Publishers Group UK.

First edition cover and text design by Susan Van Horn
Second edition production by Michael Cutter
Cover photography by Stephen Olejnik

Library of Congress Cataloging-in-Publication Data

Nist-Olejnik, Sherrie, 1946–
College rules! : how to study, survive, and succeed in college / Sherrie Nist-Olejnik, and Jodi Patrick Holschuh. — 2nd ed.
p. cm.
Includes index.
ISBN-13: 978-1-58008-838-1 (pbk.)
ISBN-10: 1-58008-838-4 (pbk.)
1. College student orientation—United States. 2. Study skills—United States. 3. College students—United States—Conduct of life. I. Holschuh, Jodi. II. Title.
LB2343.32.N57 2007
378.1'98—dc22   2006101169

Printed in the United States of America

First printing, 2007
1 2 3 4 5 6 7 8 9 10 — 11 10 09 08 07

DEDICATION

To our husbands, Steve and Doug, and to our children, Kama, Maia, and Sam, with love.

ACKNOWLEDGMENTS

For Sherrie Nist, the second edition of *College Rules!*—written late in her tenure (actually completed right after retirement)—represents a career-spanning culmination of her many interactions with mentors, colleagues, students, and teachers. For Jodi Holschuh, this book—written midtenure (actually, right after she received tenure)—represents a means to put into practice the research on college-student learning that she had been reading about and conducting. One professor emerita, one associate professor—neither of whom would have been able to accomplish her goal of writing *College Rules!* without the help and support of many individuals.

First, our heartfelt thanks to Barbara Collins-Rosenberg, our agent, who encouraged us to revisit *College Rules!* to update it with the most current information on college learning.

Second, thanks to everyone at Ten Speed Press: Lorena Jones, who decided that *College Rules!* deserved a second edition; Meghan Keeffe, whose energy and effort helped keep this book appealing and cool while adding some heady stuff to it; Jane Merryman, Elisabeth Beller, and Ken DellaPenta, who in various and wonderful ways, helped spruce up *College Rules!* for its readers.

Third, there's not a "thank you" big enough for our mentors, colleagues, and teachers, both past and current, who taught us to be teachers, researchers, writers, and questioners. These individuals, although too numerous to mention, also gave us the self-confidence and skills to be successful in the sometimes treacherous world of academe.

Fourth, a special thanks to Dr. Deborah Martin, Dr. Ian Lukas, and Dr. David Zehr for allowing us to share parts of their syllabi with our readers (and their potential future students) and to Dr. Janet Frick for sharing some sad-but-true stories.

Fifth, this book could not have existed without our students. We have learned as much from them—even more, perhaps—than they have ever learned from us. For both of us, teaching and other interactions with students continue to breathe new life into our research and other writing. It adds meaning to what we do and on many a day simply makes us smile.

Sixth, thanks go to our parents, Charlene and Roy Miller and Mary and Stanley Patrick, who instilled in us the love and pleasure of learning. Their curiosity and love of learning helped us recognize these characteristics in ourselves. For that, we are eternally grateful.

But most of all, we thank our spouses and children: Steve and Kama; Doug, Maia, and Sam. Our husbands, Steve Olejnik and Doug Holschuh, encouraged us to write this book and believed in our idea that if students knew how to learn in college right from the start, they would ultimately have an easier and more enjoyable college experience. They were also very understanding when dinner was late (or was take-out sushi or pizza) as we were wrapping up the final chapters. Our children, Kama, Maia, and Sam, had very different roles. Kama drew on her own college experiences to offer advice and guidance. Maia and Sam helped us remember the beginnings of learning—from learning to walk to beginning to read. They make the learning process seem transparent and fun—which is what we hope for you in college.

CONTENTS

Contents

INTRODUCTION

We introduce you to *College Rules!* by telling you some of our deep, dark, secrets—the confessions of two professors who (in all honesty) didn't have the most stellar beginnings as college students. For the first year-and-a-half of college, each of us held our breath when grades came out at the end of the term; we were clueless about what it took to be successful students. We both felt guilty about our lack of attention to schoolwork—we did sort of want to learn something—but not guilty enough to make any real changes. But did we have fun! If we could have earned grades in social life, both of us would have made A+s.

Sherrie began to turn things around when she received an ultimatum from her dad. She remembers his words clearly: "I'm not paying for Cs—or worse—anymore. You made good grades in high school; you either do better in college or you come home." Talk about a dose of reality. It had never occurred to Sherrie, who had always done well in school, that she might not make it in college unless she made some real changes. It had never occurred to her that she had to discipline herself and rethink the way she approached learning. The possibility of having to return home without a degree in hand was a big wake-up call.

Jodi remembers walking into her first large-lecture college class, Introduction to Sociology. She filed into the auditorium with three hundred other students. The professor started class by stating that he did not care whether students came to class or not—he'd teach the same material either way. "Great," thought Jodi. "I'll get to sleep in on Tuesdays and Thursdays." She kept the mindset that class was optional until she noticed that her friends who were doing well in college were doing things differently. They were going to class every day and they were studying most evenings, and as a result of their efforts, they were much less stressed out about the workload. Once Jodi decided to adopt this strategy, things (and grades) improved greatly. Jodi wished she had realized what to do before she entered college.

Now you might say, so what? It ended up great for you guys. You must have done all right. After all, you got into graduate school, earned Ph.D.'s, and have great careers. Life is sweet. But although we ended up in academe, we seriously wish we had been better students right from the start. Honestly. In fact, we believe that we chose to study the ways students make the transition from high school to college learning because we did not do such good jobs ourselves. Which brings us to why we wrote *College Rules!*.... If we had known then what we know now, well, let's just say we wouldn't have had so much catching up to do. We want you to learn from our mistakes and our successes.

We know you're smart. You know you're smart. You wouldn't have been accepted to college if you weren't. So why do you need *College Rules!*? Because this book draws on our years of experience as both students and professors to bring you the very best advice on how to have a successful college career.

Your high school probably did a fairly decent job of teaching you information; you'll go off to college armed with lots of facts. What might give you a bit of a challenge, however, is how to turn these facts into knowledge. In other words, do you know how to think critically and learn actively? Do you know how to manage your time? Are you self-disciplined? Can you synthesize, analyze, critique? Do you know how to take good notes in a lecture or discussion class? Can you learn lots of new information quickly? Do you know the best ways to prepare for and take college-level exams? Yikes. Lots of questions to answer. But if you don't think about them before you start college, you might just spend the first year (or at least the first semester) trying to figure out what college is all about and how to maintain the grades you made in high school.

Take Maggie for example. We remember Maggie because she reminded us so much of ourselves. She was a good student in high school, but we could tell she didn't think that how she studied and learned would have to change in college. She pledged a sorority her first semester and had an active social life. And although she enrolled in some tough courses, Maggie stuck to what worked in high school, which translated into studying (or what she called studying—flipping through the pages in her textbook and notes to memorize key terms) about four hours a week. To make a long story short, by the end of her freshman year, Maggie had dug herself into an academic hole that was difficult for her to climb out of. She realized that getting into college is the easy part; staying in is more difficult.

So how can you avoid these mistakes and start out on the right track? Enter *College Rules!*. Although we have written several "how to learn" textbooks that are used in college courses nationwide, we firmly believe that the message of active learning needs to be in your hands before you begin college. We also believe that it's important to demystify learning by letting you in on the secrets of postsecondary academic expectations. And we believe in the importance of emphasizing academics as a way for you to have a satisfying and well-rounded college experience. By this we mean that, all else aside, your college experience will suffer if you are in trouble academically, plain and simple. Poor grades simply make you spiral downward both socially and psychologically.

College Rules! focuses on how you can do well academically, thereby opening the door for you to enrich your life in other ways. We expect (and want) you to have a full social life, and we encourage you to become involved in campus groups and organizations. We want you to understand the importance of knowledge and how you must be the one responsible for gaining it. We want you to seek purpose in your knowledge quest and to have the self-discipline to make learning happen. Perhaps most important, we want you to be able to make good choices. We want you to do it all and make good grades. We expect lots from you but probably no more than you expect from yourself.

We realize that there are lots of "college success" books out there, so what makes *College Rules!* different? Unlike some, this book does not tell you how to keep your underwear from turning pink (don't wash it with a red T-shirt). It does not tell you how to buy football tickets (get your order in early) or how to get a fake ID (just don't even go there). It does not tell you how to get along with weird roommates nor does it suggest how to get around the system. What it does provide are "rules" on studying and learning that will help you be both efficient and effective in achieving academic success in college. We attempt to paint a realistic picture of what you should expect academically and what your college will expect from you. Attending college can be a life-changing experience. It can also be a great adventure. We hope that *College Rules!* will introduce you to lots of ideas that will help you make the most of the experience.

What's New in Edition Two?

In this second edition, we have given the entire book an updating and an overhaul to bring you the newest information on college learning. We have added three new chapters: Chapter 11, "Can You Believe That?," discusses how beliefs about knowledge impact college success; Chapter 20, "Everything You Wanted to Know about Research and Presentations but Were Afraid to Ask," discusses writing and presenting academic work; and Chapter 24, "Just the FAQs: Frequently Asked Questions," answers burning student questions that weren't completely answered in other *College Rules!* chapters. These new chapters round out the already excellent advice from the first edition and make the second edition a more comprehensive look at college success.

In addition, we decided to make computers and technology integral to all chapters rather than having this information in a separate chapter as was the case in the first edition. The impact of technology on all aspects of college life is one of the many changes that struck us while writing the second edition. We have included our favorite websites and software where appropriate and added advice on how to make the most of technology in your own learning.

We have also introduced some new features and sidebars to help you achieve college success:

- **If So, Read On**—Each chapter begins with questions that ask you to reflect on yourself as a learner. These questions pave the way for what you will read in the chapter.

- **Get It Together**—This sidebar is aimed at students who are struggling academically but perhaps deep down want to be good students (but it has good motivational advice for all students).

- **If You Read Nothing Else, Read This**—Each chapter ends with a list highlighting the important points from the chapter. Although, we want you to read the entire text, these lists give you the key ideas that will help you focus on the most important ideas in the chapter.

Continuing Features from Edition One

Even though *College Rules!* is new and improved, we have maintained the excellent features from the first edition. If you thumb through the chapters (a good strategy to use with any book—see chapter 16), you will notice there are lots of sidebars offering first-rate advice. Here's what you'll see:

- **Sad but True**—These student stories focus on some of the troubles that are common to students regardless of what type of college they attend. Although you might find some of these stories difficult to believe, we have actually encountered all these students over our careers. (The names have been changed to protect the innocent.) Hopefully, you can learn from their mistakes so you don't fall into these traps.

- **The Inside Scoop**—These sidebars provide advice for being successful based on actual research that has been conducted on learning and studying.

- **Listen Up**—These sidebars give you tried-and-true study tips to help make your learning more efficient and effective.

- **Do Your Homework**—These sidebars give advice on things you should do routinely outside of class.

- **For Adults Only**—These sidebars give advice to nontraditional students—those who are heading back to college after several years in the workforce. But, there's good advice here for students entering straight from high school as well.

- **Get Wired**—These sidebars give tips for maximizing learning through the use of computers and other technology. Because technology has become so pervasive in college, it seemed to make more sense to incorporate these tips throughout *College Rules!* 2nd Edition rather than keep them in a separate chapter as we did in the first edition. We also refer you to specific websites or software programs that we have found to be good resources.

- **Urban Legend**—These sidebars focus on a variety of untrue stories that have been circulating around college campuses for years. They are sort of like computer hoaxes. They sound probable, but really aren't true.

How to Use College Rules!

Although the primary audience for *College Rules!* is students heading off to campus, we certainly wouldn't discourage sophomores, juniors, or seniors from reading it (we even know some graduate students who would benefit). We believe there is valuable information here for students at any point in their college career. However, our major goal is helping college freshmen make the often treacherous transition from learning in high school to learning in college.

To this end, approach reading *College Rules!* in any way that suits your needs. You can read it the traditional way—start at chapter 1 and read through to chapter 24 in consecutive order. If you're a high school student who will be starting college, this ordered approach might be the best. Read a chapter or two every day and then, once you get to college, go back and reread chapters that piqued your interest or that did not quite sink in.

You can also use *College Rules!* as an at-your-fingertips reference for college success. If you're a bit hesitant as you're packing up your stuff to head off to campus, read chapter 6 and chapter 9. If you're getting ready to take your first college exams (and you haven't even opened this book yet), read chapters 21, 22, and 23. If you can't manage your time worth a hoot, read chapter 7. In other words, read (or reread) the chapters you think will benefit you at any particular time.

With the second approach, we offer a few words of caution, however. We know for a fact that learning in college is a complex process. Being successful is not about doing this or that. Being successful is usually about doing this *and* that (and then doing some more). There's no one particular suggestion in *College Rules!* that's guaranteed to make you a better student. There are no "magic beans" for college success. Rather, we have provided you with a comprehensive guide to help you hit the campus running at least ten paces ahead of your fellow students. So though you can read *College Rules!* on an as-needed basis, if you want to get the most out of the book, you should read all of it—not necessarily in the order in which the chapters are presented, but do give it a good, comprehensive read.

We wish you the very best of luck as you begin your college journey and hope that, as so many students who had success with the first edition did, you email us and let us know what you think. We are so excited for you! Enjoy yourself (and get your work done too!).

CHAPTER 1

YOU'RE IN THE BIG TIME NOW

- Worried about some of the adjustments you will need to make as you head off to college?
- Think that college is simply grade 13?
- Concerned that you can't have a social life and a respectable GPA at the same time?

If so, read on . . .

Collège—you've dreamed about what it would be like for years now. Perhaps you envisioned four (or five) years of partying, whirlwind social events, and fun. Or maybe you thought just the opposite—that college would be nothing but hard work—classes, exams, papers, never having your nose out of a book. Yikes.

But most of you probably don't think in such extremes. Instead, you anticipate making new friends, learning lots of new things, and of course experiencing some good old-fashioned college fun.

Success in college requires a considerable amount of hard work, determination, motivation, and just plain luck. It also requires you to make some changes, because one thing we know for certain: college is different from high school, plain and simple. You may have the idea that college is high school with a little more freedom. In some ways that's true, but in the classroom, college is very different from high school. Sure, you have more freedom, but you also have more responsibility, harder courses, more reading, and longer hours of studying. Academic responsibilities can often conflict with the P-A-R-T-Y part of the college experience. Although we think both are important to a well-rounded college experience, you can get in trouble if you begin college unaware of the academic adjustments you'll have to make.

Your college years can end up being the best of your life if you begin with the understanding that some things will change—in fact, change dramatically—and if you become a savvy student and an efficient, effective learner.

THE INSIDE SCOOP

Research suggests that students often enter college lacking the study strategies they need to be successful. Not much of a surprise. What is a bit surprising, however, is the reason why. It seems that in high school many students aren't challenged to any great degree. Tests in high school may not be very demanding, so students really don't have to use studying techniques that require them to think at higher levels. And (SHOCK), they can even get by without reading their textbooks. This could explain why students have a difficult time adjusting to the academic demands of college.

Doing College

In high school you may not have had to work very hard to make decent grades. You listened to what the teachers said, dutifully wrote down the information they put on the board, and answered all the questions they gave you on a study guide. Because that same information was on the exam, you may never have had to take your textbooks home at all and you still aced the test. Your teacher was probably deeply committed to making sure that everyone learned in her classroom. If you were having trouble, she probably

The university is not engaged in making ideas safe for students. It is engaged in making students safe for ideas.

—Clark Kerr

8

took time to help you (or to find you help). And if you showed real aptitude in her subject, she was very encouraging as well.

When you get to college, though, it's as if the rules you've spent twelve years mastering have changed. Gone are flipping through study guides and memorizing facts as accepted ways of learning.

If you can't use the standbys, just what do you need to do to be successful once you are in college? According to the thousands of students we've interacted with, you need at least some of the following—not everything, mind you—just some.

- **Self-discipline.** You have probably thought about this already. In college you need to find ways to make yourself do the things you need to do every day. But sometimes finding the discipline you need is tough—especially when assignments pile up and you would rather be outside shooting hoops than reading yet another chapter of history. (In fact, you would rather walk on hot coals than read another word of history.) Self-discipline is a skill that you must develop even if you don't have it to begin with. Hmm. Looks as though you have to develop self-discipline even if you currently don't have any. But you can do it. We know you can. Think of developing self-discipline as a challenge rather than torture. Sometimes just having a goal to get work done is the best first step. It won't happen overnight, but with a little effort you will establish the self-discipline you need.

- **Motivation.** Just as you must nurture self-discipline, you must find motivation for learning, which often means finding something positive in a course you really don't like. Contrary to what you might think, there's something about every discipline that can be interesting and motivating if you look for it. In some instances, you might even have to look hard! As you will learn later, you are always motivated to do something, even if it's just sleeping. The trick is to motivate yourself to do the tasks involved in college. Then you can do anything you want.

- **A game plan.** Everyone needs a plan of action, and this is especially true for college students, who often have lots of commitments to keep track of (like assignments, meetings, social obligations, and so on). To create a game plan, you must figure out exactly what you need to do, then set aside time to get it all done.

● **Patience.** One way in which college prepares you for the world of work is by insisting that every student graduates having gone through his share of frustrating and oftentimes incomprehensible experiences commonly referred to as "red tape"—filling out forms; getting your ID; meeting with your advisor to register for classes; setting up your campus email account; waiting in endless lines to buy books, parking passes, or concert tickets. When it happens to you, take deep breaths, say something to yourself to make yourself laugh, or count to ten. Your grandmother is right. Patience is a virtue, one best learned when you are young.

🦻 LISTEN UP

If you do not have a system for managing your time, the first thing you should do is run to your campus bookstore or nearest office-supply store to buy a daily planner to keep track of assignments, readings, exams, and all the other things you need to do each day. If you're short on cash, a plain old desk calendar with large blocks for writing will do just fine.

● **A bunch of effective learning strategies.** Many students begin college using strategies that have worked for them in the past, such as rereading a text or relying only on information supplied by the teacher. To succeed in college you'll need to change your strategies to meet the new challenges. You'll need to create a learning cycle, which means knowing lots of different ways to approach learning.

If you have already started college, think about the changes you have made. Were there any that you weren't expecting? If you are getting ready to enter college, think about the changes you are anticipating. How will you cope with these new situations?

🖐 GET IT TOGETHER

Starting out strong is really the best advice we can give you. The way you use your time during the first few weeks of classes is often indicative of the way you will manage yourself and your time throughout your first year. So start with a plan to get your assignments done, do your reading right from the first day of classes, and keep up with assignments, and you will find yourself in good shape! If you are already behind, give yourself one week to catch up.

But What If I Wasn't the World's Greatest High School Student?

Let's face it, not everyone leaves high school with a great GPA (or great college entrance exam scores). You may be worried that if you were a slacker in high school, you will never make it through college. Although this is a legitimate concern, don't let this fear keep you from pursuing your goal of getting that college degree. If your high school record isn't stellar, you may not be able to get into Harvard, but like most students, you probably can get in somewhere, and maybe even transfer to Harvard.

We've found that many students blossom academically once they get to college. They may feel challenged for the first time or they may suddenly become motivated to reach their goals. Almost overnight, some students decide to take responsibility for their own actions and want to prove they can succeed academically. Whatever the case, we have seen this happen over and over again. We call it the clean slate phenomenon. Students who start out believing that their weak academic slate has been wiped clean tend to do better than those who are carrying around the baggage of their high school record.

Another thing you should realize about the grades in college is that just because students made outstanding grades in high school, it doesn't necessarily mean those same high grades will follow them in college. It's much harder to earn top grades in college, and so a good many of those high achievers in high school have to get used to getting a B (or even, gasp, a C) here and there in college. So while you may think of it as having nowhere to go but up, other students are stressed out from the start worrying about trying to make all As.

To give yourself a clean slate, you need to believe that you are capable of college work. Picture yourself acing that first exam or in a cap and gown marching up to get your diploma—whatever works for you. You'll also need to make some changes in how you set your priorities, manage your time, and study for classes. This book shows you how. Of course, you already know that if you messed up in high school, you will have to work hard to make it through college—but it probably helps to realize that so will everyone else.

Six Ways College Differs from High School

You may already have considered how college is different from high school. Perhaps you've talked to relatives or friends about their experiences. Chances are you've seen lots of college scenes in movies and on television (trust us—college really isn't like *Animal House*), so you have a mental picture of what college is like and how it differs from your previous school experiences. To get you thinking a little more about this, here are six ways in which you can expect college to be different from high school. (You'll probably think of more from your own personal experience, but these six generally apply to just about every college student.)

⊗ FOR ADULTS ONLY

If you are returning to college after some years away from schooling, you may find that you are experiencing just the opposite of what many freshman go through: it may have been quite a while since anyone told you what to do and how to do it. You may find the deadlines and bureaucracy of college frustrating, especially if you are juggling a full-time job and family responsibilities as well. We suggest you meet with your professors or your advisor to speak about these concerns.

1. GREATER RESPONSIBILITY

In high school, most of your time is usually planned by others. Someone is always bossing you around—telling you when to go to class, when to do homework, and maybe even when you can go out with friends. In college, you not only set your own class schedule, but you also manage your own free time. You can no longer count on your teacher or your parents to remind you when something is due or when you have to be somewhere. Even if you have so-called helicopter parents (does this sound like your parents—always "hovering" over you, doing everything for you?), they won't call you to wake you up in the morning to be sure you get to class on time. You set your own priorities and manage all your new responsibilities. It may also be the first time you have lived away from home; this means you have the additional responsibility of fending for yourself—eating properly, doing laundry, managing money, getting medical attention, and studying when you should. Even though mom and dad are only an email or cell phone call away, more responsibility will definitely fall on your shoulders.

2. DIFFERENT CLASS STRUCTURE AND INSTRUCTION

Unlike high school classes, college classes generally don't meet every day. Usually, college classes meet on either a Monday-Wednesday-Friday or Tuesday-Thursday schedule, and you don't necessarily go from one class directly to the next. You will also spend less time in class each week—usually just twelve to fifteen hours, depending on how many courses you're taking. This is quite a change from the thirty-plus hours you spent in high school classes.

You will also find that class sizes are much different in college. You may be in a class with as few as five students (although this is extremely rare, it does happen occasionally) or you may find yourself in a classroom with more than three hundred fellow students. If you are in one of the large lecture sections, you will find that the professor probably will not even attempt to learn students' names.

You may find that the way you are taught differs. Your professors will often make assignments (such as reading the text or completing practice problems) and then not check them. They assume you are responsible and you are eager to do the work. On top of that, they assume that, if you don't ask any questions, you must understand the information. Unlike your high school teachers, your college professors usually don't approach you if you are experiencing trouble in the course. Instead, they expect you to seek them out if you need any extra assistance (which, in most cases, they are happy to supply during their office hours). Nor will your professor approach you if you miss a class. In high school, your teachers probably gave you the information you missed (handouts, notes, assignments), but in college you will need to get notes from a classmate and ask the professor for any other assignments or important information you may have missed.

DO YOUR HOMEWORK

Actually, that's our advice: do your homework. If your precalculus professor tells you it would be a good idea to do certain problems and you know for a fact that she will never in a million years collect them, do the problems anyway. It will help you in the long run as you prepare to take the exam.

We must add another word about assignments. More than likely, professors won't remind you about impending due dates. Instead, they expect you to consult your syllabus regularly and turn in assignments on the proper dates.

3. FASTER PACE

You will soon notice that instruction moves at a much faster pace in college. The amount of material you may have covered in a year in high school may take up only one semester's worth of college work. Not only that, professors lecture nonstop during class time, especially in the introductory courses that first-year students have to take. Your professors have high expectations of you; they expect you to be able to keep up with what they are saying and to take good, comprehensive notes. Whew. Also, any professors worth their salt don't lecture straight from the text. Instead, they expect you to be able to relate text information to the lecture topics without discussing it in class. Of course, this activity is always done on your own time. Finally, it's also reasonable to expect to cover three or more text chapters in one week. At first you may feel like one of those little hamsters in a wheel, running faster and faster and not getting anywhere, but most students eventually adjust to the pace.

4. NEW (AND IMPROVED) KINDS OF STUDYING

Many students begin college thinking they just need to study more. This is not particularly surprising, since according to a recent study, the average high school student studies less than two hours a week. Are you surprised? Although it's correct to assume that you will need to study longer, it's also important to understand that you need to study differently. You need to be able to connect new information with what you already know and with other content. You are also responsible for learning large amounts of information with very little guidance. We will talk about this issue in greater depth throughout *College Rules!*. For now, know that you will have to spend some time each day studying for your classes and that the way you approach studying will change.

5. FEWER EXAMS

In college there are fewer exams—often only two or three per semester, per course. Although this initially sounds like a good thing, it actually makes your life tougher. Because there are so few exams, each one covers a great deal of information. Do the math. If you have only three tests in a fifteen-week semester, each test covers five weeks' worth of reading and lecture notes. In a heavy reading course such as psychology or political science that can translate into reading hundreds of pages and remembering even more information presented in lectures. In addition, many college exams are cumulative, which means that the test covers all the information taught in the class during that term. If you make a poor grade on an exam in high school, it's not a particularly big deal because you have a lot of other opportunities for grades and your teacher is likely to drop (or just not count) a bad grade if the rest of your grades are good. In college, however, grading works a bit differently.

This urban legend has been going around college campuses for several years. Although we don't know if this ever really happened, it does say a lot about how students can feel unknown in their classes.

 URBAN LEGEND

Professor Jones looks out over his three hundred students taking their biology final exam. His eye catches a student in the upper-left-hand side of the classroom who is sneakily looking at the floor beneath his desk, then quickly bubbling in an answer on his test. "Gee," thinks Professor Jones, "this student must have some kind of cheat sheet."

When the student brings his test up to the front to leave it in the pile accumulating on the lectern, Professor Jones shakes his head. "You can't turn that in," he says. "You were cheating. I saw you."

The student looks the professor directly in the eye and demands, "Do you know who I am? Do you even know my name?"

Professor Jones replies, "Of course not. There are over three hundred students in this class."

The student smiles, shoves his test into the middle of the pile, and runs out of the room.

6. FEWER GRADES

In high school it might have seemed as though you were being graded on every move you made. But in college you are often assigned work that is not graded. Usually, only the scores on exams, papers, computer assignments, projects—the big things—make up what counts in your overall course grade. There are also far fewer opportunities (make that almost no opportunities) to receive extra credit in college, so you need to do well on the few graded assignments you have.

In addition, in high school you may have been rewarded for "effort"; in other words, as long as the teacher thought you were trying hard to learn, at a bare-bones minimum you would pass. In college, however, not only is your professor largely unaware of the effort you make, but she also actually expects you to be working hard and working smart. Therefore, when computing your final course grade, most professors rely solely on your exam scores, papers, and other major projects.

Don't Mess Up

Starting off on the right foot is important for your future success in college. You really can't "blow off" a semester before you get serious about your academics, no matter what anyone tells you. Students who take too long "adjusting" to the demands of college learning and studying can find themselves in a deep academic pit that's very difficult to get out of. That's why it's important to start out strong. As with other challenges in life, you can always lighten up, but it's much more difficult to tighten up.

Getting off on the right foot isn't too difficult if you understand some fundamentals. Think of it as basic training for newbies. If you can get through the first few weeks by following the advice of our former students, you should be on your way to smooth sailing.

It is well to remember that the entire population of the universe, with one trifling exception, is composed of others.

—John Andrew Holmes

🔊 LISTEN UP

If you have a diagnosed learning disability (or think you may have a learning disability), getting the help you need also works differently in college. Chances are you won't have special tutors or teachers and your instructors probably won't call you at home. You are responsible for your own success. You are also responsible for working out the accommodations you're entitled to with your professors. However, be sure to check with the disabilities services office on your campus to find out what you need to do. Sometimes there are deadlines for accommodations such as requesting extended testing time, and colleges will provide the accommodation only if it is requested before the deadline. Colleges are ready to give you the support you need, but you must seek it out and ask for help.

KEEP UP

We often ask our students at the end of a term to give advice to the next class concerning what it takes to be successful at our university. The number one answer each and every time is . . . keep up with your work. Most college students find themselves behind in their work at one time or another. This isn't much of an issue when it happens occasionally, but you can get into big trouble if it becomes a way of life. You can avoid the stress that goes with getting behind by establishing a reading and studying schedule and following it each day.

GO TO CLASS

Our students also say that it's important to attend class every day. You may have heard the rumor that professors don't care whether you are in class. Or you think that because they post their lecture notes on the Web, they are giving you the message that class attendance isn't important. However, in our experience this is simply not true. In fact, some professors—even those with more than two hundred students in their class—take attendance every day because they feel so strongly about the importance of students' being in class. Even professors who don't take attendance want you to be there. So get off your duff and go to class. Get all the information that you (or your parents) are paying for.

TAKE A BALANCED COURSE LOAD

Taking a balanced course load means taking a range of courses that are a combination of subjects you are interested in and subjects that don't require too much of the same type of task. In other words, don't take four (or worse yet, five) courses that all require tons of reading (such as history, biology, sociology, psychology, literature) or writing (such as English, political science, comparative literature) or problem sets (such as mathematics, statistics, chemistry) all in one semester. Mix it up a bit—take a heavy reading course, a course that requires writing, another where you are problem solving, and a course that interests you that you can use as an elective.

BE AWARE OF YOUR STATUS

Another good piece of advice that we hear from students is the importance of monitoring your status in every course. Know where you stand and be honest with yourself. If you have made a C– on your last two chemistry tests, don't delude yourself into

> The dictionary is the only place in which success comes before work.
>
> —Author unknown

thinking that you can get an A in the course when you have only one test left. It's not going to happen! If you have already missed three English classes and your grade is docked points if you miss any more, be sure to roust yourself out of bed and get to class. Many of your classmates will be in denial about where they stand. Don't let it happen to you.

Use this advice from our former students to help get yourself started on the right foot. Remember, once you enter college you are, for the most part, in control of the experience you will have.

☹ SAD BUT TRUE

Many students hear stories of what college is like from friends and family, but some of these tales contain misinformation that can actually hurt your college performance. For example, Andrew, one of our students, recently missed class because he was running late and heard from his brother that you shouldn't bother to even go to class if you will be more than ten minutes late. He told Andrew that professors don't let anyone in when they are so late. Although this may be true for some classes, it was not for ours, and Andrew missed some very important information (and was not able to turn in an assignment due that day, so he also lost some points). The moral of this story is to find out your professors' rules for attendance and follow them—don't take for granted that the rules are the same in all cases, and don't rely on another student's "expertise." Go to the source of the information you want.

If You Read Nothing Else, Read This

○ Prepare to make some changes in how you think about school, learning, and studying. Doing college right means thinking about (and maybe improving) your motivation, self-discipline, and strategies for learning.

○ College requires greater personal responsibility. You, rather than your parents, must keep track of all the many things you need to do as a college student.

○ To stay strong, start out strong. Keep up with your assignments and (please) go to class every day.

CHAPTER 2

WHERE TO FIND THE HELP YOU NEED

- Worried about finding good, cheap (FREE) help for your classes if you don't know a Bunsen burner from a flask?
- Concerned that you won't know when or if you actually need assistance?
- Think you'll come down with the flu or the plague and have no one to turn to?

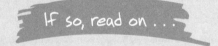

If so, read on . . .

An article by humorist Dave Barry reminded us of the importance of devoting a chapter in *College Rules!* to seeking help. Mr. Barry's teenage son was going to Europe for a few weeks of backpacking. Being an experienced father (and also having been a teenager himself eons ago), Mr. Barry "reminded" his son several times about being careful with his passport. The last thing he said to his son before he boarded the plane was, "Don't lose your passport." His son rolled his eyes, confident that everything would be fine. Unfortunately, his passport and all his traveler's checks were stolen before he even got off the plane. So he ended up in a foreign country where he couldn't speak the language and he didn't have the foggiest idea

19

what to do. He hadn't thought ahead because he was certain that nothing like that would happen to him.

As a college student, no matter how independent you are, you're going to need help at some point in time. You might need help finding out about financial aid, lining up a tutor for an impossibly difficult chemistry course, seeing a doctor when you are too sick to die, locating the counseling center when your life is falling apart, or connecting with the registrar when you're sure a terrible mistake has been made on your transcript. Our advice: be proactive. Know whom to contact in a variety of situations before you actually need the service, and know how to get what you need in the least stressful way.

Why is it important to be proactive? Because college students are busy, involved people. And when busy, involved people have anything more, different, or out of the ordinary added to an already hectic schedule, they tend not to handle it very well. Let's take a simple example, one that is guaranteed to happen to you sometime in your college career: illness—more specifically, the dreaded flu. On our campus it usually hits about six or eight weeks into the semester (it seems not to matter whether it's fall or spring semester). You wake up one morning. You can't breathe. Your throat feels like a piece of raw meat. You're coughing so hard that your ribs ache. And, oh my gosh, you have tests to prepare for, you're behind in your reading, you're supposed to put in three hours of service learning, you have a fraternity/sorority/team meeting, you have library books due today. . . . The list goes on.

DO YOUR HOMEWORK

Early in the term, think about all the services you might need to know about. Write down phone numbers or email addresses. Tack the information up on your bulletin board or store it in your email address book. Find out where offices are located on campus. Ask questions. Don't wait until you need something to start tracking it down. That approach can only lead to unnecessary frustration.

How would you handle this? Do you know the procedure for getting medical attention on your campus? Can you get an excused absence for today's classes? How will you get the notes you missed? Whom can you contact about not participating in the service learning? What happens if your library books aren't returned today? If you have to try to find out all the answers to these questions while you are as sick as you've ever been in your life, we guarantee that you will not be a happy camper. But you can prevent yourself from getting into this situation.

20

I Need Help!

The first step in getting the assistance you need is admitting that you need it. We can pretty much assure you that unless your residence hall is on fire, no one is going to come knocking on your door asking if you need help with something. But for some reason, a large portion of college students would rather ignore the fact that a problem exists than get some relief from what's bogging them down. Depending on what your problem is, you may be able to do one-stop shopping or you may have to go to several offices to get it taken care of. A glance at some of the offices available on most campuses will give you an idea of the services they traditionally offer. The extent of services varies greatly, as does the quality, but nearly all campuses offer them. Once you begin college, you may want to write down the phone numbers of each office and keep them in a handy place, bookmark their websites, or have their email addresses in your address book just in case you need them.

GET WIRED

Most college websites have links to a variety of student services on campus. Look for links to services such as the counseling center, health center, tutoring, learning center, financial aid office, library—any office that might be able to help you.

Counseling center. Does your life feel out of control? Did your girlfriend or boyfriend just dump you? Do you think you have a drug or alcohol problem? Are you having trouble adjusting to living away from home? Are you depressed or just unhappy? On a scale of 1 to 10, is your motivation level a 0? These are but a handful of the problems that students bring to college counseling centers every day. Friends are good for the little things, but it's better to get professional help if you know your academics are suffering because of emotional havoc. The counseling may be provided in a freestanding center, as part of the health center or learning center, or through a student-success program.

Health center. The campus health center may be minimal—a couple of rooms staffed by a

> No student knows his subject: the most he knows is where and how to find out the things he does not know.
>
> —Woodrow Wilson

21

nurse and a part-time doctor—or as large as a small hospital, capable of treating ailments way beyond colds and flu. On our campus, for example, the health center is staffed by many full-time doctors, nurses, and other support staff; it even includes a dentist and a travel clinic. As soon as you reach campus, find out how to navigate the rules and regulations of the health center. For example: What are the hours? Do you need to make an appointment or can you just walk in? How much do you pay per visit? More than likely you'll have to pay a health fee when you enroll, so you should know what services are covered by your fee.

THE INSIDE SCOOP

It has been shown time and time again that students who seek out help when they first begin to struggle academically make a comeback and do well. Those who don't seek the assistance they need tend to spiral downward, earning poor grades and low GPAs. So remember, it's good to ask for help early in the game.

Tutorial center or learning center. Like other services, those that help students academically may be limited or expansive. Most campuses offer some form of peer tutoring and assistance through a learning center. Many also offer brief academic workshops focusing on topics such as time management or study skills. Sometimes you can get one-on-one tutoring or drop-in tutoring for difficult courses. The college or university generally funds these services, so they are usually free. When you are struggling academically and trying to locate help, the trick is figuring out what these programs are called. Look for titles such as "Student Success," "Academic Assistance," "Learning Center," or "Tutoring Program."

Registrar. Need a transcript? Have a beef about your records? It's important to know what kinds of records are kept in the registrar's office on your campus and then how to get access to them. On our campus, for example, when students are first admitted their records are handled by the Admissions Office. Once the students have taken their placement tests during orientation, the records are transferred to the Office of the Registrar.

Financial aid office. If you want information on the types of financial assistance that are available to you or whether you might qualify for such aid, visit one of the financial aid officers. Most students don't know that a considerable amount of scholarship money goes unused every year, mainly because the students don't

have any idea that it's available. If
you already receive financial aid,
you'll need to stay in close contact
with this office so you know in a
timely fashion that your aid money
has arrived, whom to talk with if
there are problems, and when you
have to reapply for aid.

Police and fire departments. These
require little explanation. Although we hope you never need the assistance of
either department, keep their phone numbers handy. If you live in an apartment,
store both numbers either on speed dial or close to your bedroom phone, particularly if there is no 911 access.

Email addresses and phone numbers of your professors. Although you see your professors each class day, it's still important to know how to contact them should
the need arise. Most professors provide methods of contact on the syllabus, as
well as the situations in which they want you to contact them. For example,
some profs want you to email them if you are going to miss class; others don't
care. Almost every professor wants to be contacted if you are unable to show up
for a test. Know your professors' rules and contact preferences.

Your advisor. On most campuses you must have a face-to-face conversation with your
advisor once a term so she can clear you for registration. If this is the case on
your campus, you should have ready access to your advisor's phone number or
email address so you can make an appointment (they tend to have tight schedules around registration time). Try to find out if your campus has online advising, which allows you to talk with your advisor via email. Many large campuses
are moving to this method; although it is somewhat impersonal, it is also very
convenient for students. Find out what method is used on your campus and add
the contact information to your list.

Library. At the very least, you should have the main webpage of your campus library
bookmarked on your computer. From this page, you can find out all the information you need about library hours, access to online systems, and how to search

databases. Another piece of good advice concerning the library: don't wait until two days before your first paper is due to find out how to use library resources. If you have checked out the library early, you'll be able to get right down to work, making the most of those resources.

😣 SAD BUT TRUE

Elizabeth had always been an outstanding student in high school. She was from a small town and a small high school so she knew her teachers well. She worked hard and was rewarded with high grades. In fact, Elizabeth was the valedictorian of her high school, graduating with a perfect 4.0 grade-point average. She decided to attend a very large public university that had a top-notch reputation in the area of business. Her first semester she took fifteen hours, an average load for a freshman, but she had an extremely difficult time in not only keeping up but also understanding all the information that seemed to be thrown at her from all directions. There were lots of different offices on campus where Elizabeth could have gotten help (she learned about many of them at Freshman Orientation), but she was too embarrassed to ask. On top of not doing well on her first exams, she started feeling bad about herself, thinking that maybe she didn't belong in college. About three-fourths of the way through the first semester, she swallowed her pride and started seeking a tutor, and her grades improved although she barely eked out Cs that first semester. She did, however, learn a valuable lesson. During her second semester, she regrouped and did better by seeking out help early on.

This list of services is not necessarily comprehensive; many campuses provide other specialized services that students should be aware of. Check things out on your own campus once you arrive and at least begin to identify those offices you might need to contact.

Getting Hassle-Free Help

We hear horror stories from students about how difficult it is to get a straight answer to their questions when they call certain offices on campus. Let's face it, a college campus—whether big or small, public or private, two- or four-year institution—is a bureaucracy. You should expect a certain amount of red tape—instances in which you get the runaround or someone can't or won't help you—but if you know which office handles which kinds of problems, you can avoid a lot of frustration. Remember, one way to find out who does what on your campus is to examine each office's website for those services you know you'll probably need. These days, most every campus office lists pertinent information on its website, perhaps to avoid getting unrelated phone calls or emails.

You can also reduce the hassle of finding information by being as clear as you possibly can be about the questions you want answered or the information needed. Before you send an email, make a phone call, or physically go to an office on campus, try to put yourself in the other person's shoes. Ask yourself: If I were on the receiving end, would I understand this question? Am I explaining the problem clearly? Is it even plausible that this office handles problems such as this? If you can't communicate your problems or needs very clearly, you may feel as if you're getting the runaround when in fact the person you're asking simply can't figure out what it is you want or need.

> **GET IT TOGETHER**
>
> Interestingly, the students who are struggling and would appear to need help the most are the ones who don't take advantage of all the services offered by colleges. Then these students find themselves on academic probation or worse. We are not sure why this phenomenon occurs, but we don't want it to happen to you. If you need help, get it sooner rather than later.

If you have done your homework and contact exactly the right office for the information you need but you still get the runaround (grrrrrrrrrrrr), here are some tips that may help in a pinch.

Be persistent but patient. If someone says, "We don't handle that," respond with something like this: "Well, on your website it says that (whatever it is you need) is handled through your office. Could you look with me in the FAQ (frequently asked questions) section to see if I'm misunderstanding something?" If the person still believes you have the wrong office, ask politely to speak with a supervisor or ask if she can transfer you to the office that does handle your needs. And always, always, always politely ask for the name of the person you are talking with.

Try your best to remain pleasant. It's not always the easiest thing to do, we know. (It's not easy for us either when we think we are getting the runaround.) Although we won't guarantee that keeping your temper at bay will get you a straight answer, we can tell you with a fair degree of certainty that if you are rude to individuals on the other end of the phone or computer or, heaven forbid, in person (now they know what you look like!), they will be rude to you as well. Perhaps even worse, they will simply ignore you—you know, hit the delete button on email and pretend you don't exist. Keep in mind that you stand a much better chance of getting someone to help you if you keep a positive attitude.

SAD BUT TRUE

In our division (the Division of Academic Enhancement), we have received requests for transcripts (handled through the Registrar's Office), questions about transfer credit (handled through the Admissions Office), questions about disability services (handled through Disability Services), the requirements of almost every conceivable major (handled through the respective academic departments), questions about meal plans (handled through Food Services), and even a request from a student in a foreign country for help obtaining a visa. Although we attempt to answer emails and phone calls and to point students in the right direction, we get a bit miffed sometimes (only a bit—we are really nice people). If any of these students had taken the time to look at our website, they would have known that our division does not and cannot handle any of these requests.

Enlist help. Ask your advisor, friends, or professors to help you find the answers to your questions. You're probably not the first student who has had trouble finding information; if you live in a residence hall, ask your RA or others on your hall. Perhaps they can provide insights that will help you get what you need quickly. If you are on a smaller campus, information might be available at a help desk in a place that is centrally located, such as the student union.

It takes a village to raise a child.

—African proverb

In the big scheme of things, using the three Ps—persistence, patience, and pleasantness—will go a long way in helping you get answers to your questions.

If You Read Nothing Else, Read This

○ Be proactive, not reactive. Seek out assistance when you first recognize you might need it, not when the alligators are nipping at your heels.

○ Know what services are available on your campus. Every campus staffs a variety of offices that generally provide help. Make friends with these folks.

○ Get the help you need with the least amount of hassle. Articulate what you need clearly and be persistent, patient, and pleasant.

CHAPTER 3

A FEW WORDS ABOUT PROFESSORS

- Worried that you will have intimidating professors?
- Concerned that your professors won't have any time for you?
- Think you won't know what to say if you actually do make an appointment to talk with your professor about how you're doing?

If so, read on . . .

magine that you are sitting in a class with 150 other students, listening to your professor discussing existential philosophy. She seamlessly interweaves Latin, Arabic, and French into her lecture. And most amazingly, she is able to lecture on this difficult material for fifty minutes without using any notes! Who is this person, anyway? How did she get so smart? Will all the stuff in Latin be on the exam?

Your professors may seem like brilliant, unapproachable figures (especially if you find yourself in very large classes), but most faculty enjoy interacting with students. In fact, we actually hope to convince you to get to know some of your professors very well. We believe that understanding what professors do and who they are will help you learn better in all your classes.

Just What the Heck Do Professors Do?

Regardless of whether you're attending a two-year community college, a public four-year university, or a small, private liberal arts school, your professors will have obligations that go beyond teaching. Unlike your high school teachers, who may teach as many as seven classes a day, your college professors may actually be in class as few as six hours per week.

"Great!" you say. "More time for him to sit patiently in his office and wait for me to stop by." On most campuses, however, that's not the case. Sure, all professors are supposed to hold office hours—times when they are available to meet with students, either through appointments or on a drop-in basis. But professors do have other obligations—tasks that are often carried out away from the office or even off campus.

Most faculty at four-year colleges are expected to "engage in creative activities." This means that they are expected to conduct research, write for professional journals, publish books, present papers at professional meetings, create portfolios of art or music compositions, interpret historical events, write poetry, find a cure for cancer, invent amazing products—the list goes on and on. The types of creative activities that faculty need to pursue depend on their discipline—obviously a biology professor working in a lab on a cure for diabetes wouldn't be expected to write poetry—but all faculty must consistently show involvement in creative activity or they risk losing their jobs (you may have heard of the publish or perish rule). As you probably know, creativity takes time, so at least part of a faculty member's time is spent figuring out how much of this creativity she has to produce in order to be promoted and then (and this is the hard part) actually producing something.

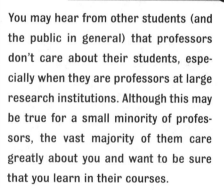

THE INSIDE SCOOP

You may hear from other students (and the public in general) that professors don't care about their students, especially when they are professors at large research institutions. Although this may be true for a small minority of professors, the vast majority of them care greatly about you and want to be sure that you learn in their courses.

DO YOUR HOMEWORK

As a way of getting to know your professors a bit even before you go to class on the first day, check to see if they have webpages. If so, take time to visit them. Webpages often present a less formal image of your professor than you will see in class. You can often find out their hobbies (my prof has a Harley), research interests (the life cycle of the cockroach—yuck!), or whether they are dog or cat people.

GET WIRED

Some professors have virtual office hours. This means that they will be online to answer your questions at a certain time of day—a great service, especially when you are studying for an exam. In addition, you can ask questions in email if it is more convenient than going to a professor's office.

All faculty, regardless of institution type, are also required to perform "service" activities. No, they don't have to sign on for a stint in the military. Service in this setting means serving on a variety of committees, acting as student advisors, providing services to their profession by reviewing scholarly papers, holding offices in professional organizations, and attending professional meetings. And because colleges tend to have faculty committees for everything, many professors end up spending a tremendous amount of time in service-related activities.

Which brings us back to the issue of your professor's schedule. Most professors will be glad to meet with you, but it's up to you to figure out how to arrange that meeting. Start by looking at your syllabus; it should provide your professor's office hours and procedures for seeing him. Some professors will see you only if you have an appointment; others have set office hours each week during which you can simply stop by to ask questions, get clarification, or discuss your grade.

I Have an Appointment with One of "Them"—Now What?

Before we discuss the nuts and bolts of talking with professors, we want to make the radical suggestion that you get to know some of them well—very well. In fact, make a pledge to yourself that you will get to know at least one professor a year; two, if you can. Right now, you can probably remember a teacher in your past who had a tremendous impact on you. If you make the effort to get to know some of your college teachers, we guarantee that years later you will still profit from the relationships. Having good relationships with college faculty members, especially those who teach in your major, can open many doors. They may have connections for jobs after graduation and they can write letters of recom-

> The mediocre teacher tells. The good teacher explains. The superior teacher demonstrates. The great teacher inspires.
>
> —William Arthur Ward

mendation for jobs or graduate school. Perhaps more important, they can stimulate your curiosity beyond the classroom and help you establish lifelong connections to your institution. Some campuses have mentoring programs that pair students (if they choose) with a faculty mentor at the beginning of their freshman year. The mentor meets with the student in a variety of settings over the course of the term. It could be a casual setting, such as having lunch, or a more formal setting in which students get additional one-on-one attention for writing papers or discussing books. If your campus offers such a program, sign up pronto.

You're ready to get to know your professors. But where do you start? Well, you have to begin by calling them something. It was easy in high school; you called your teachers Ms. Jones or Mr. Smith or Coach. In college it gets a bit more complicated.

Here's the quick and dirty on the pecking order for college profs, especially at larger colleges and universities. With the exception of instructors, those in the ranks most likely will have doctorates, that is, Ph.D.'s. Translate that into lots of years of schooling.

- *Instructors* sometimes teach only part-time and (at large four-year colleges, anyway) must have at least a master's degree.

- New profs, or those with only a couple of years of experience, are *assistant professors*. They are fairly easy to spot—they're the ones with bloodshot eyes from staying up late engaging in creative activities or trying to stay one step ahead of their students in terms of class preparation. These folks are working toward getting promoted and being tenured, so they never seem to have enough time.

- When profs get promoted (the first time), they are called *associate professors*.

🎧 LISTEN UP

Over the years, many female professors have found that students address them as "Ms." or "Mrs." even though they have a Ph.D. For some reason, students are more likely to address male faculty as "Dr." or Professor. In order to avoid this faux pas, it is always a safe bet to call your professor . . . well . . . Professor.

This means that they have met the requirements at their college or university to merit this promotion. At larger institutions, they have probably written some articles and gotten them published, or maybe they've written books—perhaps even the books you're using for their courses. At all levels of institutions, they generally had success in the classroom (good teaching ratings) or provided lots of service to the school and community. Usually, along with promotion to associate professor comes tenure. Simply defined, tenure means that your prof has a job at the college for life (if she wants it). Pretty good, huh? It takes an assistant professor six or seven years to get to this point. (One of the authors of this book falls into this category.)

- Finally, there are the big guns—*professors*, sometimes called full professors. These folks have been around the block a few times and have done lots of things right in order to achieve this goal. It's hard to get promoted to professor. They're usually easy to spot too: wrinkled brow, old leather briefcase, offices filled with years of stuff accumulated from years of teaching. (The other author falls into this category, wrinkled brow and all.)

With the exception of instructors who do not have Ph.D.'s, to whom you would refer much as you did your high school teachers (Ms. or Mr. Whomever), other faculty should be referred to as Dr. or Professor Whomever, until they tell you otherwise. Either title is a safe bet, but check out your syllabus to see if there is any indication

I not only use all of the brains I have, but all I can borrow.

—Woodrow Wilson

what he would like to be called. We know one professor who, on the first day of class, belts out very loudly—"I'm Professor Kelly" (not his real name). No doubt about what he wants to be called! Even if you have no idea in the world what your professor wants to be called, under no circumstances should you refer to him (or her) as "dude."

Now that you know how to address your profs, there are still a few things you need to know if you're going to get off on the right foot with them. Because professors are just ordinary people, no two are the same. What wows and works for one will fail miserably on the next. But here's some standard advice for dealing with profs, at least on the first meeting. We'll get you through that; the rest is up to you.

1. **Make an appointment.** Even if professors have drop-in office hours, we still think it's best to set up a time. You can either approach your professor before or after class or send her an email. Try to have several times that would work so you can be flexible in scheduling the appointment. And don't forget to have your daily planner with you when you make the appointment so you can write down the time and the place. (We sometimes have students show up in the classroom when we've arranged to meet them in our offices.)

2. **Show up on time.** Tardiness is a pet peeve of many professors (including one of the authors of this book), and you're not going to earn any points by showing up late or not at all. If you have to cancel the appointment, try to give your prof some notice in advance.

3. **Be brief and to the point.** Why have you made the appointment? Is it to get help with something you don't understand? To discuss a grade? To get some studying advice? We know this may make us sound stuffy—maybe even uptight—but it doesn't hurt to have a jot list and begin your meeting by saying something such as "I made this list of questions to be certain I asked you everything." Your professor will be impressed that you have thought the issue through before coming to her office. If you really feel lost and can't clearly verbalize your problem, tell her that as well so she may more easily help you figure it out.

4. **Ask questions or make points appropriately.** Let's say you've made an appointment to discuss your grade on your first history test. You didn't do nearly as well as you thought; in fact, you believe you deserve a much higher grade than the C– you earned. How do you approach the professor? Trust us on this one, it's best not to talk to your professor in a hostile or disrespectful way. And in no way should you swear at him, even under your breath. We know. It's odd that we should even have to mention this, but it happens more often than you think. Try

to put yourself in your professor's shoes. What if someone came into your room and was hostile with you? How would you feel?

If you're angry about a grade or something else a professor has said or done, walk away and count to ten. Count to one hundred if you have to. Think things through and take a deep breath, particularly if you tend to say things that you regret later. Even if you believe the grading was terribly unfair, be as positive as you can and communicate that you want to understand why you earned a low C so you can improve for the next test: "I thought I did much better than this. Can we talk for a few minutes about my strengths and weaknesses on this exam so I can do better next time?" or "I understand why I had points taken off here, but how could this part of my essay have been stronger?" Professors sometimes have the belief that all students are there just to "grade grub"—if you try not to present yourself as a grubber, your professor will be much more willing to work with you.

> A poor surgeon hurts one person at a time. A poor teacher hurts 130.
>
> —Ernest Boyer

With just a little thought and planning, meetings with professors can be almost pleasant. In fact, you just might learn something interesting.

Hangin' with Your Profs

We're not the only ones who believe that one of the smartest things you can do is get to know some of your professors well. In the past few years, there has been more of a push nationwide for professors to interact with undergraduate students in informal settings. In fact, on our campus there is a fund set aside for faculty to use to entertain students in their homes. Students who participate in these informal social activities usually have positive things to say about the experience because they have been able to see their professors in a different light. So if your professor invites you over for pizza or a five-course meal, put on a clean shirt and go. You will probably end up having a good time.

There are lots of ways to get to know your professors better. Many students get involved with student government, join clubs that have faculty sponsors, take small

Leslie looked back on almost three years of college and smiled. She had met so many interesting people and made a ton of friends, mostly her sorority sisters and others in campus organizations she participated in. As she reflected on her whole college experience to date, she thought she was in good shape—a more than respectable GPA, a working knowledge of print journalism (her major), and a good social network. Life was good. As she neared the end of her third year, her next big hurdle was finding a good internship to round out her college experience, to think about a topic for her senior project, and to finish up a bit of course work so she could graduate on time. To her credit, she started looking at internship opportunities early so she could submit the necessary paperwork and get the best possible internship—preferably one with a top-notch fashion magazine. As she scrutinized the huge bulletin board loaded with internship possibilities, she found five that seemed perfect for her . . . except for one thing. Every single one of them wanted recommendations from at least two of her professors. Three would be better. Leslie was panic-stricken. Although she went to class and had good grades, she really never made an effort to connect with any of her teachers, even those who seemed to take an interest in her. She wasn't even sure how this had happened or why she'd never realized how important this was. Her friends always seemed to be able to get some prof they hardly knew at all to write for them, but more often than not, those recommendations were only lukewarm, which may do more harm than good. So, Leslie was faced with the possibility of not being able to apply for any of the top internships because no faculty members knew her well enough to write her a recommendation. She went ahead and applied for the internships she wanted and also for some that didn't require letters from her professor. In the end, she barely managed to snag a position using letters of recommendation from a former high school teacher and her program advisor, but it wasn't what she wanted, and it wasn't a particularly positive experience for her. Don't be like Leslie. Make an effort to get to know some of your profs. It will serve you well down the line.

classes whenever possible, or get a part-time job working for a professor who shares a common interest. It's a real plus to put yourself in situations where you can meet and interact with faculty, where you can get to know them as people, and where they can get to know you.

What Do Your Profs Think about You?

You'll be better able to interact more comfortably with your professors and get to know them if you understand some of their general perceptions about students, particularly freshmen. Take these tidbits for what they are: generalizations that college faculty have in mind when they look out over the sea of faces. Right or wrong, faculty make assumptions like these.

You're in college to get an education. So if you're a slacker or come to your profs with lame excuses about why you didn't complete your paper on time ("I went to save my forty-page paper and I lost everything" or "I was sitting out by the pool with my laptop working on my paper and this dude threw me in the pool, laptop and all"), your words will probably fall on deaf ears. They have heard more excuses than you can dream up. They do expect you to anticipate the best but plan for the worst so when the worst occurs, you actually have some extra time to finish assignments that were given way in advance.

You're interested in whatever it is they teach. And if you're not interested, you'll get interested. At the very least, you'll pretend you're interested. Falling asleep in class, responding to email on your laptop, or talking to the person next to you will not endear you to your professors. Remember, showing up is only half the battle.

You're self-motivated. No matter what obstacles professors throw in your path, they're sure you can handle it because you are highly motivated. Never mind that you're taking four other classes and have the reading load of ten graduate students. You're motivated and you can do it.

You know how to study and manage your time. Profs expect you to be a studying machine and know all sorts of effective ways to learn their material. They also expect you to be just like them—you know, get to class on time and submit your work three days before it's due. Take this assumption as a compliment.

You can do more with course material than simply memorize it. Your profs expect you to think critically. This means that when they lecture on some topic that seems almost unintelligible they expect you to magically understand everything they have said. Sure, some memorizing is necessary, but they expect you to go beyond that. They expect you to be able to think about their topic as an expert would. Unrealistic? Maybe, but it is a reality that they think you're pretty smart, so you should be able to think about ideas logically and critically.

You catch on easily to class rules and respect the rights of others. As mentioned earlier, each professor has her quirks, often little rules that she expects you to follow without being told twice. We know profs who insist that students not wear baseball caps during class, or require that students must quietly take a seat in the back if they are late, or who actually single out students who nod off during class. But every professor we know is totally annoyed when cell phones go off during class. Profs look at it as disrespectful to them and to other students. So get used to turning off the cell phone as you walk into classes or events.

Your professors are actually just regular folks who happen to have lots of education. When they look out over the sea of faces in a class, they see students who are bright, capable, and have a real desire to learn.

If You Read Nothing Else, Read This

○ **Professors do lots of things in addition to teaching—research, writing, advising.**

○ **When you need to see your professor, make an appointment and be prepared.**

○ **Profs come in three types: assistant, associate, and full.**

○ **Get to know some of your profs very well. They can help you out down the line.**

○ **Your profs think you are bright and want to learn. (Don't disappoint them.)**

CHAPTER 4

ZEN AND THE ART OF COURSE SELECTION

- Worried about graduating on time because you can't get into required courses?
- Concerned that you don't really understand how to compute your GPA?
- Think you could use some tips about staying on top of your course requirements and balancing your course selections at the same time?

If so, read on . . .

You've been staring at a course catalog the size of a small telephone book for days now. How do you know which courses to take? You're not even sure what you are going to major in yet. (Don't worry. The next chapter will help you sort out your interests to determine the kinds of careers that suit you best.) You've talked to your advisor and are armed with a list of four possible courses to start with. You figure out how to get into the computer registration system but find that all the courses you've planned to take this term are filled, and it seems that the only courses left have titles like Baroque Art for Physicists or they begin at 7:50 in the morning! Before you decide to quit college and work full-time at a fast-food joint, try taking a different approach to course selection.

Racking Up the Credits: How Many Courses Should You Take?

The first thing you need to decide is how many courses you want to take each term. In most colleges, twelve hours (or four courses) is considered full-time under a semester system. At colleges using a quarter system, nine hours (or three courses) is usually considered full-time. If you are receiving scholarship or student loan funds, you may need to register for a full load to receive the money. And if you want to complete your degree in four years, you should plan on taking more than full-time credit hours. You will probably need to take fifteen hours (or five courses) if you are under a semester system or twelve hours (four courses) under a quarter system—and if you end up dropping a course, maybe even some summer hours (we will talk more about the reasons for dropping a course later in this chapter).

However, there are many reasons you might choose to enroll part-time. For example, if you are working full-time or are returning to school after a long absence, it might be more realistic to

start out with a part-time load to determine how many courses you can handle. In fact, any entering student may feel this way for the first term and decide to start out slowly.

Ohmmmm: Creating a Balance

Selecting courses should be easy. You just pick any four or five that you need, stir gently, and you have an instant course schedule, right? Actually, you need to ask yourself some questions as you create your course schedule each semester—and be honest with yourself. Are you really going to wake up early to make it to an 8 A.M. class? Is the only course section offered this semester taught by the professor who made your roommate so nervous she broke out in hives? Will you have to run at breakneck speed from one end of campus to the other in the fifteen minutes between classes? To create a balanced schedule, you need to consider the following issues.

BALANCING TASKS

When choosing courses, think about the tasks you will be required to do. You really don't want to take four courses that all require heavy reading, like literature, sociology, history, philosophy, or biology. Likewise, you don't want to be doing only mathematics problems all term either (no matter how much you enjoy them). Instead, try to create a balance between heavy reading courses and those that require less reading, courses that involve problem solving and those that do not.

BALANCING INTERESTS

It would be great if you could be interested in each and every course you take in college (we hope you will find something interesting in every course). However, most colleges require a core of courses, some of which may not be your favorites. Instead of waiting until the last possible semester to take these dreaded courses, it is a much better idea to spread them out over your college career. Try to balance each term with some courses you find highly interesting, something in your major, and a course that focuses on topics you've always wanted to know more about. For example, one of the authors of this book took an elective course on King Arthur legends as an undergrad that was not part of her major but was the highlight of that semester.

BALANCING TIME

It is not enough to offer a smorgasbord of courses. We must insure that students are not just eating at one end of the table.

—A. Bartlett Giamatti

When creating your course schedule, you should also consider when each class meets. If you know you have grave difficulty just finding the shower early in the morning (let alone trying to make your brain function), avoid 8 A.M. classes like the plague. In addition, resist the urge to overload your schedule. We have known students who have attempted to take all their courses on Tuesdays

SAD BUT TRUE

Josh, a senior ecology major, had always hated taking literature courses. He really couldn't see where his teachers got all that stuff about theme and metaphor—yuck! So in his years as a college student he just avoided them, even though he was required to take two lit courses to graduate. (Maybe he thought if he ignored them, they'd just go away.) Now, as he registers for his final semester in school, he finds that he needs to squeeze in both lit courses on top of his very tough senior-level ecology courses. He thinks to himself, If only I'd gotten these lit courses out of the way earlier, I could've really enjoyed this last semester in school.

The moral of Josh's tale: don't wait to take the courses you are not crazy about. Instead, distribute them over your college years—who knows, you may end up liking them more than you think. At the very least, you won't have to face them all at once.

and Thursdays and were in class from 9 A.M. until after 6 P.M. Unless you are extremely disciplined, you will soon find this kind of schedule grueling. Also, try to schedule the courses you are least interested in at your personal peak times. This way you are more likely to make it to class every day. (Later in the book we'll have a more in-depth discussion of time management.) Creating a balance in your schedule can often mean the difference between a great semester and a lousy one. Take the time to consider these factors each time you make your course schedule.

Working with Your Advisor

If you listen to people talking on campus, everyone knows someone in Keisha's situation. Advisors get a bum rap because it seems they are always getting blamed for misguiding students. It may be that a course the student needs is not offered or that a prerequisite

SAD BUT TRUE

Keisha thought she would be graduating spring semester with a degree in marketing. However, when she registered for classes she found out that she needed one more economics course that would not be offered again until the fall. Keisha is really angry with her advisor for not making sure she had this course. Now she won't graduate in four years and she won't be able to begin interviewing until next year.

course is needed before the student can register for a course that's required for graduation or that the student took extra courses not needed for the major. Although we strongly believe that advisors should be up on things, we also know that it is very difficult for them to keep up with the many curriculum requirement changes that occur at most colleges—especially if advising is not the advisor's full-time job. In fact, often colleges require faculty to advise students; given all that your professors have to do, it is no wonder that some of them do not invest much time in their advising duties.

No matter who your advisor is, it is your responsibility to be sure you get the guidance you need. We're not saying that you need to familiarize yourself with the entire course catalogue, but you should ask lots of questions and seek answers from more than one source as you set your course load each term, particularly if something seems fishy to you. For example, at our college there was a rumor that students could not use scholarship money to take summer courses. Students said they heard this from their advisors, but upon checking with the Registrar's Office they found this was simply not true.

Here are some basic questions to ask your advisor:

1. Which courses are required for graduating with a major in _____ (fill in the blank)?

2. Are there prerequisite courses for any of these requirements? (You may want to ask this question every time you meet with your advisor.)

3. How often are these courses offered—and are there any that are only offered occasionally? On most campuses, courses are planned almost a year in advance (or at least tentatively planned), so your advisor should be able to find out what will be offered the following semester or two.

4. Are there any requirements governing how I must choose to use my elective credit hours? Some colleges require that you take some electives in the humanities, sciences, and so on. Others have no such requirements for electives, and you can use them as you choose.

5. Is there a particular order to follow when signing up for the courses in my major?

6. Are there any courses that need to be taken at the same time?

Advisors can do more than just help you plan your course schedule. They often have the inside scoop on internships, summer jobs, or special learning opportunities (like study abroad). Advisors can also be great resources if you are not sure where to go with an issue or a question. For example, if you want to find out about deciding on a minor, getting help in your chemistry class, or applying for a scholarship, your advisor can help you find out which office to contact.

Choosing Your Professors

Many students tell us that selecting professors is even more important than selecting courses. Ask your friends, your advisor, and students in your major which professors they'd suggest. Try to get some specifics about the professor. What is his general style of teaching? What kinds of tests does he give? How large is the class? What are the grading procedures? What is the overall level of difficulty? (Remember that an easy course is not always a blessing—especially if you need to really learn the information for your future career.) You may even want to talk to the professor through email or during his office hours to find out a little more about a course before signing up.

In general, seeking help from advisors, peers, and professors can help you create a course schedule you can live with (and even learn to love).

Making a Plan

Once you have decided on a major (we aren't rushing you—for many students this may not happen until the end of sophomore year), you should map out a general college course plan. Your plan should include both the courses you are required to take and some electives you want to take. Taking the time to do this will help you figure out how long it will take you to get your degree. Most colleges have a form to help you—if you didn't get one, ask your advisor. In fact, some colleges will ask you to submit your course plan when you officially declare your major. However, let's assume

> Not doing more than the average is what keeps the average down.
>
> —William M. Winans

that you do not have such guidance. How do you make your own college course plan?

Check out the course catalogue. Most colleges now have their "undergraduate bulletin" online or they will send you a copy along with your acceptance letter. Others may give it out at orientation. It's always a good idea to go over the undergraduate bulletin before you go to register so you can see the many fascinating courses that await you. Examine the courses offered for your major and then take a look at any electives that seem interesting to you. If some of the courses are specialty courses (like that King Arthur legends course), you should contact the appropriate departments to find out when the classes will be offered again or if nonmajors are permitted to enroll. Sometimes departments list courses that have not been taught in years or are taught only once every few years; finding out this information will save you from building a course into your college plan only to find later that it won't be offered until after you've graduated.

LISTEN UP

It's not always easy to find out about the best, most interesting electives to take. Students have told us they didn't catch on to how to do this until their junior year, when it was largely too late. Our advice? Ask around. In fact, ask everyone—a professor you found interesting, your friends, advisors, people you meet at the library. In addition, skim through the course catalogue and mark the things that look interesting. Remember to search outside your major or college—there's good stuff out there you might never have even considered.

Figure out how long it will take to get your degree. Most students assume they will finish a bachelor's degree in four years or an associate's degree in two. But the reality is that it is becoming more and more common for it to take longer. If your goal is to finish in four years, your college plan must take this into account.

Make a time line. Plot out the courses you will take each term. Be sure to give yourself some wiggle room in case a course you'd like to take is not offered during the term you've set out in your time line. Double-check your plan to be sure you have created a balanced course load for each term.

For example, here is Ben's sample course time line for his first two years toward completing a degree in botany (see opposite page).

Notice how Ben has created a balance of the types of courses he plans to take, while still taking at least one course per term that relates to his major—and often also fulfills a general curriculum requirement. He has also planned to start out his first semester with fewer credit hours so he can ramp up to the challenge of college.

Once you are enrolled in college, try to plan out at least your first two semesters. What do you envision your courses will be like? Remember, if you are not sure what your major will be, focus on fulfilling your general requirements first; these courses just might help you decide.

TERM	COURSE	CREDITS
Fall 2007	Intro Biology I w/lab	3
	Intro Psychology	3
	Freshman seminar	1
	Racquetball	2
	Precalc	3
Spring 2008	Intro Biology II w/lab	3
	Freshman English	3
	Music Appreciation	3
	Spanish I	3
	Speech Communications	3
Fall 2008	Plant Biology	3
	History I	3
	Intro to Chemistry	3
	Calculus	3
	Spanish II	3
Spring 2009	Developmental Biology	3
	Cell Biology	3
	Sophomore English	3
	Human Geography	3
	Spanish III	3

Some students think that taking courses during the summer session is like attending summer school in high school—a penalty for falling behind during the regular school year. But in college, summer session courses are just like courses given in the fall and spring terms, except they are usually compressed into a shorter period of time. They are not a punishment; they are another opportunity to help you complete your college career in a timely fashion. And, many students like the smaller class sizes that summer session usually offers.

Withdrawal Symptoms

There's a pretty good chance that, sooner or later, you will want (or need) to withdraw from a course. The reasons vary; as a general rule, if you do not think you can successfully complete a course, it is often best to drop it. Talk to your professor and advisor before you withdraw from a course to get their advice. You'll probably need their signatures too, because at some colleges, withdrawing can be an exercise in filling out lots of paperwork.

Students often hang onto courses they cannot pass and end up with a GPA that can get them into trouble. These students may feel that withdrawing from a course is quitting and that quitting is a greater failure than seeing the course through to the end. The decision to withdraw is difficult, but it is often the best choice. On the other hand, choose wisely because if you have withdrawn from more courses than you've completed, graduation may not occur until you're old enough to retire.

DO YOUR HOMEWORK

It is becoming more and more common for students to enter college with AP (Advanced Placement) credit, joint enrollment credit, or both. On our campus, currently about one-third of new freshmen have earned some college credit prior to their official college matriculation. Everyone seems to be an overachiever these days! If you already have some college credit, it is up to you to be sure your institution receives confirmation of what you have taken. It's also important to keep this in mind as you plan your schedule. You don't want to have to take courses that you already have credit for.

Some colleges set limits on the number of courses you can withdraw from over your college career. If your college falls into this category, you will need to be careful because you don't want to use up all your withdrawals in the first two years. In addition, withdrawal deadlines can vary greatly (check your college catalogue or website for these policies so you don't miss the drop date).

When should you withdraw from a course? There are two good indicators:

1. You are feeling overwhelmed with the number of courses you are taking and believe you would do better in all your other courses if you just got rid of one. Dump the course that is giving you the most problems or the one that seems to be consuming way too much time.

2. You are failing a course and believe you cannot pull up your grade by the end of the term. However, we must note that some professors will let you withdraw only if you are passing the course. Be sure to check your syllabus before attempting to withdraw—you may need to make your decision before the first exam.

URBAN LEGEND

A freshman writes the following letter to her parents. . . .

Dear Mom and Dad,

I am sorry I have not written sooner, but this has been quite a semester. Before you read on, you might want to sit down.

First, you should know that the concussion I received by jumping from my dorm window during a fire in my room is healing nicely. I only spent five days in the hospital and my vision is almost back to normal. The headaches are almost gone too.

Fortunately, a guy in the floor below called the ambulance and the fire department. He visited me in the hospital every day, and we are deeply in love. He was kind enough to let me share his room (after mine burned) and we plan to get married before my pregnancy starts to show.

Well, now that I have caught you up, I want to tell you that there was no dorm fire, I did not have a concussion, and I am not pregnant or getting married. However, I am getting a D in chemistry and an F in accounting, but wanted you to see these grades in their proper perspective.

Sincerely,

Your loving daughter

Know Thy GPA

Most students think they have only one GPA (grade point average), but actually your GPA is calculated in several ways. First, you have a term GPA: your average for the courses you are taking in a particular semester or quarter. It is calculated by dividing the grade points earned that term by the total number of credit hours attempted that semester. Second, you have a cumulative GPA: your average for all the courses you have taken so far. Your cumulative GPA is calculated by dividing your total number of grade points by the total number of credits you have earned.

Because we are discussing how to figure out your grades, it is important to note that although grades are important, if you focus only on grades:

- You're not learning for your own sake. If you are concerned only with the grade you'll earn, you'll find that you are working to please the professor instead of learning to please yourself.

- You become less interested in the course if you do not make the grade you desire. Students have told us that when they work for a grade and they don't do as well as they would have liked, they end up feeling frustrated and often just give up. Generally, grades alone are not enough to sustain your motivation.

- You find that you put responsibility for learning on others. Students who are worried about grades tend to blame others for any failures: "I didn't do well on the test because the professor didn't go over half the material in class." Remember, you are in charge of your own learning.

What is a grade point, anyway? A grade point is the number assigned to each letter grade. Most colleges use the point system shown on page 49. (Note: If your college does not use plusses or minuses, use only the full letter grades when calculating your GPA. Check your college's policy on grading in the course catalogue.)

Basically, to improve your GPA you need to make above-average grades, As or Bs. However, when you begin college it is very important to get off to a good start. This is why you need to know both your term GPA and your cumulative GPA. The more credits you have earned each term, the harder it is to improve your cumulative

GPA. In addition, for some majors there are minimum GPA requirements for admission. You'll need to keep track of your GPA to be sure you meet these standards. And we should also mention that most colleges do not include AP credit or grades in your GPA. Your GPA is generally a reflection of just the courses you take following your acceptance and enrollment.

We suggest you figure out your GPA every semester. In addition, keep track of your grades in each course so you'll know where you stand at all times. Some students keep a record in the front of their binder for each course.

A	4.0
A–	3.7
B+	3.3
B	3.0
B–	2.7
C+	2.3
C	2.0
C–	1.7
D	1.0
F	0.0

GET WIRED ⚡

Many colleges offer "what if?" calculators on their websites. These sites help you figure out the exact grades you will need to earn to get the GPA you desire.

DO YOUR HOMEWORK 🖥

Pop Quiz: Sam is taking four courses in his first semester in college—English, Math, Spanish, and Psychology. He wants to end the semester with at least a 3.0 cumulative GPA. If he gets a B– in English, a C in math, an A in Spanish, and an A– in psychology, will he reach this goal?

Course	Grade	Grade Points x	Number of Credits =	Total Points
Engl 101	B–	2.7	3	8.1
Math 101	C	2.0	3	6.0
Span 101	A	4.0	4	16.0
Psych 101	A–	3.7	3	11.1
		Total	13	41.2

To calculate the GPA, you divide total points by total credits. Sam's 41.2 points divided by 13 credits produces a 3.17 GPA. So Sam did reach his goal this term. Way to go, Sam!

Sometimes you enroll in a course that just isn't what you thought it would be. In fact, you hate this course! The reading is dry, dull, and boring; the prof is not much better. The first test was impossible, and the list goes on. What to do? First and foremost, be sure you understand what your school's policy is on withdrawing from classes as well as withdrawal deadlines. Then, if you can, we recommend withdrawal, rather than self-destruction. Withdrawing from an occasional course usually doesn't have a negative impact on you, but several poor grades on your transcript certainly do.

If You Read Nothing Else, Read This

O   Take only as many courses as you can handle. When you are choosing courses, aim to balance interests, tasks, requirements, and electives.

O   Work with your advisor. Ask questions about course and degree requirements (even if you haven't decided on your major yet) and about which professors to take.

O   Have a plan. Don't just chip away at course requirements; map out what you are going to take over the next four (or more) years. Try to take at least one course you think you will enjoy each semester

O   Figure out your GPA. Stay on top of both your term (semester) grades and your cumulative (overall) GPA.

CHAPTER 5

MAJOR DECISIONS: SELECTING A FIELD OF STUDY

- Worried about making good decisions regarding selecting your major? (Psst: more students start out in pre-law or premed than end up in either of those fields.)
- Concerned about finding out about all your choices?
- Worried that your major will have absolutely nothing to do with the things you are really interested in?

If so, read on . . .

You may enter college knowing exactly what you want to major in, or you may be one of an ever-growing number of students who begin with no idea what they will end up doing. Let's say you are in the second category. Some studies indicate that up to 75 percent of entering freshmen are uncertain of their choice of major, so you are in good company. To make the choice, you begin by figuring out the career you want for the rest of your life, right? Not really. Selecting a major is quite different from selecting a career. College majors often lead to a variety of career choices. And while you are in college, you may learn of interesting careers that you have never thought about or even heard of.

Help! I Don't Know What I Want to Do When I Grow Up

When selecting a major, there's a lot to think about. Some students try to look to the future and select a major that will allow them to have a variety of options careerwise. Others are very focused and select a major that will prepare them for more limited careers. Whatever your approach, there are a few basic steps to follow so you can select the major that is right for you.

RELAX

This is an important decision, but don't let it stress you out. Selecting a major does not mean you are cutting off other options. You will still have a chance to change your mind—many students do. So take a deep breath and read on. And by the way, if your parents are worried because they think you have no direction in your life, have them read this chapter too.

ASSESS YOUR STRENGTHS AND INTERESTS

What do you like to do? Do you enjoy working with people? Do you like to read for information? Do you like working with numbers? What hobbies currently interest you? Do you prefer to work indoors or outdoors? What activities do you know you do not like to do? To determine what you do like to do, see the exercise on figuring out your interests later in this chapter.

FIND OUT HOW YOUR INTERESTS RELATE TO COLLEGE MAJORS

If you enjoy working with people, you may want to pursue a degree that allows you to teach or provide guidance to others. If you are mechanically inclined and would rather deal with things than with people, consider degrees such as engineering or forestry that allow you to work at building or "doing." If you are artistic, seek majors that encourage those talents, such as graphic arts or music. If you love kids, there are lots of other majors besides early childhood education—look for those that apply to a career as a speech therapist, museum director for children's activities, pediatric nurse, social worker.

We know what we are, but know not what we may be.

-William Shakespeare

52

James, a senior accounting major, recently came to a startling realization. He discovered he did not like accounting. Nope, he didn't like any part of it—not solving problems using accounting models, not balancing budgets, not figuring out credits and debits—not any of the tasks he had been taught to do in college. The more he thought about it, the more he discovered he wished he had majored in something that allowed him to be more creative, like advertising, or something that really interested him, like history. James had chosen accounting at the end of his freshman year for two reasons: it led to a clear career path with a good potential for making money, and his parents seemed to think it would be a good career choice. After all, his dad was an accountant. Looking back on that decision, James says ruefully, "I mean, what would you do with a degree in history? At least with accounting I knew—or thought I knew—what I was getting into." The moral of James's story: don't allow others to pressure you into making your decision too early (psst . . . not even your parents). Your strengths and interests often develop and change during your first years in college, so take your time when making this very important choice. It is also important to note that a college degree can lead you to almost any career—if James did an internship in advertising the summer after college, there you go—a beginning to a career in advertising.

Many colleges offer website questionnaires designed to help you discover how your interests relate to college majors and future careers. Also check out your college's career planning office. Such offices usually offer a combination of support services that may include assessments, one-on-one counseling, workshops, and even courses on choosing a major and a career. Or check out mindtools.com for some good advice on careers, stress management, time management, and lots of other good stuff.

FIND OUT HOW POTENTIAL MAJORS RELATE TO CAREER OPTIONS

Some majors relate directly to specific careers; others are more general. Basically, there are three categories of majors:

- **Career-specific.** These majors prepare you for a specific job, for example, accounting, education, engineering, and nursing. After earning a degree in many of these fields, you must pass some kind of license or certification test before you can either practice or advance in your career.

- **Career-oriented.** These majors lead you to a general field of employment but not to a specific job. Some good examples are degrees in marketing, public relations, communications, biology, and social work. These degrees prepare students for a variety of entry-level positions within these fields.

- **Noncareer-specific.** These majors do not directly prepare you for a job. Some examples are comparative literature, history, psychology, sociology, and political science. Often students choosing these majors go on for an advanced degree or seek internships or other career-related experiences while enrolled in college.

X FOR ADULTS ONLY

If you are returning to college to start a career or to change careers, the career-planning office often has special resources that can help you determine ways to combine previous experiences with your current major to lead to a variety of career opportunities. Be sure to take advantage of their services.

TAKE ADVANTAGE OF CAMPUS RESOURCES

Most colleges offer some kind of career-planning services. Whether you have entered college knowing your major and career path or not, you should familiarize yourself with this valuable campus resource early in your college career. In addition to offering personalized career counseling, career-discovery inventories, and computer resources to help you determine a good career or major, they can also help you build a resume, find an internship, or even teach you how to interview for a job.

SEEK OUT INTERNSHIPS

An internship is a short-term career-related job—some students have full-time summer internships and others do part-time internships during the school year. Some internships are paid positions and some are unpaid. Most internships have some kind of academic component where you can earn college credit for your work. Internship experience looks great on a resume and can also help you figure out what you do (and don't) want to do with your life. Internships are so valuable that some majors even require them.

DO A REALITY CHECK

Your college major will, in essence, be your full-time job for the next four (or five) years. Think about the kinds of courses you will be expected to take in the major and the types of careers that can be pursued with your degree. If you like the kinds of tasks that you will be asked to do in your major and you look forward to the types of careers this major will lead to, you are on the right path. What if, on the other hand, you are a premed major who can't stand the sight of blood, an interior design major who can't draw a straight line, or a computer science major who hates solving math problems? Are you in love with the idea of your major, but not with the realities of what completing that major would entail? Periodically ask yourself, "Can I see myself doing these kinds of tasks in my career?" It's time to reevaluate your major and career goals if your answer is "No!" more often than "Yes!"

For most students, choosing a major is not an easy decision. Our best advice is to arm yourself with as much information as you can before you make your choice. If you decide too early and then switch your major later on, you may end up needing to take more courses (and additional semesters) if some of the courses you've taken don't count for anything in your new major.

So Many Choices!

Most people want a major and a career that are tied into their interests. But sometimes determining what those interests are is more challenging than you'd expect. Most career counselors use six generally accepted categories created by John Holland and explained in *Making Vocational Choices: A Theory of Vocational Personalities and Work Environments*, 3rd ed. (Odessa, FL: Psychological Assessment Resources, 1997) to determine interests for future careers and majors. See which categories you fall into. Note: most people fit into more than one category.

Artistic. Artistic people usually like unstructured tasks in a creative environment. They like to use their imagination and enjoy work that fosters creativity. Artistic types may enjoy majoring in interior design, music, literature, advertising, drama, or other creative fields.

Enterprising. These types like to take initiative and often assume a leadership position. They enjoy persuading or influencing others. Enterprising types may enjoy majoring in marketing, speech communication, political science, business, or other fields that encourage leadership, communication, and persuasion.

Social. Social people like to work with others. They enjoy teaching, informing, curing, or other activities that help people. They value social situations and interpersonal relationships. Social types may enjoy majoring in education, speech communications, psychology, nursing, social work, or similar fields that encourage helping and working with others.

Realistic. These types tend to be mechanically inclined and are often athletic. They may enjoy dealing with things rather than people. They are likely to enjoy working outdoors or with machines or building and fixing things. Realistic types may enjoy majoring in engineering, agriculture, or other fields that emphasize the technical or mechanical.

Investigative. These are thinking types who like to solve problems through analyzing or using data. They see themselves as scholarly and intellectually capable and may prefer working alone. Investigative types may enjoy majoring in science, mathematics, philosophy, computer science, or other fields that encourage their intellectual spirit.

Conventional. These types are orderly and precise. They are practical and neat; they like to work in structured situations in which they know what is expected of them and where accuracy counts. Conventional types may enjoy majoring in accounting, business, management, finance, computer science, or other fields where precision and accuracy are valued.

How can you figure out where you fit among these types? Take this little test by placing a check mark next to each activity you enjoy (check as many as apply).

To figure out your interests, total the number of items you have checked in each category. Remember that most people fall into more than one category. To get the broadest view of your interests, select the top three categories that describe you. So

ARTISTIC

☐ Work in flexible settings

☐ Think creatively

☐ Play a musical instrument, sing, compose, or act

☐ Write stories, poetry, or essays

☐ Communicate ideas

☐ Sketch, draw, paint, or sculpt

ENTERPRISING

☐ Make decisions

☐ Give talks or speeches

☐ Organize activities and events

☐ Sell things

☐ Be in charge, take a leadership role

☐ Lead a group

SOCIAL

☐ Work in groups

☐ Help people with problems

☐ Participate in meetings

☐ Lead a group discussion

☐ Teach or train others

REALISTIC

☐ Build things

☐ Work outdoors

☐ Be active

☐ Work with plants or animals

☐ Work with my hands

☐ Work on cars

INVESTIGATIVE

☐ Investigate ideas

☐ Use computers

☐ Work alone

☐ Work in a lab

☐ Solve math problems

CONVENTIONAL

☐ Follow procedures

☐ Keep records and organize paperwork

☐ Work with numbers

☐ Organize data

☐ Create databases of information

☐ Be responsible for details

you may be enterprising, artistic, and social; or conventional, realistic, and investigative; or any combination of these six categories. This information can help guide you not only in choosing a major and a career, but also in selecting courses that match your broader interests. For example, if you find that you are social, realistic, and enterprising you might like to take some courses that will allow you to complete some group projects (many business and computer science courses are run this way) so you can work with people to solve real problems in a creative way—who knows, you might even find a major in the process.

Double (or Even Triple) Majors

Most colleges offer double majors in areas that are closely tied together (such as computer science and mathematics) or even in areas that seem unrelated (like sociology and agriculture). For example, if you love to learn languages, yet you know you want a career that will earn a good living and allow you to travel, your ticket to success may be a double major in language and business.

Remember, if you choose to seek a double major, you will have to fulfill the requirements of both majors in order to graduate. You will probably need to take a heavier course load than your classmates most semesters, especially if you hope to finish in four years. However, for most students who choose to double major, this challenge is worth the extra effort because it brings their interests together. If you double major, it's important to use your electives wisely. In fact, you may end up with very few "free" electives because an elective credit in one major may fulfill a required course in the other major.

> When you have to make a choice and don't make it, that in itself is a choice.
>
> —William James

SAD BUT TRUE

Stacy felt pressured to declare her major before she really knew what she wanted to do. Because she'd always done well in science in high school, she chose to major in chemistry, figuring that maybe she'd go on to become a pharmacist. As she finished her sophomore year, she decided that her true passion was not working in a lab, but working with people. Stacy wanted to switch over to science education. Unfortunately, because she had taken so many chemistry requirements that were not a part of the science education curriculum, changing her major now would mean spending at least one extra year in college. If only she had waited and taken more general course requirements instead of rushing to declare a major.

You may be wondering who in their right mind would want to pursue a double major. Some students believe this path will lead them to a better job or more job options after college. They may be right—but it depends on what those two majors are. There's another good reason: if you know you are going to apply for an advanced degree (say, medical school), a double major in chemistry and biology will certainly be helpful. On the other hand, sometimes a single major with very strong grades and a minor in your secondary interest can serve you just as well, without the added pressure. Check with your advisor and talk to students majoring in both areas before you make your final decision.

Major Assistance Is Out There

Choosing a major is obviously not an easy decision. In fact, most college students change majors at least once. Take advantage of the many resources available to help you make this very important decision. These resources include the following:

- **Your college's course catalogue.** This book contains a wealth of information about the courses you need to take and may introduce you to some specialized or interesting majors you've never heard of before.

- **Your professors and your academic advisor.** Many of your professors have worked in the field in which they teach and may be able to tell you about career options. In addition, when you take a course in a field you find interesting and worth pursuing further, talk to the professor and your advisor about it.

- **Your friends** (and your friends' friends). Even talk to your parents' friends. Ask people about their majors and how they came to make their choices. Talk to students with the majors you are considering and to folks going through the job-interview process to gather as much information as you can.

- **Your college career-planning and placement center.** We don't know why students don't just flock to these places. Helping students choose majors and then find jobs is the career choice of those who work in career centers. And yet these centers are some of the most underused places on campus. Don't wait until your senior year to visit; go there in your very first semester. You can often find out about internships, summer jobs, and other opportunities that will help you reach your long-term goals.

● **Specialized websites.** Our college hosts a website where students can explore all the different majors offered. In addition, the website provides information about careers associated with certain majors, beginning salaries, and the prospects for employment opportunities in that field. What a great resource! Check out what's offered online at your own institution.

● **Your family.** Is there someone in your family who has a job you'd just love to do? Talk to that person about choosing a major and try to visit her at her place of employment to learn more about what it entails. Heck, she might even be able to help you find an internship or summer employment in her field.

These suggestions are just to help you begin to think about the resources available to you. But don't stop there. Every time you read about someone in a newspaper or watch something on TV and think, "Gee, that person has a great job," consider how you could get on a track that leads to a career like that.

Why Choosing a Major ≠ Choosing a Career

If you have chosen to major in philosophy, everyone you meet probably asks, "What in the world are you going to do with that?" In fact, majoring in fields such as philosophy, drama, literature, history, or psychology can lead to careers in business, teaching, writing, or research. Just because there is no clearly defined end-point career doesn't mean there are no jobs available for you. In fact, in a study asking college graduates what they'd do differently if they could do college over again, many responded that they would seek a liberal arts education to build a broader background.

On the other hand, if you have decided to become a lawyer, that doesn't mean you need to major in pre-law. Depending on what kind of law you'd like to practice, a major in business, history, literature, or language can serve you just as well. For exam-

> Anyone who stops learning is old, whether at twenty or eighty. Anyone who keeps learning stays young. The greatest thing in life is to keep your mind young."
>
> —Henry Ford

Many of our first-year students say they are premed, pre-law, pre-business—just about anything they can "pre." However, by the second year, an overwhelming majority have changed majors. This is not necessarily a bad thing. There is no shame in figuring out that you **don't** want to do something. In fact, these changes are what can guide you to what you do want to do.

ple, if you are interested in pursuing environmental law, then a bachelor's degree in ecology may be very helpful. However, it is important to know what the admissions requirements for professional schools are. Therefore, if you are planning to go to pharmacy, vet, medical, or law school, find out as much information as you can about what it takes to gain admission.

There's a common misperception that choosing a major is equivalent to choosing a career. However, recent research has indicated that only 50 percent of college graduates report a close connection between their major and their job. This means that getting a bachelor's degree can prepare you for a variety of careers.

We don't know any better than you do what the job market will look like in the future. Jobs that are plentiful now may become obsolete as we find new ways of getting things done. For example, as we finish *College Rules!* we know quite a few business majors having a difficult time finding the job they'd hoped for. New opportunities will arise that no one can predict—could anyone in your parents' generation have predicted the number of jobs created by the Internet? So our best advice is to use your college years to build skills that will apply to a variety of possible careers—skills such as written and verbal communication, computing, organizing, and problem solving.

If You Read Nothing Else, Read This

○ Figure out your interests and strengths before you choose a major. Use the resources available to you on campus and on the Internet to help make your decision.

○ Choosing a major does not mean you are stuck in only one career path. Rather than focusing on your eventual career, focus on choosing a major that requires you to do the things you enjoy (such as writing, painting, solving problems, working in a lab).

○ Talk to everyone you can about your choice of major before you decide. And don't let anyone pressure you to settle too quickly. Take your time as you make your choice.

CHAPTER 6

CLASSES, WORK, AND PLAY: ADJUSTING TO THE DEMANDS OF COLLEGE

- Worried that you'll have to make a gazillion adjustments to succeed in college?
- Concerned that you'll never have time to play?
- Think that you'll need to have your nose in a book all the time?

If so, read on . . .

Your professors may have different beliefs than you do about why you are in college in the first place. Most likely, your professors have the almost idealistic belief that you actually want to get an education, that you hang on their every word, that you are inspired by their infinite wisdom (college professors tend to have rather large egos), that your major goal is to learn as much _____ (whatever it is they are teaching—you fill in the blank) as possible, no matter how much time and effort it takes. Do these people think you have no life?

You, on the other hand, have only a slightly different view of why you are in college: to land a good job and make a gazillion bucks by the time you're twenty-five.

Sure, it's important to learn stuff in college, but in the end you believe that it's the grade that counts and the job you'll get and the money you'll make—not how much you've really learned. Besides, if you took things as seriously as some of your professors, you'd be like a monk—locked up in your room studying from sunrise to sunset, leaving your room only to go to class and be enlightened by one of those ego-ridden professors. Not your idea of fun, right?

Okay, okay, both of these beliefs are extreme. There is a happy medium among getting an education (actually learning something—learning a lot, even), playing and having a social life, and working if you choose or need to. But before you can think about balancing everything, it's important to put the demands of college into perspective and to think a little about the changes you may need to make in order to make a smooth adjustment to college. Think of it as training for the real world—that day when you have to transition all over again into the world of work.

> The unfortunate thing about this world is that the good habits are much easier to give up than the bad ones.
>
> —W. Somerset Maugham

Lots of Changes

We said in the first chapter that college is different from high school. College requires you to think differently, act differently, deal with things differently. Once you understand that you are probably going to have to make some changes in most aspects of managing your life, you have half the battle won. It doesn't matter whether you are an eighteen-year-old going away to school, an older student returning to school, or someone testing the waters at the local community college; it's important to understand that you will need to make adjustments. It's time to grow up, just a little bit.

THE ROLLER-COASTER RIDE: EMOTIONAL ADJUSTMENTS

If you have mixed emotions as you arrive on campus and try to find your way, don't think you're alone. On the one hand, you're so excited about all the freedom you'll have that you can hardly stand it. On the other hand, the idea that it's time to cut the cord, take on additional responsibility, and not have mom and dad right there to bail you out of jams may be a bit scary. Even for students who actually like the idea of having "helicopter parents," being on their own can be an exhilarating feeling. For eighteen-year-olds heading off to college, the first term in school can be an emotional roller coaster—trying (and expected) to be an adult (or at least act like one), but still wanting (and needing) to be a kid. If you are returning to college after some years in the workforce, you may feel out of place (read: old) surrounded by all those young faces or guilty about spending time away from your family.

Your emotions during those first few weeks on campus will range from raw fear to sheer elation. Almost all new students are nervous about meeting their roommates, finding out where their classes are, figuring out how everything is done, making good grades, fitting in—the list goes on and on. Understand that (1) thousands—no, millions—of students have done this before you and survived; and (2) you are not alone.

FOR ADULTS ONLY X

Starting or returning to college after several years of raising a family or being in the workplace poses special concerns and adjustments. Few older students are prepared for the amount of adjusting they'll need to make. For some, this adjustment is easier, especially if family members help out or the student doesn't have a full-time job. But even if you don't have the ideal situation, don't despair. Many campuses offer special support groups for nontraditional students that can be very beneficial.

PARTY ON . . . SOMETIMES: SOCIAL ADJUSTMENTS

It's important to have a good social network in college. Most of you reading *College Rules!* have probably been in the same social situation for quite a long time. You have gone to high school with the same group of people and have friends that you hang out and interact with socially—maybe even since kindergarten. This changes, however, once you head to college. Students who attend school away from home and live in a residence hall with lots of other students may have the most difficult time adjusting socially. New students may feel afraid that they won't fit in or that they will have a difficult time making friends. On the other hand, returning students may feel they have little in common with students fresh out of high school. Students who feel socially isolated often lack the support system that is necessary to being successful in college. To make adjusting socially a little easier, here are some tips; and remember, somewhere out there on campus, there are students who are like you in some way. You just have to find them.

- If you're living on campus, get in touch with your roommate before you move in. Most schools try to match students who have some general things in common; others have roommate-matching websites where you can find students with whom you might be compatible. Usually, you will feel better once you have talked to your future roommate before arriving on campus. (Of course, this can backfire. If you talk with your future roommate either by phone or through email and she comes across as a real freak, you may have more anxiety than you did before.)

> Experience is a hard teacher because she gives the test first, the lesson afterwards.
>
> —Vernon Saunders Law

- Think about joining a club or community service organization where other members share common interests. Some students "go Greek" just because they stand a good chance of meeting others with similar beliefs and interests. Other students find clubs that sound interesting and join them just to find out more (for example, there is a Zen meditation club on our campus). Still others become involved in residence life or student government. Just remember, no matter how small or large your campus, there is something for everyone.

- If you live in a residence hall, get involved. Dorms offer both academic and social programs. These are good places to meet new people. If you don't live on campus, become part of other student groups or check out the campus newspaper to see what kinds of events are going on.

- If your campus has a peer mentor or faculty mentor program, sign up. Such programs provide great opportunities for not only adjusting socially but also making important connections with faculty, which can help you down the line.

- Be open-minded. Be willing to try new things. College represents new beginnings—a place to reinvent yourself and discover other interests.

- Join a study group. Although study groups shouldn't be social groups per se, they can help you meet other students. And they actually work better for studying when they don't include your good friends.

Knowing where you are going is all you need to get there.

—Carl Frederick

- Don't forget about the play and fun part of college and be sure you build it into your schedule. It's almost as important as study time.

Whatever ways you choose to become socially connected, get to know other students. Find a group of students to hang out with. Students who have social support also tend to do better academically.

SAD BUT TRUE

Paula was having a very difficult time adjusting to being away from home. She had left a boyfriend behind, one who was several years older than she and had decided that college just wasn't for him, at least not at this time. Since home was only a short two-hour drive away, Paula would make the drive to see her boyfriend and hometown friends every Friday afternoon and then return to campus each Sunday evening. During the week, she pretty much kept to herself and failed to make friends from her dorm or her classes. She said she just wanted to concentrate on studying during the week so she wouldn't have to worry about getting schoolwork done over the weekend when she was with her boyfriend. But by midterm, Paula was miserable. Her feelings of not wanting to be in school in the first place only increased and it became harder and harder for her to keep her mind on her courses. She lived for the weekends, when she could go home and be with friends. She made a feeble attempt at making friends with others on her hall, but they had already formed social groups and were active in a variety of things on campus. When they invited her to join them, she turned them down because she either had to study or wasn't going to be there on the weekends. So they quit asking, and she was pretty much alone all week. To Paula's credit, she did keep up her grades that first semester but then withdrew from the university and went home to attend a community college so she could be closer to her boyfriend and high school friends.

SHOW ME THE $: FINANCIAL ADJUSTMENTS

We include a few words about financial adjustments mainly because we've seen too many students run amok academically because they have managed to get themselves into financial binds.

The money-management challenges of college are as vast and varied as the number of students attending. Some of you will continue to be supported by your parents; they will pay for your tuition, room, and board and provide you with spending money. You guys are really lucky. Others will have partial support and be expected to take out student loans for the remainder or to work part-time. You guys probably have to watch your pennies. Still others will have to work full-time to pay for school and other expenses and can go to school only part-time. You guys really have to watch your pennies.

Our goal here is not to give you a crash course on how to manage your finances. We simply want to warn you about a problem that is becoming more pervasive on college campuses: students are graduating with a degree, sometimes hefty student loans to repay, and thousands of dollars of credit card debt. In fact, we'd bet if you walked across your campus right now, you would see at least two companies offering T-shirts (or some other junk) for signing up for a credit card.

A word to the wise: whatever your financial situation in college, learn early on how to manage your money wisely. You can use your college years to establish credit by getting one credit card with a low credit limit and paying it off monthly. Don't spend what you don't have. Aim to live within your means, not for instant gratification. If you begin college by using a credit card judiciously, you will probably continue to do so throughout your college career and beyond. We know this is easier said than done. And as with most things, you'll need to use self-control. Credit card companies want you to spend beyond your means (that's how they stay in business), but don't fall for it.

As dorky as it may sound, the best way to keep yourself in sound financial health is to set up a budget and stick to it. For example, if you budget $100 per month for credit card expenditures, you really have to resist going out and spending double that for a new outfit just because you want it. If you let want rather than need rule your budget, you will constantly be in the hole. So figure out how much it costs you to live and then live within your means.

There are all kinds of nifty websites or free software available for you to download that will frankly discuss everything you should know about managing credit cards while in college. Check out edfund.org for information on handling finances and also great information about student loans. It is best to get a handle on responsible credit card use before you attend your first college class. Until recently, this has been one life skill that's rarely taught in high school.

BUT WHO'S GOING TO WAKE ME UP OR WASH MY CLOTHES?: LIVING ADJUSTMENTS

For some of you, life before college was pretty cushy. Your parents cooked your meals, made sure you ate right, and did your laundry. They kicked your butt out of bed in the morning and maybe even cleaned your room. Life was easy. Life was good. But you didn't realize it at the time. Now you're in charge of just about everything.

We realize that what we are about to say may seem like a no-brainer. I mean, how difficult can it be to do your own laundry, especially when everything you need is in the basement of your residence hall? Light colors with light, dark colors with dark. How hard can it be to eat right when you still have someone preparing most of your meals and you have such a big selection of food to choose from? Just eat something from each of the food groups and go light on the fats. And how hard can it be to keep a very small dorm room cleaned up? A place for everything and everything in its place.

Well, at times it can be pretty hard. It's not that doing laundry is so difficult—insert enough quarters into machine, fill washer, add clothes and

If you find yourself having money problems, don't be in denial about it. Things will only get worse and wind up affecting you academically and emotionally. Seek out assistance if you need to. Many campuses offer financial literacy courses often taught by peer counselors. Such courses are usually designed primarily for entering freshmen; these courses discuss the principles of managing your money—with considerable emphasis on responsible credit card use. If your campus offers such a course, sign yourself up, especially if you have never really had to manage money before or if you have and you weren't very good at it.

soap—easy enough. It's somehow finding the time (and motivation) that's the hard part. And eating—going to the dining hall and finding something good to eat is not the hard part. (Isn't pizza one of the major food groups?) What's hard is eating in a healthy way so you don't put on the dreaded "freshman fifteen," which really is very common. And the hard part about keeping a very small dorm room clean is that it is, well, small. There's no place to put all that stuff you need on a daily basis.

We mention this because all these little things add up to other ways you'll have to adjust. In early phone calls or emails, most students tell their mom and dad, "I never realized before how much you do for me!" (Note: try to wait until the second call home to ask for more money.) The good news is that most students figure out how to do all these things for themselves. They find time between all their studying and other activities to get the laundry done. Some even turn this chore into a studying session. After putting on a few pounds, they learn that the only way not to pork up is to eat less, eat healthier, and get some regular exercise. And they find creative ways to cram all their stuff into a small space. On our campus, for example, there are more loft companies than you can shake a stick at.

THE INSIDE SCOOP

Ever heard of the Buckley Amendment? What about FERPA (Federal Education Rights and Privacy Act)? According to the Buckley Amendment and FERPA, once you are enrolled in college, you are considered an adult, regardless of your chronological age. What this means is that your parents cannot get information about your progress in college without your permission. Your grades are sent to you, and any other information about test scores, fees, and so forth is also sent to you. (P.S. You may want to pass this tidbit on to your parents, especially if they are, you know, clingy.)

HITTING THE BOOKS: ACADEMIC ADJUSTMENTS

Academic adjustments may be more difficult to make than any of the others, although all the other changes influence academics. One of the first adjustments you will have to make is to realize that everyone on your campus is smart—maybe even smarter than you. Remember those geeks in high school who always did their homework, aced the tests, learned effortlessly (or so it seemed), and didn't work nearly as hard as you did? Well, guess who's sitting next to you in History, English, and Precalculus? The very same. So what does this mean? It means the competition for good grades is high—and in order to be competitive, you're going to have to make some academic adjustments. This isn't high school anymore. Although we'll discuss this idea in more detail later in the book (our focus in *College Rules!* is on academics), we'll briefly list some of these academic adjustments here:

- Assuming greater responsibility for your own learning

- Being more open-minded and receptive to new (different) ideas

- Doing lots of reading that you will be held accountable for

- Adjusting to stiffer competition

- Setting goals and working toward achieving them

- Having and sustaining motivation

- Developing time-management skills

- Understanding that it's not just about studying more, it's about studying smarter

Some students make these adjustments quickly, but it takes a while for the average student to get it together. The best way to balance all the things you have to do is to take it a little at a time. Make small changes first and stick with them. You'll wake up one morning and find that you can handle this college thing pretty well.

Characteristics of Well-Rounded Students

In order to get the most out of college, you need to have experiences beyond the classroom. The student who graduates with only a degree and an impressive grade point average has missed out on a lot. There's so much to experience in college these days that it's hard to imagine why any student wouldn't want to get involved. The students we know who have been most successful—both as undergraduate and graduate students and in the world of work—are those who make the most of what college has to offer, both in and out of the classroom. These students are happy with themselves in many respects and feel allegiance to their school. They believe they have gotten their money's worth out of a college education and that it has prepared them for the world in many respects. Many of the friends they make are friends for life. What do these students have in common?

- Not only do they earn good grades, but they also actually like to learn.

- They know that learning and studying require effort and they are willing to put in that effort.

- They balance academics, work, and play.

- They are involved in extracurricular activities, including some sort of volunteer work—"service learning" as it is currently referred to.

- They set and reach goals.

- They have strong networks of friends and family to help support them emotionally.

- They have connected with several faculty members.

- They enjoy being students.

- They have a variety of interests and hobbies.

- They take time for themselves.

- They budget their time (and their money) wisely.

- They take responsibility for their actions.

- They take care of their health.

- They are help-seekers.

- And sometimes they just have to make some noise to let off steam.

Getting the most out of college and being academically successful requires you to maintain balance in your life. If the only thing you do is stay cooped up in your room and study all the time, you'll be unhappy. If all you do is socialize, you may be happy for a while, but you won't stay in school very long. So work it out. All college students need to work hard, play hard, and have some downtime.

Brent had looked forward to going off to college ever since he could remember. His older brother, Sid, had just graduated and had lots of stories about how much fun it had been. Sid had also warned Brent that he would have to prioritize. There was so much to get involved in that it was easy not to study. Brent paid attention to all the fun things his brother had told him and sort of ignored the studying part. Brent wanted to be part of a fraternity and pledged one of the most social frats on campus during his first semester. He loved it! Lots of parties. Lots of new friends to hang with. It seemed as if something was going on every night. His social life was full, and he was having a blast. Before he knew it, midterm was upon him and he slowed down enough to take stock of how he was doing in his classes. He had started the semester with five three-credit courses and was doing so horribly that he withdrew from two of them. He was down to nine hours and had a respectable grade in only one of his classes. Now Brent started getting anxious, but he wasn't going to let this interfere with his social life. Besides, he knew he'd be able to pull it out in the end . . . just as he had always done.

Brent's story brings to light the importance of balancing your life as a college student. Majoring in partying may be fun for a while, but know that it can't go on forever. At some point you have to be accountable for your actions—the good ones and those that aren't so good. But you can have it all. You just have to work at it a bit.

If You Read Nothing Else, Read This

○ Transitioning to college means lots of change and adjustments. You'll have to adjust emotionally, socially, financially, domestically, and academically. Tough, we know. But you can do it.

○ Well-rounded students take advantage of what their college has to offer both inside and outside of the classroom. Being a well-rounded student means more than just hitting the books.

CHAPTER 7

TIMELY TIPS: THE ABC (& D)S OF TIME MANAGEMENT

- Worried that you'll never have enough time to get all your work done and still have a life?
- Concerned that you'll have to study eight days a week in order to make good grades?
- Think that you'll be so stressed out and overworked that you won't ever be able to just relax?

If so, read on . . .

The only thing you have in common with every other college student is the same number of hours in a day to get everything done—24 big ones. That's 24 hours in a day, 168 hours in a week, 672 hours in a month (give or take a few). Sounds like lots of time to get things done, doesn't it? It should be plenty of time, as long as you are not a master at the art of procrastination—and as long as you can make a pledge to spend forty hours a week at your job, which for the next four years or so is being a college student.

The Forty-Hour Mindset

One of the most difficult adjustment issues that students face when they enter college is learning to effectively and efficiently manage their time. Students and professors alike believe that lack of time-management skills leads many students down dangerous paths. If you are entering college right out of high school, most of your time has probably been managed for you. You were in school all day, and when you came home, your parents may have made sure you did your homework and fulfilled many other responsibilities. If you had a job, you probably worked a limited number of hours. It's likely that someone else also took care of your basic needs for food, shelter, and so forth. It's quite possible that you really didn't have to worry very much about finding time to get things done and that many things were actually done for you.

In college, things are different. You will be in class only a few hours each day (and perhaps not at all on some days), no one will be watching over your shoulder to make sure you get things done, and no one will clean your room or do your laundry for you. At first glance, this may seem like the ideal situation—that you will have loads of free time. You can live in as big a mess as you

DO YOUR HOMEWORK

Try making a schedule of all the things you have to do in a complete seven-day week. Put in your classes; work and family obligations; time to eat, sleep, get dressed, and so on; and other commitments. Count up the number of hours per week that you have already committed. How many of the 168 hours do you have left? Are you doing your job—being a student—for forty hours a week? You'll need to know this information as we progress through this chapter.

FOR ADULTS ONLY Ⓧ

If you are a returning student or one who has to work twenty or more hours a week, you may think that the forty-hour rule doesn't apply to you. How could it? Where in the world will you find forty hours to devote to academics if you have a family and also work, even part-time? You may have some decisions to make, because if you plan on taking a full load (usually twelve or fifteen hours) you will have to follow the forty-hour mindset. That may mean getting fewer hours of sleep, spending less time with your family, and eating more fast food. The alternative is to ease into college life. Take a lighter load as a way of adjusting, and see how it goes.

😞 **SAD BUT TRUE**

Angela was having a tremendously difficult time fitting everything into her schedule. She just couldn't understand where all the time went and why she never seemed to complete anything on time—or, if she did, she knew it wasn't her best work. After some encouragement, she made an appointment to talk with one of us. Angela's busy schedule and courses were indeed demanding, but it seemed as though she should have ample time for everything. So, to find out just what the heck she was doing with her time, she was instructed to write down how she spent her time (every waking minute) for a week and then come back for a second appointment.

When she returned (on time) for the next appointment, she had an almost embarrassed look on her face. She confessed, "You won't believe this, but I think I'm spending five hours a day eating. Well, not really eating but just sitting in the dining hall after I've finished and talking with friends, socializing. Most days I'm okay at breakfast but spend anywhere from two to three hours for lunch and another couple hours at dinner. I never realized I was doing this." Angela had diagnosed her own problem, but could she do something about it? It was really hard for her, but she stuck to it, making small changes at first, and eventually salvaging almost three hours daily that she could then spend getting other things done. It made a tremendous difference in so many areas of her life.

want to, you can wear dirty underwear, and, best of all, there's no one to bug you about stuff. It should be easy to get everything done in a relaxed, orderly fashion. Well, think again. Fitting everything into a reasonable schedule is the number-one problem many college students have.

So where do you start? We suggest that you take a pledge to get into the forty-hour mindset. Please repeat: "I pledge to put at least forty hours a week into being a student. Cross my heart and hope to die." Why forty hours?

It's the standard number of hours in a traditional work week, and it's probably the least number of hours per week that you will be expected to spend on the job once you graduate from college. But anyone who has a full-time job will tell you that sometimes you have to spend more than forty hours a week, because some tasks require more time and effort than others and you have to work until the job gets done. That's why we call it a mindset: start with forty hours in mind, but adjust the time so you can get your job—being a successful student—done right. Remember, these forty hours (or so) include your time in class, reading and study time, meeting with study groups, doing library research—anything that has to do with your academics.

With the exception of the hours you spend in class, which are fixed, you can "be a student" at any other time during the week that suits you. You can study at 2:00 in the afternoon or 4:00 in the morning. You can go to the library on Saturday or Sunday afternoon or 10:00 Wednesday night. Once you figure out your prime time for studying

Perhaps the most valuable result of all education is the ability to make yourself do the thing you have to do, when it ought to be done, whether you like it or not.

—Aldous Huxley

and learning, your schedule can be quite flexible. The world will be your oyster. Your busy life can be quite manageable and fairly stress-free. Ah—if it were only that easy.

The Alphabet Approach: ABC (& D)s of Managing Your Life

Three truisms about time management should be etched in your memory as you begin your college career:

- Truism #1: Time flies.

- Truism #2: Everything takes longer than you think it will.

- Truism #3: No matter what you are doing at this minute, in most cases, you would rather be doing something else.

Now that we have that out of the way, think about how you can use the 168 hours you have each week in such a way that you can meet all your academic requirements and still have plenty of time for sleep, play, and perhaps even work, not to mention those all-important out-of-the-classroom experiences that make your time in college so rich. (Remember, you've pledged to spend only about one-quarter of those 168 hours being a student.)

Managing your time (and yourself) is as easy as A, B, C, and, well, D. All you need to do is

- A = Anticipate and plan.
- B = Break tasks down.
- C = Cross things off.
- D = Don't procrastinate.

A = ANTICIPATE AND PLAN

No student (not a single, solitary one) should be without some sort of tool to keep track of her busy life. It can be as simple as a paper daily planner or calendar or as high-tech as a Blackberry. Whatever the cost or complexity, it needs to be something portable enough to carry with you. And you need to be able to see at least a week at a time so projects or tests or papers don't sneak up on you. Be sure you have it on the first day of class, because the planning for the rest of the term will begin on day one. Trying to catch up on time management is like trying to catch up on sleep—it's almost impossible to do.

Remember what we said about everything taking longer than you think? That's why the first rule of managing your life is to anticipate and plan. If you think about things in advance and try to at least plan out the certainties, you will have enough flexibility and wiggle room in your schedule to handle unexpected happenings like illness, a family crisis, or an additional paper being thrown at you at the last minute. Would you wait until Friday to try to get a date for your fraternity formal on Saturday? Would you try to plan a surprise birthday party for your best friend two days before her birthday? Chances are, if you did, things wouldn't work out very well.

The best way to attack the academic planning thing is to do the following:

LISTEN UP

You may have heard through the grapevine that you should spend at least two hours out of class (studying) for every hour you spend in class. This advice is not particularly accurate, although it's probably not a bad rule of thumb. For example, if you are taking a three-hour course that is really difficult for you, you may need to spend considerably more than six hours per week studying the material outside of class. On the other hand, if you're taking a three-hour course that is a piece of cake, it wouldn't be very efficient to spend six hours hitting the books. So use common sense. Difficult courses require more time; easy courses require less. Be flexible.

- Once you have your class schedule for the term set (and you've finished adding and dropping courses), block out those class times in your planner for the whole semester.

- Carefully go through the syllabus for each course and note test dates or dates on which projects or papers are due. If the professor changes the date, be sure to change it in your planner as well. (We recommend writing in pencil in case things do change.)

- If there are other certainties in your life that you know you will have to consider in planning your forty hours a week as a student, note those as well. For example, if you are a member of an organization that meets at the same time every week or month, block out those periods of time. If you work, block out the hours you work as soon as you know them. If you exercise every day at 2:00, block that out as well.

Now you're ready to block out reading, study, and test-preparation time. If you have fifteen hours of class per week, that leaves you around twenty-five hours to be a student in other ways. Ask yourself these questions as you plan this time:

- When are you most alert? Are you a morning or an evening person? If you try to study at 8:00 A.M. and you don't become human until noon, you'll just be wasting time.

- Are you going to be able to study where you live or will you need to go somewhere that has fewer distractions, such as the library or a study room in your dorm?

- Are you going to be able to discipline yourself to study on weekends or should you just plan on getting all your schoolwork done during the week? Are there other nights when you know you just won't hit the books? On our campus, for example, Thursday is a big party night. If you know you will want to go out along with everyone else on Thursday, be honest about it and adjust your schedule accordingly.

- How difficult are your courses this term? If you have a couple of really hard courses, you may have to put in more than forty hours a week being a student, unless you have an easier course to balance things out. Keep in mind that the forty-hour thing is a mindset, not a hard-and-fast rule.

- When do you have blocks of time you can use for extended studying? Ten minutes here and ten minutes there is fine for reviewing. But studying for ten minutes at a clip won't turn you into a scholar. Studying every day for a good block of time may.

- Do you already know you have a procrastination problem? If so, what small steps can you take today to start fixing the problem?

Once you have answered these questions, you should have an idea of which courses will require more work and which will require less, be able to set reasonable goals for getting your work done on time, and be able to block out some quality study time. By "quality," we mean that you'll be alert and geared up for learning and that you'll be in a place relatively distraction-free. Set up study blocks of two to three hours with short breaks (five or ten minutes every hour or so) planned into them. Block out these times the first week of class and see how it goes. The good thing about anticipating and planning is that you can continue to tweak your schedule so it works for you. Just stick to the forty-hour mindset. Remember, you made a pledge. We know it seems as if we're asking a lot here, but once you get the hang of it, it gets easier.

B = BREAK TASKS DOWN

Whether you're faced with a really huge task, such as completing your degree in four years, or a much smaller task, such as studying for a psychology exam, it's easier to muster the will to stick to it if you break it down into smaller, manageable parts. Even keeping up with your reading assignments can be much less painful if you read half the pages of a chapter in one sitting and the rest in a second sitting later in the same day. Students tell us one of the terrible consequences of procrastinating is that when you finally get around to doing a task, it seems insurmountable. And when things seem insurmountable, they are generally done less than adequately or not at all.

As you decide how you will spend your forty hours per week, think about the things you will have to complete over the semester and, right from the start, break them down into smaller tasks. For example, suppose you have a project due for your anthropology class at midterm. You have to write an eight-page paper and then do a fifteen-minute PowerPoint presentation to the class on the highlights. This type of assignment is actually more difficult and will require more time than you may believe. Always remember: everything takes longer than you think it will. You have

If you have been using a hands-off approach to time management, you may have some trouble adjusting to using a schedule. Some students say they just don't want the bother of having to keep track of everything. However, when we talk to students in academic trouble, time (and self-) management is the number-one cause of their problems. They just can't seem to bring everything they need to class, keep up with assignments, or even pay bills on time. But trust us, a schedule can really help—and you will probably feel less stressed as well. To adjust to keeping a schedule, start with a two-week span. Write down everything you need to do for the next two weeks and then consult your schedule at least once a day. You will be amazed at how much you can get done once you know what you have to do.

to select a relatively narrow topic, spend time in the library and on the Web finding information, synthesize what you find, write an outline and a couple of drafts, and be sure to have your citations done correctly—and all that's before you've even started making the PowerPoint slides and practicing your class presentation. That's a lot. Unless you start breaking this large task down into smaller pieces and getting started way before the due date, you will be burning the midnight oil trying to put together something acceptable to meet the deadline. But you want to do better than just acceptable work. You want to be exceptional. So break tasks down. Here's how.

1. Look at the big picture first. Be sure you clearly understand what the end product is supposed to look like. Ask your prof to show you some examples from previous classes.

2. Look at the parts. What pieces will enable you to get to the whole? Figure out step-by-step what you need to do—it's not going to happen through magic.

3. Think about the logical order of completing the pieces. What should you do first, second, last?

4. Put yourself on a time line for completing the task. Most students find it helpful to work backward. Put in the date the project is due first and then set your deadline dates from there.

5. Have a plan to help you stay on track. Put the time you will spend on the project into your study schedule so you can set aside the hours for it. And then stick

with it, stick with it, stick with it. Overkill, you say? Maybe, but a plan is good only if you see it through.

6. Complete it early enough to have some time left for a final go-through and cleanup.

Keep in mind that you can even break smaller, less overwhelming tasks, such as reading assignments, into manageable parts. This strategy works particularly well for courses that require heavy reading, such as history. On our campus, students enrolled in an introductory history course have an average of one hundred pages to read a week in this class alone! That's more than some of you may have read in a month in high school. But if you take those one hundred pages and break them down with the plan of reading some history six out of seven days in a week, you would only have to read about sixteen pages per day. So what would you rather do, read sixteen pages per day or be eight hundred pages behind by the time the first exam rolls around?

⚡ **GET WIRED**

Many students like to use an online calendar so they know they can access it from wherever they are at the moment. Often colleges will have a calendar program for students to download and use. Or check out Microsoft Outlook or another software program to help you keep track of your time. And from our perspective, Google's calendar feature is awesome. Once you have a calendar (online or paper) that you like, take a look at 43folders.com for excellent tips about time management and getting things done. It is all about improving organization and improving your ability to be productive while you work so you can enjoy the rest of your day.

C = CROSS THINGS OFF

We are both "to-do" list freaks. In fact, everyone we know who manages their time effectively uses some form of list where they can cross things off as they are completed. Making to-do lists serves a couple of purposes. First, and most obvious, it lets you see what you need to get accomplished. It serves as a sort of memory-jogger so you don't forget things that have to get done. Students are busy people with a variety of commitments, and to-do lists can help keep life more manageable. Second, to-do lists act as psychological boosters because as you do the things you have listed, you cross them off. This gives you a feeling of accomplishment.

You can make all kinds of to-do lists. Perhaps the most common type—and maybe even the type that is the most helpful—is the immediate to-do list. As the name implies, it's a listing of things you need to get done within a brief period of time: a day, a few days, maybe even as long as a week. Often, immediate to-do lists include minor sorts of tasks that don't take much time but are easily forgotten. These lists can include both classroom and nonclassroom activities. A list might look something like this:

TO DO THURSDAY:

Read history pp. 230-253

Do laundry!!!! (at least 2 loads)

Meet with biology study group 8-9 P.M.

12 Statistics problems—ch. 8

As you get things finished, cross them off. Add other things to the list as they come up. You can keep a running list for a week or so and then start fresh.

But to-do lists can also be more long term as well. You can make a list at the beginning of the term that covers major projects you need to complete by the end of the term. Also included on this type of list are smaller things that need to be done by a later date but not immediately. List each item, along with the date it is due, beginning with what needs to be completed first. As each is taken care of, cross it off. A long-term list might look something like this.

TO DO:	DATE DUE:
History term paper	April 16
Plan Dad's surprise party	February 1
MIS project	April 17
	(weekly meetings Tues. 8 p.m.)
Talk to friends about spring-break plans	by February 15

One final comment about lists: once you make a list, clip it in a convenient place in your daily planner, somewhere you are sure to look at. Each time you make a new list, put it in the same place so you know where to look for it. Making lists and then not using them will hardly lead to good time-management skills.

Dan, a junior genetics major, was a hard-core procrastinator who followed the usual pattern. He consistently (and consciously) put off changing his behavior "until tomorrow." He even joked about the problem with his friends. While he usually managed to pull things off at the last minute, earning low Cs on exams and eking out passing grades on papers and projects, Dan found that his stress level was becoming almost unmanageable. He was taking a couple of really hard courses in his major, and he had slid by for so long that now he didn't even know where to start. He couldn't keep up at all, not even enough to get by. On top of the stress, he started feeling extremely guilty about his shoddy work habits. He knew he could do better, and he really was interested in some of his courses. The crowning blow came the morning he overslept and almost missed a major exam because he had stayed up late trying to cram. He made it to the test but made a low D.

Now Dan decided to get some help with his procrastination problems. He went to a couple of workshops, talked with an academic counselor in the learning center, and made a real attempt to change his ways. At first it was really difficult. He continued to make some low grades, but he stuck with it. Much to his surprise, his grades improved somewhat and he began feeling better about himself. Although procrastination may always be a problem for Dan, his deciding to make even small changes influenced him positively in a number of ways.

D = DON'T PROCRASTINATE

If for most of your life you have followed the credo "Always put off until tomorrow what you don't have to do today," you stand a good chance of taking this attitude off to college with you. Procrastination is a major problem for many, many college students. Just ask any student on any campus. Procrastinating can get you into academic hot water and affect other aspects of your life. At worst, it can cause you to be a weak student and, at best, a mediocre one. Unfortunately, it may be the most difficult problem to mend, because for some people procrastination is simply a way of life. Procrastinators not only tend to put things off, but they also tend to be late for everything—classes, meetings, dates. Although some people will tell you they thrive on the stress that

> Things may come to those who wait, but only the things left by those who hustle.
>
> —Abraham Lincoln

procrastination brings, we don't believe them for one minute. We all nee
iety and stress in our lives, not more.

In a nutshell, procrastinators tend not to use their time wisely, particularly small pockets of time. The ten to fifteen minutes between classes or time spent grabbing a snack could instead be spent reviewing lecture notes or practicing vocabulary for French class. These small blocks can add up in the long run. If you review your lecture notes for economics fifteen minutes each day, you add seventy-five minutes of extra study time to this course each week. That's significant.

We see students like Dan all the time. The scenario usually goes something like this: Student feels guilty (often very guilty) for getting behind in her work. She wakes up in the morning panic-stricken about all the things she has to do and vows that "tonight's the night!" Tonight comes and she sits down at her desk and looks for any excuse possible not to study (usually this is unconscious behavior): Can't find the book. Need to make just one phone call. Something cold to drink might help. Then the real excuse arrives: someone bursts into her room inviting her to go get pizza. "Yes," she says and promises herself (again) that she'll start on her studying routine tomorrow night. Don't let procrastination be a way of life for you. Manage your time right from the start. Make it a habit to take care of business first. Then go out and party down.

The Advantages of Excelling at Time Management

We return to the idea we presented at the beginning of this chapter: the only thing every college student has in common is a day with twenty-four hours in it. It is your choice how you use those hours. You can be productive and stay on top of things and still have ample time for those out-of-classroom learning experiences that are also important. The alternative is that you squander your time, have little to show for it, and end up feeling bad about yourself.

You probably already know the advantages of managing your time effectively, but we list a few here as a way of further convincing you of the importance of starting college on the right foot. Even if you have been the world's worst

It is more than probable that the average man could, with no injury to his health, increase his efficiency fifty percent.

—Walter Scott

procrastinator, you have a chance to make a fresh start in college. If you can learn to manage your time and your life, you will

- **Have less stress in your life.** Less stress is always good.

- **Have more time for the things you want to do.** Fun is good too. It's hard to go out and have fun if you're worried about all the things you haven't done.

- **Be a more well-rounded student.** Remember, well-rounded students (those who have lots of different experiences) get the most out of college.

- **Be able to spend more time with friends.** Social connections are important, and everyone needs to have time to laugh with friends.

- **Learn more.** Efficient learners get more from their classes than those who keep trying to figure out how to study and learn effectively.

- **Play more.** Everyone loves to play. No one has ever said on his or her deathbed, "Gee, I regret that I didn't work more."

- **Feel good about yourself.** When you feel good about your academic accomplishments, it spills over into other parts of your life and gives you confidence.

- **Be envied by all.** Absolutely.

We can't stress strongly enough the importance of managing your time. Entire books have been written on the subject, and businesses spend huge sums of money to provide time-management training to their employees. It's a skill you will need for life.

If You Read Nothing Else, Read This

- O **Follow the forty-hour mindset if you want to succeed academically. Be involved in academics at least forty hours a week and you should do well.**

- O **Follow the ABC (& D)s of time management: anticipate and plan, break tasks down, cross things off, and don't procrastinate.**

- O **The advantages of effective time management are great, including having less stress in your life and feeling good about yourself.**

CHAPTER 8

"I THINK I CAN, I THINK I CAN": GETTING AND STAYING MOTIVATED

- Concerned about your motivation level?
- Worried that you never seem to reach the goals you set for yourself?
- Think that you need big, fat rewards in order to complete even the smallest task?

If so, read on . . .

Believe it or not, you are always motivated to do something. It may be only to watch TV, talk on the phone, or sleep, but you are motivated toward something (right now, you are motivated to read *College Rules!*). For a college student, however, the key is to be motivated to do the right things at the right time. Although it is tempting to blame a lack of motivation on others (a really dull professor, your roommate who parties all the time, a lack of sleep), you are responsible for your own motivation. That's right. No one else can motivate you to do anything if you do not have your own internal motivation. Because of this and because motivation can be so fleeting—here one minute, gone the next—you need strategies for staying motivated, even in courses you don't like.

We have said it time and time again: "Show us a student who's motivated and is willing to work smart, and we'll show you a successful student." Because motivation is so important to college success, it has been called the academic glue that holds everything together. This means that even in classes that are difficult for you, even if you aren't exactly using the most effective strategies for learning the information, even if you have had the worst day, you'll make it through (often exceedingly well) if you are motivated.

So how do you motivate yourself? The easiest place to begin is by thinking about your goals.

⊘ THE INSIDE SCOOP

Students are more motivated to do things when they are given choices and when the tasks are challenging but not overwhelming. Motivation is also higher when you can work with others and when you feel you have some control over reaching your learning goals. This explains why you may be very motivated to learn in one class and totally unmotivated in another. And if you are feeling unmotivated, you might want to think about how you can create a feeling of control to get yourself back on track.

Setting Goals You Can Accomplish

Students who set goals—both short-term and longer-term goals—are more motivated to complete those goals. Just think about anything you have accomplished: maybe learning to play soccer or guitar, finishing a challenging computer game, pulling off a successful surprise party, or planning a spring break vacation. You were probably very motivated to do that activity and you probably even set goals to achieve whatever it was you set out to do. In fact, although you might not have even been aware that you were setting and reaching goals, there is a very strong connection between motivation and goal setting. Chances are, you

> Even if you're on the right track, you'll get run over if you just sit there.
>
> —Arthur Godfrey

already set goals for personal things like losing weight or exercising, but you can and should set academic goals as well.

Having defined goals can help you become motivated even in courses you don't particularly like. But the way you set goals can also help you. Saying "I want to get an A in calculus" may not be enough. Instead, try to set smaller goals that will help you reach the ultimate goal of every college student—getting a degree.

Often we set goals that we never achieve. It may be human nature to do so or (more likely) it may be because of the kinds of goals we set. Saying "I want to be a better person" is great. But how will you ever know whether that goal has been achieved? Try this activity—jot down three academic goals you would like to reach within the next three months:

1. _____

2. _____

3. _____

Now check your goals to see if they meet the following criteria: are they specific, measurable, realistic, and flexible?

- **Specific.** Are your goals clearly defined? "I want to read twenty pages of history a night" is specific; "I want to read more" is not. In fact, if you find that you are unmotivated, make your goals ultraspecific. For example, instead of saying that you want to read twenty pages a night, create a specific reading schedule by defining exactly which pages you will read each night for a week. Setting specific goals will help you keep your eyes on the prize. But when goals are not specific, people tend to lose focus on achieving them.

- **Measurable.** Your goals should also be easily measured. It is easy to know whether or not you have reached your goal of reading those twenty pages of history, but it would be difficult to measure a goal of "reading more." Setting measurable goals helps you track your progress and keeps your motivation high.

> You are free to do whatever you like. You only need to face the consequences.
>
> —Sheldon Kopp

- **Realistic.** Can your goals be reached? Often people set goals that are unrealistic. For example, a student who wants to raise his cumulative GPA from a 2.0 to a 3.0 in one semester (or even one year) may find this goal is not even mathematically possible. A better goal may be to focus on earning better grades during the current semester.

- **Flexible.** Don't be too rigid in trying to achieve the goals you set. Sometimes when we're midway to our goals we realize we need to make adjustments. Suppose you had set a goal of achieving an A in chemistry. But you get very sick and miss two weeks of class, and after taking the first two exams, you realize you will be lucky to get out of the class with a passing grade. Rather than beating yourself up about not achieving everything you've set out to do, be flexible with your goals and set your sights on catching up on what you missed and understanding the course content instead of focusing solely on the grade.

SHORT-TERM, INTERMEDIATE, AND LONG-TERM GOALS

To keep your motivation up, it is important that you set three kinds of goals: short-term, intermediate, and long-term goals. Most people are good at setting long-term goals, like getting a college degree, finding true love, and making a lot of money. But it is the short-term and intermediate goals that will help you get there. A short-term goal might be to do fifteen practice problems in statistics each night. An intermediate goal might be to learn the basics of French this year.

SET PROCESS GOALS

Most of us do a fine job at setting outcome goals. That is, we set goals related to what we hope to achieve—getting a degree, speaking French, losing weight. But we rarely set process goals, or goals that describe what we will do to reach the desired outcome. Process goals are based on skills or knowledge you can acquire. A process goal might be to select key quotes as you read to help you write your English paper or to make vocabulary cards to help you learn French. Process goals help you reach your short-term and intermediate goals on the way to your long-term goals by helping you recognize how you will get there.

Haven't you heard? Smart is the new dumb. Seriously. In college, smart is the way to go. Recently, we asked our students to report to the class their progress on their goals for the semester, and anytime they said something even remotely academic or on target (related to goal setting), they would apologize. "I'm sorry I'm so geeky, but this really worked . . ." or "I know this is really anal, but checking things off a list helped. . . ." Every student saw the advantage of goal setting, but it seemed that all were reluctant to admit they cared. We say, embrace your inner smart person (or at least set some helpful goals).

SET YOUR GOALS AT THE RIGHT LEVEL

Your goals should be set at a level that may be a tiny bit beyond your grasp but not so far that they are completely out of reach. The ability to set goals at the right level (neither too low nor too high) is a skill that takes some practice. You need to consider such factors as tiredness, family and social commitments, and other outside influences when you set your goals. But don't set your goals too low, because there's little satisfaction in achieving goals you knew were too easy to begin with. Give yourself a challenge. Reaching goals that are slightly challenging can do wonders for your motivation and your confidence.

Take a look at the three goals you set earlier in this chapter. What changes, if any, do you need to make to these goals so you can successfully reach

Research has indicated that people who regularly set goals are more self-confident, concentrate better, and perform better. But the types of goals you set are also important in keeping your motivation up. So remember to set short-term, intermediate, and long-term goals.

There are several free Internet resources that will help you set and reach your goals. Many offer good advice on goal setting for things not academic (which is important too!). We like mygoals.com because they will send you email reminders (on the day and time you said you would be working on said goal) and help you track your progress toward your goal. You gotta love how technology can even help you achieve your goals.

them? Should they be more specific, more realistic, more challenging? Goal setting is intricately linked to motivation: the better you set (and reach) your goals, the more motivated you will be.

Getting Motivated

Whenever we ask our students to give advice to incoming freshman on how to get motivated, their responses always have something to do with staying on top of things or, as they often put it, "keeping up." There is nothing more unmotivating than falling behind. But it's easier to say we'll keep up than to do it. It is amazing how quickly schoolwork can pile up. Following are some simple suggestions to help you stay motivated.

Break big assignments into smaller chunks. Sometimes thinking about writing that big term paper is overwhelming. But if you break such a task into smaller, more manageable bits, it is much less intimidating. Selecting a topic early, making an outline, planning to visit the library several times, reading the papers of students who've taken the course in the past—all will help you avoid having to write the whole thing at the last minute. (See chapter 20 for more on writing research papers.)

Use the five-minute rule. The hardest part of tackling schoolwork is just getting started. The five-minute rule can really help with this. Simply put, tell yourself you will study for five minutes (you can do anything for five minutes, right?). At the end of that time, if you still are not motivated, you can stop. Most often, once you get started you will find that you won't stop after the set time.

Set goals for each study session. Goals for study sessions are even smaller than your short-term goals—in fact, consider these goals to be the kind that will help you achieve your short-term goals. Instead of planning to "study," which is not very specific, set a goal—to learn the material on cellular respiration in biology or to review the information on merchandising operations from last week's notes in accounting. Every time you sit down to study you should plan out exactly what you want to accomplish (learn) that session.

Reward yourself. One way to get yourself motivated to do something you may not want to do is to plan how you will reward yourself for getting the job done. Often students find this is a good way to begin a long hard task. The reward doesn't

SAD BUT TRUE ☹

Kyle, a freshman, just couldn't seem to get started on his schoolwork. Every day he'd come home from classes tired from a long day of thinking. There was no way, he thought, he could get right down to studying then. He'd hang out with his dorm-mates in the common room watching TV, listening to music, whatever. Around 6:30 the whole group would go to dinner, and usually they'd linger there till around 8:00 talking and generally having a good time. Because the weather had been so nice, Kyle and his friends usually played some ball after dinner—football, basketball, whatever struck their mood that evening. Often Kyle wouldn't get back to his room until around 11:00, when he was far too tired to study. Kyle had gotten into this pattern during the first few weeks of classes when there wasn't much reading or studying to do. Now that the semester was in full swing he knew he needed to make some changes, but he didn't want to miss out on the fun. Kyle had formed some habits that could really hurt his chances for success in college. Our advice to Kyle was to take an hour break after classes (relaxing with his friends) and then use the five-minute rule to get started studying. Although this helped some, Kyle also needed to reassess his motivation for being a college student: was it to hang out and play ball or to get a degree?

really have to be anything too extensive—maybe checking your email, going out with friends, or watching a movie. It just needs to be something you can look forward to doing or having after you study. But the only way the reward system can work is if you really get your work done (no skimping) before you give yourself the reward.

Seek help if you need it. If you use all these strategies but find you are still unmotivated, it may be that you need some help with the content. Often we meet students who say they have no motivation when in reality they just do not understand the course material. Sometimes the best way to get motivated is to find someone who can help you understand the information or find some interest in the topic. Don't just give up. Most colleges offer tutoring (often for free), so you can get a tutor, talk to the professor, or ask a classmate to help you. You just might find your motivation.

And Staying Motivated

Once you get motivated, the key to success is being able to stay motivated. We know that motivation ebbs and flows; what motivates you one day may not motivate you the next day. So use the following suggestions to help maintain your motivation to learn.

Use both intrinsic and extrinsic motivation. You probably have heard somewhere that only intrinsic (or internal) motivation is good and that extrinsic (or external) motivation, such as money or even grades, is not. We believe this really oversimplifies the complex concept of motivation. Usually people need both kinds of motivation to make it through school, and you need to use both to your advantage. For example, if you are enrolled in a class you don't really find interesting, you may initially focus on the external forces (testing, grades, and rewards) to get you going, but as you read and learn more about the topic, you may find yourself increasingly focused on the material. By the end of the semester, you may consider taking another course in the topic because now you are internally motivated to learn. Internal motivation is always more desirable because you usually learn more deeply, but extrinsic motivators can often lead you on this path.

Add variety. Change how long you study or even where you choose to study. Change the order of the topics you plan to study if you find you are getting bored (don't always start with math, then do history, then literature). Note, however, that some people do best by not adding variety to their studying. If you find that changing things throws you off task, keep your current routine for studying and add variety to your life in other ways—take a walk after studying or phone a friend instead of turning on the TV.

Organize a study group. Working with others can be very motivating. Create a study group to help you reach your goals. You may want to start out with one study partner instead of trying to work with several people. Have a plan for what you will do when you meet—maybe working sample problems or predicting (and answering) test questions.

Keep a schedule. We discussed the merits of good time management in the last chapter, but a schedule can help your motivation too. If you find your motivation slipping (this usually happens at least once a semester—around midterm or when the weather finally breaks), try hard to stick to your schedule. You'll find that it helps you recapture your motivation to get things done.

Use positive self-talk. When you speak positively to yourself ("I can do this"), you are much more successful than when you speak negatively ("I'll never get through this"). Every time you find you are telling yourself negative things, stop and try to turn them into something positive. Instead of telling yourself, "Everyone else is smarter than I am," say, "I know that with enough hard work, I can succeed on the next test." If you

FOR ADULTS ONLY ⊗

Returning students often find their motivation weakens as the semester goes on because they feel unconnected to college life (especially if they are attending part-time). Forming a study group will not only help your grades, but it can also help you feel part of the social scene at school. If you don't have time for a face-to-face group meeting, try organizing an online study group.

have gotten into the habit of speaking negatively to yourself, this process can take some time, but after "correcting" your thoughts for a while, speaking positively to yourself will become a habit and you'll find your motivation will increase.

Take breaks. It is easy to burn out in college. Combining a lot of schoolwork with an active social life can be disastrous to motivation. But it doesn't have to be. Try not to overextend yourself either academically or socially. Take frequent breaks while studying. Some people need a short break every thirty minutes, and others can study longer before needing to rest. Get to know yourself as a learner. If you need to stop after thirty minutes, then stop. Don't just sit there wasting time for another thirty minutes if you can't focus. In general, try to study for an hour and then take a short break (five to ten minutes) before getting back to work. Don't plan to study for three hours with no breaks—you'll find that you can't keep it up.

Maintaining your motivation is something you will need to think about again and again. Unfortunately, there is no quick fix for motivation problems, but using the strategies we've discussed should help you keep the motivation you've got.

Reviving Your Motivation

What if you are already unmotivated? How can you get yourself back on track? First, you need to think about what the problem might be. A lack of motivation does not necessarily mean you are lazy. There are lots of barriers to motivation.

☹ **SAD BUT TRUE**

Recently, one of our students came to talk to us about her lack of motivation. Salma was concerned about her grades and felt that if she could just get more motivated everything would be fine. As we talked to her, we discovered all the pressures Salma was under. She lived at home and had an hour commute to school and back every day. She felt she was missing out on a social life at school because her parents expected her to be home each night and every weekend. She also had a part-time job, which was cutting into her study (and free) time. In addition, Salma had been arguing with her boyfriend (whom she could not even tell her parents about because they did not think she should be dating, even though she was eighteen years old and in college—really). Is it any wonder she felt unmotivated? But motivation, or lack of it, was not really Salma's problem. We helped her set up an appointment with a counselor on campus to talk about the stress these other issues were causing in her life. Once she could see that other issues were getting in the way of her schoolwork (and once she started working through them with a counselor), she began to be able to separate her school life from her home life— which helped her make it through the semester.

Think about things that may be hurting your motivation, such as procrastination, low self-esteem or self-confidence, bad study habits (or no studying at all), stress, fears and worries, or lack of interest. Are these getting in the way of your reaching your goals? Students who can't seem to put a finger on what's causing them to be unmotivated tend to spiral downward—the wrong direction, for sure. Use the following suggestions to recharge your motivation.

Reevaluate your goals. Have your goals met the criteria we stated earlier in this chapter, or are they unrealistic or too vague? If so, this lack of direction could be causing you to feel unmotivated. Sometimes you can reclaim your motivation just by reworking your goals to be more specific and realistic.

Add more choice to your life. Are you feeling negative about college in general or the tasks you are required to do? How can you add more choice to your life? A lot of what you have to do in college is prescribed for you—the courses you need to get your degree, the tasks you must do to pass those courses, even when the classes meet. But you usually have a choice of professor, and you can always choose how you will approach learning in your courses (sometimes students choose not to study at all). Consider the choices you are making. Are they getting in the way of your success or are they helping you reach your goals?

Relate schoolwork to your life. Does what you are doing in college seem unconnected with your future goals? How can you relate your schoolwork with your personal interests? The better you can do this, amazingly, the more interesting the topic will become. You might even want to go talk to the professor to find out more about how his course relates to life—the prof may be able to discuss some links between his course and the wider world that you'd never think of.

LISTEN UP

We often hear students saying, "Why do I need to learn this? I will never use this in my life." When students feel this way, they are not able to connect what they are studying to their everyday life. But at the risk of sounding like your professors, let us assure you that you will use the information you learn (even in the courses you don't like) in ways you cannot even imagine today. For example, if you pay attention in statistics class today, you will be better equipped to evaluate the information you hear on the news about political polls or some implausible-sounding medical breakthrough. In addition, college teaches you the process of learning, so although you may not have to use calculus in the field of nursing, you will have to use the ability to problem solve. That skill will serve you throughout your life.

Seek professional help if you need it. Are personal problems interfering with school? Are you feeling depressed? If you think that is what is making you unmotivated, seek some help from a counselor or psychologist on campus or talk to your friends or family. There are usually a lot of folks you can talk to who can really help you. But the worst thing you can do with a personal problem is just ignore it, hoping it will go away.

Don't hibernate. Often when we feel unmotivated, all we want to do is curl up under the covers hoping it will all go away. However, the best way to overcome a lack of motivation is to do just the opposite. Instead, try to get more involved. Go out with some friends, join a campus group, go to a concert or a movie. Do something that gets you out and about. And, by all means, attend all your courses. Skipping classes will just compound the problem. If you find you just can't go out or all you want to do is sleep and avoid everything, you may actually suffer from a more serious problem than the lack of motivation. If you suspect a bigger issue, get help from a professional.

Prioritize. Sometimes motivation slips because there are just too many things that need to be done. Students can feel overwhelmed and lose their motivation to get any of it accomplished. One good solution to this problem is to make a list of what needs to be done and then organize the tasks. Which ones need to be finished first? Which ones can wait until next week? By writing them all down, you can prioritize the tasks, put your workload into perspective, and get it all done in a timely fashion.

Try to recognize when your motivation breaks down. What kinds of things lead you to become unmotivated? Once you are able to see what affects your motivation, you will be better able to make adjustments (sometimes these will be very minor changes) to keep your motivation up.

> There are no uninteresting things; there are only uninterested people.
>
> —Gilbert K. Chesterton

If You Read Nothing Else, Read This

○ You are always motivated to do something during every moment of your life. The trick is to be motivated to do the right things at the right time.

○ Set short-term and intermediate goals to help you reach your long-term goals. These goals should be specific, measurable, realistic, and flexible.

○ Use both intrinsic and extrinsic rewards to help you stay motivated. Although internal rewards are best for lifelong learning, external rewards (going shopping, seeing a movie, hanging out with friends) can help you stay motivated.

CHAPTER 9

ARRRRRRGH! AND OTHER WAYS TO HANDLE STRESS

- Concerned that the stress in college will be all-consuming and that you'll run screaming into the night?
- Worried that your reactions to stress may be, well, weird?
- Think you need some better coping strategies to help you deal with stress?

If so, read on . . .

This week you have a political science paper due, a calculus quiz, and an entire 350-page novel to read for literature class. Oh my. To top it off, you just had a fight with your roommate and got a letter from the bank that you bounced a check and they're going to charge you $30.00 to "process" it. You feel so stressed out that you are about to explode. Sometimes life is so complicated. Could anything else go wrong?

There are many new kinds of stresses that you face in college, including social demands, academic pressures, financial responsibilities, and career anxieties. One thing you need to be aware of is that some stress is good for you. Yes, that's right. Without any stress at all life would seem dull and we would hardly be able to drag ourselves out of bed each morning. However, too much stress can be damaging. What you need to be able to do is figure out when you are experiencing too much stress and then find ways to cope with it.

THE INSIDE SCOOP

Researchers have found that students who have good social-support networks from family and friends perceive and handle stressful situations more effectively. So when you are feeling stressed out, call home or talk to a friend. It may not solve all your problems, but it will help you begin to feel better.

Good Stress/Bad Stress

Stress is defined as a response made by your body to a demand placed on it. It is impossible to live through even one day stress free. But not all stress is bad for you. Some stressors actually make life worth living. For example, you can feel a great accomplishment after running a 5K race or passing a difficult exam. Stress allows you to be creative and expand your experiences. However, stress becomes bad when it results from an overload of demands placed on you.

What Causes College Stress?

There is no doubt that college students feel stress. When you are new to college, you may feel stress about new responsibilities or living away from home. Returning students may feel stress about the time away from their family or balancing a full-time job with schoolwork. You may feel stress because it seems as if all your professors got together to schedule exams and papers for the same week (or worse, the same day).

One of the most common reasons college students are stressed out is because they are having trouble dealing with all the changes they have experienced in such a short time. Think about it. You are in a new place (maybe even away from

There are two times I feel stress—day and night.

—Anonymous

😃 GOOD STRESS	😦 BAD STRESS
Feeling slightly nervous before a big exam	Forgetting all the information you learned as soon as you enter the classroom to take the test
Joining a sorority or fraternity or playing intramural sports	Freaking out because you have a club or team meeting every single night and no time to do schoolwork
Keeping up with your work for each class every day	Having to read the book and write the paper the night before the assignment is due
Planning a weekend road trip with friends	Goofing off with friends all weekend and feeling like you'll never get all your schoolwork done

home for the first time), you have new responsibilities (like paying your cell phone bill on time or dragging yourself to class at 8 A.M.), you are meeting new people, and you are dealing with a lot of schoolwork. You may not know one person on campus. Compare this situation with the comfortable setting you're used to. It is no wonder you may be feeling a bit stressed. Stress is caused by all sorts of things.

Academic Stress

There are several kinds of academic stress. You may feel anxiety when taking a test, giving a speech, or writing a paper. Or you may feel a general level of stress all the time because you are anxious about doing well in your classes. A little stress is probably good for your performance on these tasks. If you feel no stress at all when going in to take an exam, you may not be gearing yourself up enough to do as well as you could. But (and this is a big one), if your stress is getting in the way of your academic

Make haste slowly.

–Latin proverb

101

☹ **SAD BUT TRUE**

Kristen seemed to have it all together—beautiful, friendly, and smart—but when she turned in an assignment that she copied from a classmate, things got pretty rough for her. It turns out that this was Kristen's second academic dishonesty offense—automatic expulsion from college if found guilty. In an initial meeting with the professor, she acknowledged her dishonesty but then changed her claim (which was within her rights) so the case would go to an academic honesty panel. But Kristen said she could not meet until the end of the summer because she had an internship and would not be on campus. Her professor accepted this story and agreed to the delay, but then was shocked to see Kristen walking down the hall in a classroom building on the first day of summer school. It turns out Kristen was taking four courses during summer semester (hmmm . . . the exact number of credits she needed to graduate). Not only was Kristen academically dishonest, but she was trying to "beat" the system and actually thought she could graduate before the expulsion would occur (we are speechless, really). When the university found out about this wrinkle to the story, they scheduled the panel hearing immediately.

Kristen was expelled and she now has a permanent transcript notation that says "expelled for academic dishonesty." Try explaining that to another college or a future employer. And all for a lousy ten-point homework assignment. HUGE mistake!

performance (for example, you know every word of the speech you are about to give, but you are too nervous to say it in class), you need to take action. Here are some common academic concerns.

Test taking, writing, or public speaking anxiety. Some students get so stressed before taking a test or writing a paper they can't even remember what they've learned. Their palms get sweaty, and their hearts beat faster. They may even get terrible headaches or colds every time they are placed in a testing situation. Usually, these students do not do as well as they could on exams because they are too anxious to truly let the exam reflect what they have learned.

Procrastination. Some professors think students who procrastinate just don't care about getting their work done, but we have met many a student who cares but just can't seem to get it together. These students feel more and more stressed as the semester progresses and they get more and more behind in their work.

High academic standards. Still others experience academic stress because they want to be the best. Maybe you were one of the top students in your high school. You always did well, and the teachers expected a lot from you. Now you are in college and realize you are surrounded by top students. Suddenly, you feel even more pressure to succeed at much higher levels.

You may experience other academic stresses, and these stresses may change throughout any given semester (and throughout your entire college career). This stress may stem from dealing with relationships (not being compatible with your roommate or breaking up with your boyfriend or girlfriend) to drug or alcohol issues to money problems. Find out what these stresses are, because academic stress is different from other stresses you will experience. Wise students make changes in their lives to minimize their academic stress whenever possible.

Nonacademic College Stress

In addition to wanting to do well in classes, there are several other common concerns college students have that can influence academics.

Financial stress. Money, money, money! College costs can really send students into a tailspin. Besides tuition, the costs of books, rent, food, and other unexpected things (like parking tickets and an expensive date night) can really cause sticker shock. Some students feel financial stress because they have just maxed out a credit card or have a $200 cell phone bill their first month away from home.

Social stress. Meeting new people can be overwhelming for some students. Could this be what is stressing you out? Suppose you are at a party with people you have never met before. Do you (1) find someone who looks interesting and start a conversation or (2) ease back into a corner and try to be invisible or simply leave ten minutes after arriving? The 2s find it difficult to cope with situations where interacting with new people is involved. Unfortunately for them, college involves lots of interaction with lots of folks. However, the 1s are not off the hook; they may feel social stress because they have overbooked their schedules with social obligations. One look at their daily planners is enough to send us all

🏫 DO YOUR HOMEWORK

Ever tell yourself, "If I ignore it, it will go away"? Many students choose to ignore the enormous social stresses that are placed on them. However, research has indicated that students who feel an overwhelming sense of social stress are less likely to complete their college degree. Take action to change the situation (see a counselor or confide in a friend) rather than drift along hoping it will change by itself.

into full anxiety mode as we try to think about how they will manage to study given all their social tasks.

Family stress. This may be the first time you are away from home, making decisions and taking responsibility for yourself. This can be stressful. Or it can be just as stressful if you are ready to take on that independence and responsibility and your parents are having a difficult time "letting go." Family stress can also occur because you want to make your family proud. Maybe you are the first in your family ever to go to college, or perhaps you have a brother who just graduated cum laude from some great school. Maybe you've left your full-time job to return to school for your college degree. Whatever your situation, chances are some pressure from family is involved. Family stress can also occur if a parent, sibling, or other close relative becomes ill. Worrying over family illness or having to miss class for several days to help care for an ailing relative can be one of the most stressful situations in a college student's life.

The first step toward dealing with your stress is to recognize what is causing it. Consider your current situation. How would you rate your stress level on a scale of 1

🔧 GET IT TOGETHER

So you're cutting class, you haven't read one word of your accounting book in three weeks and slept through your labs, you have amassed a small fortune in parking tickets (they are talking about impounding your car), and you're "thinking about" buying a paper online because there is no way you can pull one together in the next three days. We would predict that your stress level is off the scale, but let's put things in perspective. Get a grip and control the things you can because there will be plenty of things that go wrong that you can't control. Try acting on one small thing this week and another next week. We realize that slackers can't do it all overnight, but we do have confidence that you can do it.

to 10? If you're pretty stressed (say, a 5 or higher), what kinds of things are bothering you? Is your stress mostly academic or nonacademic, or is it a generous dose of both? Do academic stresses affect you differently than nonacademic ones? Once you know what kinds of stress you are facing, you will be much better able to cope with it.

What Does Stress Do to You?

Stress gets your body and mind to pay attention. You may have heard of this as a "fight or flight" response. Your heart pumps blood faster, your hearing and vision become more acute, and your body releases hormones such as adrenaline to meet the challenge. Although this might have been a great response in prehistoric times to being chased by a wolf, it is actually an overreaction for many of the daily stressors we face in modern life. And too much stress can wreak havoc on your body and your mind.

SAD BUT TRUE

Suzanne, a freshman pre-law major, realized at midpoint that she was going to have to do something to change the way she was managing her life. She was pledging a sorority, a part of the ROTC program, enrolled in eighteen hours of coursework, and under extreme pressure to keep her scholarship. She was under so much stress she literally could not sleep (a physical reaction to stress). She was in tears half the time. Her inability to sleep produced even greater stress. She couldn't focus to study in what little time she had available, so her grades took a nosedive. The harder she tried, the worse it got. It seemed as if every hour in the day was filled with something, so you would think she would be so exhausted that sleep would come. But it didn't. Exhausted and spent, Suzanne finally went to see a counselor for some help. In the end, Suzanne decided to drop out of the sorority and focus on getting her grades back up. Since she had more time, she was able to study more and eventually got her sleep cycle back on track.

There are four general categories of stress reactions. You may find that you primarily experience stress in one or two of these ways. The good news is that once you identify how you react to stress, you can do something about it. Consider your own reactions to stress. Which categories best describe how you feel under stress?

THOUGHTS	PHYSICAL REACTIONS
Loss of confidence	Sweaty palms (or general perspiration)
Fear of failure	Increased heart rate
Trouble concentrating	Dry mouth
Worrying about the future	Feeling tired
Forgetting things	Headaches
Thinking endlessly about all you have to do	Susceptibility to illness
BEHAVIORS	Nervous tics
Acting impulsively	Nausea
Becoming withdrawn	"Butterflies" in stomach
Using drugs or alcohol	**FEELINGS**
Grinding your teeth	Anxiety
Sleeping too much or too little	Irritability
Eating too much or too little	Moodiness
Crying for no apparent reason	Feeling scared

Do you recognize yourself in one or more of these categories? Some people react to stress strongly in one category (for example, thoughts), while others experience stress in several ways.

Reducing Stress Levels

You probably already have some ways to handle stress. Maybe you take a hot bath, call a good friend, attend a yoga class, or hide out and read a juicy novel. However, once you experience the added stresses of college life, you may find that these old strategies just don't cut it anymore. Maybe you have had one illness after another all semester. Perhaps you have developed a strange facial tic, or like Suzanne, you cannot sleep. Or maybe you have mild anxiety attacks that affect your breathing. Instead of abandoning the ways you used to handle stress (or giving in to stress altogether), we suggest you try some (or all) of these suggestions.

Exercise. If you experience physical reactions to stress, this may be the best solution for you. Exercise allows your body to cope with the physical symptoms of stress (such as an increased heart rate) in a healthy way. If thoughts or feelings are the way you experience stress, exercise releases hormones that will actually make you feel better and will take your mind off your troubles. You don't even have to do very vigorous exercise to reap the stress benefits—a short walk will often do the trick.

URBAN LEGEND

(Warning: This is kind of graphic, but we've heard it SO many times we felt obligated to confirm its status here as an urban legend. . . .) A student was extremely stressed out under the pressures of final exams. He was at his science final and he just couldn't take it anymore. He sat straight up in his chair, stuck a sharpened pencil in each nostril, threw his head back, and slammed it onto the desk, thrusting the pencil points into his brain. He died almost instantly. Although this story is not true, the moral of it is that you should control your stress level . . . and stay away from the pencils.

Do something for fun. Find a hobby (or rediscover one). Basically, do something just for fun. Check out the flyers posted on campus to see if there is something you might find interesting enough to pursue as a hobby.

Focus on your strengths. Each time you feel stressed or as if you can't make it, try this little activity. Instead of thinking about all the things you can't do, think about all of the things you can do. Everyone is good at something. You might even want to make a list of these things to help you remember.

Relax or meditate. Take a few minutes every day to really relax—no TV, computers, cell phone, or even conversations, just some quiet time for yourself without any distractions. You'd be amazed at what just a short quiet time can do for your stress level. Some students find meditation or yoga beneficial to help them relax and remain "centered." Whatever you do, spend time with yourself each day.

Eat well. Some people can't eat at all when they are stressed, and others tend to overeat. Recognizing your own eating patterns in relation to stress can help you make changes. Above all, don't turn to junk food (or worse yet, alcohol) to soothe your stress, because the lack of proper nutrition can send your stress level even higher.

Sleep well. When you are stressed, you may not be able to sleep, or you may be the type of person who only wants to sleep at the first sign of pressure. Either way, try to get enough good sleep every day, but don't sleep too much; wasting time can lead to greater stress levels.

Study smart. Throughout *College Rules!* we offer you strategies and tips for becoming a better studier. In general, the better prepared you are for the academic tasks you have to do, the less stressed you will feel. There is no better cure for test anxiety than knowing that you really know the information.

Just say no. Sometimes we create our own stress by becoming overcommitted. And it is amazing just how fast this can happen. A favor for a friend, an added responsibility with a social organization, and poof—suddenly you don't know how you will find the time to cram it all in. Our best advice is to pick and choose your commitments carefully. Do the things you will really enjoy and learn to turn down the things that will get in the way of achieving your goal (getting that college degree).

Practice deep breathing and visualization. These techniques really work. The next time you are feeling stressed, close your eyes and focus on your breathing. Take ten nice deep breaths of equal length (your breath in should be as long as your breath out). With each breath out think, "relax." Then, think about a time when you were truly relaxed. Where were you? What did it look like? What time of day or year was it? What did you hear and smell? Who (if anyone) was with you? Try to fully visualize the situation with as many details as you can.

There are two ways of meeting difficulties: You alter the difficulties or you alter yourself meeting them.

—Phyllis Bottome

Charge up your iPod. Put on a set of headphones, close your eyes for a few minutes, and let soothing music take you away. Some students find that classical music, light jazz, or new-age music is just the thing to help them relax. Even if you don't usually enjoy these types of music, they can be great stress reducers.

Put things in perspective. Don't build up tasks to disproportionate levels. After all, it's only a test, right? Will you even remember the grade you made on it in five years? While we don't encourage you to blow off preparing for an exam, try to keep things in perspective. The things that seem huge now may not seem so important later on. Knowing this can often help you get through the stressing event faster.

Confide in someone. Use your support system. Talk to your family or friends about how you are feeling instead of bottling it all up. Sometimes just sharing your concerns can help you overcome them.

See a counselor. Visiting a counselor gives you a chance to talk to someone who is trained to help people in your situation. Usually, there is a counselor available on campus for a small fee (or even for free). Some colleges even offer group sessions for reducing stress levels. Our advice is to get help earlier rather than later. Don't wait until your stress level has caused you a lot of trouble before getting the help you need.

The best plan for controlling and reducing your stress is to use as many of the strategies we discussed as possible. If you rely on only one or two, you may find that they don't work in really difficult situations. The key is to be flexible and try several ways to attack your stress.

> **THE INSIDE SCOOP**
>
> If you practice visualization often, when you are stressed you need only think about your relaxing memory and your body will automatically begin to relax because it has been conditioned to react that way to the memory. So make a habit of taking a mental trip to the beach, the mountains, your grandma's house, or whatever works for you.

> **GET WIRED**
>
> Go online to one of thousands of fun websites that can help you take your mind off your troubles. There are sites that will help you learn to juggle or spin a basketball, sites where you can play games, and sites that offer stress-level checks. Log on when you are feeling stressed out. And go to teachhealth.com for lots of good advice on managing and reducing stress.

If You Read Nothing Else, Read This

○ Stress comes in a variety of flavors. You may find that you experience academic stress (test anxiety, procrastination, or perfectionism) or nonacademic stress (financial, social, or family)—or both—in college.

○ People react to stress in a variety of ways. These include thoughts, feelings, behaviors, and physical reactions.

○ Reducing your stress level requires that you know both what is causing your stress and how your body reacts to stress. You need to have several strategies handy for coping with stress to help you through difficult times.

CHAPTER 10

WHAT'S IT ALL ABOUT? UNDERSTANDING HOW YOU LEARN

- Worried that you really don't like to learn?
- Concerned that you learn "differently" than most of your fellow students?
- Think you can make it through college with good grades by just "looking over" your notes?

If so, read on . . .

Have you ever stopped to think about what it means to learn? College students learn every day, yet few really think about what it means to learn and how people go about learning things. According to Webster's dictionary, learning is "modification of a behavioral tendency by experience." Huh? Simply put, learning equals a change in behavior. Some things take a long time to learn (like calculus); other lessons we learn immediately (like when a child touches a hot stove). But whether the learning takes a long period of time or a short period of time, we know that LEARNING = CHANGE.

⚡ GET WIRED

If you are interested in finding out more about your own personal style of learning, there are several assessments available on the Internet. Go to one of the major search engines and type in "learning styles." You should find several sites that offer information and assessments. You might also try to see what the learning center on your campus offers. Most centers offer online assessments of learning styles for free.

Learning occurs in many different ways. Some people talk about learning styles and say they are "auditory learners," meaning they learn best when they hear something. Others say they learn best visually; and still others say they learn best kinesthetically, or by doing things. Although we won't go as far as saying this is a bunch of hogwash (well, we might say it to ourselves, but we would never say it to you), we will say that this way of classifying how people learn is far too simplistic to be helpful.

Think about it: if you were truly only a kinesthetic learner, you would be in big trouble in most college classes, where the majority of teaching is done through lecture and reading. Everyone learns through using his or her senses (through seeing, hearing, touching, smelling, tasting), but this is just part of the picture. Many other things influence how you learn. This chapter talks about the stuff that learning is made of.

🏠 DO YOUR HOMEWORK

Think back to something you learned very easily. It may have been a sport, like playing golf or tennis, or it may have been something academic, like learning the ins and outs of computer use. Now think about something that was hard for you to learn. Why do you think it's easier for you to learn some things than others? As you begin college, it's important that you think about this. No matter what your major, some courses will always be easier for you than others.

Profiles of Amazing Students

The fact that a change occurs as a result of learning indicates that the learner is involved in some way in a complex process. Learning just doesn't happen magically or by osmosis. Learning can be easy or a struggle, and you're not always even conscious of the fact that you are learning something.

Although no two students are exactly the same when it comes to learning, there are some general traits that lead to more effective learning. When students have these characteristics, learning can be a fun-filled journey with more long straight highways than bumps in the road. So what does an amazing student have that a mediocre or poor student doesn't? Read on to see how well you fit into the amazing-student profile.

Some people never learn anything because they understand everything too soon.

–Alexander Pope

AMAZING STUDENTS ARE WILLFUL

Willfulness is perhaps the most important of all the characteristics of amazing students. Students who are willful have an enthusiasm and zest for learning. They may not love learning everything, but they have the motivation to persist, even in courses they may not like or that are particularly difficult for them. No matter the course or the topic, they see something of value in it. Willfulness also implies effort. Although we may learn lots of life's lessons without even realizing it, most school learning doesn't simply "happen." Classroom learning requires conscious effort (what is usually called studying), which in turn requires you to be an active participant—you know, to be willing to do your part.

AMAZING STUDENTS ARE SKILLFUL

Skillfulness is the ability to know what to do and how to do it in any given learning situation. Being skillful means you're more than a one-trick pony. You approach each learning task by consciously asking yourself, "What skills and strategies should I use to be successful here?" Skillfulness involves having the ability to plan your time, set learning goals you can reach, monitor and evaluate your progress, and know a variety of ways to approach lots of different kinds of knowledge and ways to learn. In short, skillfulness involves a lot. When students are making the transition to college, they may approach every course, test, or learning task the same way, using what we like to call "the rubber-stamp approach." Think about it this way: Would you wear a tuxedo to a baseball game? A strapless dress to a funeral? A bathing suit to religious services? Probably not. You know there's appropriate dress for different occasions and settings. Skillful learners know that "putting on the same clothes" won't work for every class.

They are flexible learners. They have different strategies and know when to use them. They know that you study for multiple-choice tests differently than you study for essay tests. And they not only know what to do, they also know how to do it.

AMAZING STUDENTS ARE CURIOUS

Curiosity—without it we'd still be carrying clubs and living in caves. An astronaut wouldn't have walked on the moon, certain kinds of cancer wouldn't have cures, and it would take weeks instead of hours to cross the ocean. There would be none of the things that have come to be dear to lots of college students' hearts—cell phones, computers, the Internet, and TV. Curiosity is what makes learning fun and discovery possible. It's what makes you keep searching for the solution to a difficult problem.

As we move from childhood to adulthood, we seem to lose much of our curiosity. If you've spent any time around small children, you know they ask endless questions. But as children grow into adolescents, they seem more and more reluctant to search for answers or to ask questions. Sometimes the spark of curiosity can be reignited in college. If that happens, doors open, learning becomes a quest, and college becomes a life-changing experience.

AMAZING STUDENTS ARE OPEN-MINDED

Open-mindedness is the ability to try new things, listen to the ideas of others, and possibly change your own views. When freshmen arrive on college campuses, they generally have already formulated strong opinions on certain issues, particularly those that have been discussed around their dinner table over the years or those that are community related. For example, you may have very strong opinions on controversial issues such as a woman's right to choose, political preference, evolution, capital punishment, or immigration. These opinions are very difficult to change, and we're certainly not suggesting that you should. However, one of the ways for you to get the most of your college experience is not only to listen to the views of others but also to evaluate why you have the opinions you do. Students who are able to support their views with something

> Some problems are so complex that you have to be highly intelligent and well informed just to be undecided about them.
>
> —Laurence J. Peter

SAD BUT TRUE 😟

Everyone knows at least one person like Chad. In high school, he was the guy who never cracked a book but managed to pull decent grades in spite of it. He was carefree, loved to laugh, and prioritized his life so the fun stuff was always done first. His teachers called him smart but lazy and prodded him to put more time into schoolwork. His parents did the same. They knew he was smarter than his grades reflected. Chad knew he could do better too, but he just couldn't bring himself to put more into his schoolwork. He knew what he needed to do, and he had the skill, but he lacked the will.

When he applied for college (because there's no better place to go for continued fun), his SAT scores were top-notch, but his grades only so-so. He did, however, get accepted to the school of his choice. It was a university that challenged students academically but also one that rated high on the "party scale." Chad was in paradise, at least at first. So many parties, so little time. "There will always be another test. Who knows when another party will come along?" was his motto. It didn't take long for his lack of willfulness to catch up with him, however. By midterm, his grades in all his classes were in the toilet. He went to class most of the time; he asked good questions and occasionally contributed to discussions. He would even chat with his professors after class, particularly about topics he was genuinely interested in. But he couldn't bring himself to study. Not at all. Once again, his teachers called him smart but lazy. His parents did the same. Chad managed to rally and pull all Cs his first semester. This pattern pretty much continued throughout his college career. And to his credit, he did graduate—with a 2.3 grade point average.

more than "that's just the way I was raised" stand a better chance of leaving college with the ability to look at all sides of an issue and appreciate the importance of diverse viewpoints.

AMAZING STUDENTS ARE SELF-DISCIPLINED

The ability to do the right thing at the right time regardless of what you really want to be doing is called self-discipline. When you're in college, you're in charge of your actions. No one is going to check that you go to class or that your homework is done. No one is going to ground you if you stay out all night. No one is going to prevent you from piercing any body part that you want pierced. You have to discipline yourself to take care of business, whether that business is academic or personal.

LISTEN UP

The idea of open-mindedness struck home with our students on September 11, 2001, the day the World Trade Center and the Pentagon were struck by terrorists. We were putting the final touches on the first edition of *College Rules!* and our students were gearing up to take their first exams of the semester. In our classroom discussions about what had happened, it became clear that students were having to do some heavy-duty thinking about what all this meant and how it might influence their daily lives. Many freshmen were struck by the diversity of the opinions they heard because they were used to being in settings where everyone had similar views. Some didn't know where to begin to sort it all out. But after a bit of time passed and the rawness of emotions gave way to more rational thought, most students found the different perspectives on the tragedy helpful as they tried to form their own opinions. It pays to listen to others, to evaluate what they say, and to keep an open mind, especially about events and issues that few of us understand very well.

GET IT TOGETHER

Although you may know people who appear to have it all together, no one can be self-disciplined all the time. No one is perfect. On the other end of the scale, it seems there are some people who have nothing together—they party hard, play hard, rarely hit the books, and make irresponsible choices—a lot. If this sounds like you, visualize the consequences of your behaviors and try to think rationally about why you make poor choices. Don't be in denial. Continued bad decisions can and will influence what happens to you academically. Be real.

So what does it mean to be self-disciplined? It means having the ability to read your biology assignment when everyone else on your hall is going to get pizza. It means going to the library to do research for a paper when you would rather spend the afternoon playing Frisbee on the quad. It means making an informed decision not to abuse alcohol or your body. It means understanding the consequences of the choices you make. It means setting reasonable goals for yourself and then doing what it takes to meet them. Self-discipline is just plain hard.

Learning Matters

You can probably think of a gazillion things that influence how you learn—everything from how you feel when you get up in the morning to whether you like the course material or the teacher to how things are going in your personal life. That's why there's no prescription—no magic beans—no one best way to learn. However, we do know there are some general mindsets that freshmen students bring to college with them. These are mostly things you haven't thought much about in high school, so you may be kind of surprised that they will make a difference.

WHAT YOU ALREADY KNOW, AND YOU DO KNOW LOTS

What knowledge and information are you bringing to college with you? Are you a computer whiz? Can you write poetry in your sleep? Were you a member of the debate team? Are you an American history buff? You may have been able to take tons of advanced math classes in high school, so you are well prepared to compete in higher-level math courses at the beginning of your college career. Compare yourself with someone who attended a very small high school where there were no advanced math courses offered. Which of you has more knowledge about math? Which could be predicted to enroll in higher-level math courses in college, and which could be expected to do better? Your prior educational experiences do have an influence on your performance in college.

But there is a difference between having knowledge and having information. Students who are knowledgeable can make connections between pieces of information. They can apply information in new situations, thus creating knowledge. Students who know information—who can spout off lots of facts but fail to see how things fit together—

 FOR ADULTS ONLY

Adults who are thinking about going to college after they have been out of high school for several years often experience problems with math. They may not have taken college-level math in high school, and even if they did, it's long forgotten. If you fall into this category, you may want to see what refresher math courses your college has to offer. In most instances, you probably wouldn't receive credit for taking such a course, but it is better taking that route than jumping into a course that is way over your head.

> The test of a first-rate intelligence is the ability to hold two opposed ideas at the same time, and still retain the ability to function.
>
> -F. Scott Fitzgerald

are certainly ahead of those who don't but are behind those who have figured out the knowledge thing.

Two of the major factors that influence the knowledge you bring to college are the quality of the high school you went to and the level of courses you took there. Although it differs from state to state, most high schools have a "college-prep" curriculum that prepares students for introductory college courses. The curriculum dictates the number of courses (or units) you need to take in high school. For example, most college-prep curriculums state that you need four units of English, which means you would need to take English in each of your four years in high school. And you can't just take any English; Business English wouldn't count. You would need college-prep English, honors English, or AP (advanced placement) English. In addition, if you do well in AP English, you may even be able to use that class for college credit.

☹ SAD BUT TRUE

Marlene was a pretty conscientious student in high school. She always did her homework (most of the time correctly), she studied for tests, and she made high grades. But she made one tiny mistake that came back to haunt her when she started college. In fact, she made the same mistake that lots of college-bound students make: she took the easy way out. At the advice of her older brother, Marlene decided not to enroll in the more challenging high school English classes, even though her teachers encouraged her to do so. Her brother told her it was her grade point average that mattered, not the courses that she took.

She was accepted at the college of her choice, so she was sure she had done the best thing. Everything was going fine—that is, until she went to freshman orientation and took placement tests. To her surprise (actually, to her horror), she placed into a remedial English course. According to her test results, she was not prepared to enroll in English 101. Flashback to brother's advice.

This story is repeated often on college campuses. The level of your high school courses does matter. It's important to get as much out of those high school years as possible. Don't take the easy way out. Challenge yourself in high school and you will continue to do the same in college.

Being able to take increased knowledge with you to college is one of the reasons it's important to take more advanced courses in high school rather than simply taking a course because you know it's an easy A.

How the Learning Thing REALLY Works

How much did you study in high school? Be honest now. As bizarre as it may sound when you really think about it, lots of students don't have to study hard or very much in high school and they still make exceptional grades. Students tell us all the time that cracking the book or looking over their notes for fifteen minutes before an exam was all it took to make it to the honor society because they found the work was not really challenging. We can guarantee you that considerably more effort is needed in college, even if graduating magna cum laude is not on your radar screen.

Most students new to the college studying scene have never thought about a studying cycle, the idea that there is a rhythm or a pace to learning and test preparation. First, there's the before part. When you sit down to study, you "warm up" your mind in order to make learning easier. This can be as simple as thinking about what you already know about the topics you're studying and organizing the information so it's easier to follow. Next comes the actual studying part—the part where you do more than just look over your notes for a few minutes. You rehearse the information by writing it or saying it and make connections between what you know and the new stuff you are learning. The third part of the cycle is the reviewing part—making sure that you understand the material and that it is fixed firmly in your mind. Think of it as a big loop that repeats again and again—what started off as warming up in one studying session may become review in the next.

But . . . gasp . . . there's more. Not only is it important to have a study cycle for each class you are taking, but it is also important to know that your overall study-cycle timetable will be different for each class. On any given day, you may be warming up in one course, reading your text or rehearsing for another, and reviewing for an exam in a third. Once you catch on, the cycle thing will be like second nature to you, but it's important to understand that you first have to acknowledge that a cycle exists before you get into one.

WHAT YOU ARE WILLING TO INVEST

How much time, discipline, and motivation will you put into learning in college? Have you ever heard the saying, "You reap what you sow"? Nowhere does this ring truer than in college. Those students who are willing to make a big investment in their college experience will have learned considerably more than those who are satisfied to just get by. And we don't just mean academics. That's only part of the investment. Granted, students who graduate magna cum laude have invested time and are obviously disciplined and motivated. But if you talk to students like this, they have probably also invested heavily in other aspects of the college experience. They have been active in clubs and organizations where they made connections with students and professors with similar interests. They have written for the campus newspaper, conducted research with a professor, held offices, or been active in the residence hall where they live or in community projects. All these activities have a big payoff down the road when you seek employment. It often doesn't matter to employers what you have done beyond the classroom, just that you have done something. To land the really good jobs after graduation usually requires more than good grades.

WHAT YOU WANT AS AN END RESULT

What degree do you want to earn, and what experiences are important to you? Earlier we talked about the difference between a major and a career. Remember that some majors lead to specific careers; for instance, a degree in education usually leads to a teaching career. Others prepare you more generally for a variety of careers. It may surprise you to know that some companies just want you to have a degree; they really don't care what it's in. For example, one of the authors has a daughter who is a talent agent. The firm that hired her wasn't interested in what her degree was in, although she had to have one. They were more concerned with her ability to deal with people, her social skills, and her other work experience in dealing with the public. Had she not developed those skills as a college student, she probably would not have been offered the position, no matter how good her grades were. The point is, at some point in your college career, you need to have an idea of the skills and knowledge you'll need to be successful once you graduate. If you want to spend the rest of your life developing computer software in your home, the kinds of experiences you might want to have in college will differ greatly from those you would need if you want to be a journalist for the *New York Times*. In general though, consider college the time to develop the skills to think, write, speak, and problem solve well. These skills will prepare you for just about any career.

As they head off to college, students rarely consider the importance of the factors that influence their learning, but these things do make a difference. Those who think about the big picture of learning and the more subtle things that influence it are those who are on the right track to becoming amazing students.

If You Read Nothing Else, Read This

○   Students who are amazingly successful in college are willful, skillful, curious, open-minded, and self-disciplined.

○   To be the best student possible, you need to consider how you would answer these questions: What information are you bringing to college with you? What kind of studying cycle do you need to be successful? What do you want as an end result?

CHAPTER 11

CAN YOU BELIEVE THAT?

- Concerned that your classmates seem to "get it" faster than you do?
- Think that all you'll need to do to be successful in college is to learn the facts?
- Worried that you have to be able to do your work quickly in order to get everything done?

If so, read on . . .

In the last chapter we discussed how you learn. In this chapter we address the issue of knowledge by explaining a little about beliefs. Now don't tune out on this one. It's really pretty darn interesting and might help you better understand why some of your classmates seem to breeze through classes and others are downright baffled. We'd bet that when you hear the word "beliefs" a bunch of ideas probably flood your mind—religious beliefs, moral beliefs, spiritual beliefs, political beliefs. These beliefs help shape your view of the world. In fact, some would argue that your personal beliefs impact how you experience life. And, although you may not have thought much about it before, everyone also holds beliefs about knowledge—for example, beliefs about what counts as knowledge and where knowledge comes from.

In this chapter we will discuss five factors that will explain a good deal about your own learning experiences and beliefs, ideas that you may have been largely unaware of but that can have a huge impact on college success. What do you believe learning is? How do those beliefs match up with those of your college professors? By "beliefs about knowledge," we mean

> We owe almost all of our knowledge not to those who have agreed, but to those who have differed.
>
> —Charles Caleb Colton

both the attitudes you have about what learning is and how you study based on those attitudes. These beliefs affect how you learn and how much you get out of learning.

How Certain Are You?

Some people believe knowledge is very certain and consists of facts. They believe that truth is spelled with a capital T, that there is one answer to every question. Others hold an opposite belief that knowledge is uncertain and there are few "truths" or "facts"—knowledge consists of shades of gray. But most people hold a belief somewhere in the middle: there are some things that are true—oak trees produce acorns, H_2O is water—and some things we are just not sure of—what happens at the moment of death, how can lung cancer best be treated? In terms of learning in college, students can get easily frustrated if their beliefs about the certainty of knowledge differ from those of their professors.

In general, college professors continually question assumptions and reassess what is generally believed to be true, especially in their own fields. That is how civilization moves forward—we once believed the world was flat and witches should be burned at the stake. But when people add new information to previous knowledge, it leads to new knowledge and enables people to alter their views (although there is still a Flat Earth Society).

Students, however, may actually be trained *not* to think this way through years of schooling where facts and truth are often emphasized at the expense of application and analysis. Think about your exams in high school—they probably tested you on bold-faced terms and facts found in your books. If you had read your textbooks thinking knowledge was uncertain and questioning some of the things your teacher said,

An ancient buddha said,
"Mountains are mountains;
Waters are Waters."
These words do not
mean mountains are
mountains; they mean
mountains are mountains.

—Dogen

you probably would not have done well on those exams. So over the years, you may have come to believe that learning consists of memorizing bold-faced facts only to find that your college professors don't seem to buy into that notion of learning. They want you to think about multiple theories and question assumptions—no wonder so many students get frustrated in their first few semesters!

Many students entering college equate learning with memorizing. If you believe all you have to do is to memorize the bold-faced terms in biology or the battles of the Civil War in history, you may be missing the boat—especially if the task requires you to really think about the material. Of course, some memorization is necessary. Where could we go in math without having memorized all those times tables? How would we look up words in the dictionary efficiently without memorizing the alphabet? How would we know that NaCl is ordinary table salt or that Abraham Lincoln was assassinated by John Wilkes Booth in 1865 without having memorized those facts?

But memorization is not the be-all and end-all of learning. In many classes in college, your professors will expect you to conceptualize—take the information you have memorized and put pieces of it together in a way that makes sense. In biology, for example, if you memorize these terms, which are commonly used in genetics—genotype, phenotype, homozygous, heterozygous—but you can't understand how these terms interrelate using the concepts of Mendelian genetics, you will probably run into difficulty.

Is It Really That Simple?

Some people believe knowledge is simple and consists of little chunks of information. They try to keep each bit of knowledge separate. You know, art has nothing to do with science, which of course has nothing to do with psychology. Others believe knowledge is complex and consists of highly interconnected concepts. These individuals

There is a philosophy professor on our campus who begins each semester saying, "There is no truth; there are no facts." Then the students spend the rest of the semester debating that issue. Cassi started that course with a bad attitude because she really could not see how anyone could even think that there was nothing that was true, much less base an entire course on that sentiment. So she just shut out the professor and tried to memorize the facts in the textbook. Of course, she did not do well on exams because the professor expected them to question the "knowledge" contained in their text, and Cassi was completely thrown by this task. We met Cassi a few semesters after she barely passed this philosophy course. She said when she thinks about that course she feels she missed out—not only by not learning the content of the course, but also she now understands that the professor was not trying to teach them to truly believe nothing. On the contrary, he wanted them to learn how to see multiple viewpoints and how to question assumptions. Cassi said she wished she had been able to understand what he had been trying to do because she knows it would help her learn in her other classes.

seek to find ties between pieces of knowledge. Again, most people hold a belief somewhere in the middle—that some knowledge is simple and some is complex.

Your professors probably believe that the information they teach you is vastly complex and interconnected. In fact, sometimes they know their content so well they can't understand why students *don't* see the relationships immediately. To a chemist it is natural to visualize a molecule as you think about it. That way, when you conceptualize a chemical reaction, you can actually see the changes to the molecule in your head. It is so basic to the chemistry professors (like breathing air) that they often forget to share the idea of visualizing molecules with students. So students (until they figure out the visualizing thing) try to learn chemistry by memorizing elements, formulas, and flat diagrams of single and double bonds, which makes the task much more challenging.

As with beliefs about the certainty of knowledge, the belief that knowledge is based on simple, isolated bits of information is largely established by your K-12 educational experiences. In high school you probably learned some material, took an exam over that material at the end of the week, and then were never tested on that stuff again. This leads students to believe they are better off keeping knowledge separate so they don't get new information confused with the material they previously learned. In addition, few high schools teach courses that integrate the humanities and help you better understand that history, art, music, philosophy, and so forth, all influenced one another (actually, most colleges don't offer these integrated courses either). When you study different fields in isolation, it's often difficult to see all the connections among them, thus leading you to believe they don't exist.

The effects of your personal beliefs about knowledge on learning can sometimes be cumulative. Let's say a student is taking a biology course. If he holds a strong belief that knowledge is simple and certain, he might memorize the bold-faced terms and then make no attempt to tie any of the information together. For example, he would not seek to see the similarities between plant and animal cells—he would keep that knowledge separate in his head. Suppose this same student has a professor who holds opposite beliefs—the professor believes that biology consists of knowledge where there might be more than one way to explain phenomena and she also believes that the information is based on relating ideas to one another. She would create her exams based upon these knowledge beliefs and therefore test students on their ability to pull ideas together and think about multiple explanations. The student who memorizes the terms would probably do poorly on the exam because he did not prepare for questions that integrated information. But even more troubling is that he would not even know where the questions came from because, according to his *beliefs* about knowledge, he had achieved knowledge once he had the facts memorized.

It's easy to see that students who believe learning is only about memorizing will select different approaches to learning than will those who understand the importance of pulling ideas together. Although both groups might use similar strategies to learn, perhaps by making flash cards of the definitions of terms, the memorizer would stop there. The conceptualizer might go beyond flash cards by making up problems to solve, laying out the cards to create concept maps, talking through the concepts with a study partner, and making sure he understands the relationships between ideas.

How Quick Should Learning Be?

Some people believe learning will happen quickly or not happen at all. These students get quickly frustrated in courses that are difficult or simply require more time and effort. Other people believe learning takes time—especially for things worth

SAD BUT TRUE ☹

Allison, one of our students, forwarded us an email she had received from her mother warning about an ingredient in shampoo that causes cancer. The message instructed readers to check their shampoo bottles for Sodium Laurel Sulfate (an ingredient found in most shampoos). Allison was quite nervous about the possibility that her shampoo was increasing her risk of cancer and was sending the warning to everyone she knew (as instructed by the email she received). We took one look at the message and knew it was a hoax. By typing the key phrase "shampoo causes cancer" in Google, we were able to quickly confirm that the message was completely false (there was even a page from the American Cancer Society dismissing this email as a hoax). In fact, if shampoo really caused cancer, wouldn't you expect to see it in every headline on TV, on the Internet, and in newspapers? Surely we would hear about this, right? But Internet spammers count on the fact that many people don't question what they read or hear. The moral: question what you read and don't just accept it at face value. If it seems too simple to be true, it probably is. And if you are not sure, check out websites like snopes.com to see if it is an Internet hoax.

knowing. As with the previous two components of beliefs, most people believe that some knowledge happens quickly and that some takes time.

Obviously, your professors think learning takes time—just consider how long they have spent in school! Really, some of your professors have devoted their entire working life to studying one tiny type of plankton. You might say, "Kill me now," but your professors find their areas of research fascinating and might not understand why you don't.

People usually hold some arbitrary notions about how long academic tasks should take. These notions are not completely arbitrary, however; they are usually based upon prior educational experience. In high school you were asked questions and then expected to have an answer right away. We have even heard of "speed" math or spelling quizzes where the object is to respond as fast as you can in a given period of time. In addition, the teacher generally budgeted time for you—a task was assigned and your teacher let you know when time was up. So the idea that learning should happen quickly is deeply engrained for many beginning college students. Faster is better. Be quick about it!

> Everything changes, nothing perishes.
>
> —Ovid

Learning is what most adults will do for a living in the 21st century.

—Bob Perelman

The problem comes when people hold notions about time that do not match the academic task. It may be that it took you twenty minutes to read your history textbook in high school before taking a multiple-choice or matching exam. You took the test, made an A, and moved on. Enough well-spent time. However, if you are taking history in college and are asked to think more deeply about the material for an essay exam, twenty minutes certainly isn't going to cut it! So, next time you find yourself slamming your physics book shut after trying to work one problem and saying, "I can't do this," consider that you may hold the belief that learning should be quick. It might help to think about a hobby you have—painting, sports, music—and consider the time you have invested in learning it. If you are a good musician, you know you have the ability to practice for extended periods of time to play that piece of music just right. Now, the trick is to be able to apply your stick-to-it-ness to your college classes.

LISTEN UP

Do you know how long the average high school student persists at figuring out the answer to an algebra problem? According to the experts, it's about two (that's right, two) minutes. If he can't solve it in two minutes, he gives up. Sometimes he moves on to another problem; sometimes he gives up totally. Shuts the book. End of story. Even teachers get caught up in the idea that things should happen quickly. What happens in class when your teacher asks a question and no one volunteers an answer? Usually, she'll answer the question for you if more than ten seconds go by. For some reason, even a short period of silence in the classroom is too long. But we know that some things can't be accomplished at lightning speed. When you find yourself giving up, take a deep breath and try again.

Who's in Charge?

Some people believe their professors or other authority figures are in charge of their learning. Simply put, this means they think of learning as something that is done to them—something external. It is the professor's job to "fill them up" with information but not the students' job to actively participate in learning. After all, what is my institution paying these college profs for, anyway? Others hold the belief that they themselves play a huge role in creating knowledge and therefore are responsible for much of their own learning. Again, most people hold a belief somewhere in the middle, with some knowledge being gained from external sources and some being generated by themselves.

In grade school and high school you probably felt the teacher was in charge of your learning. Not only did you believe this, but your parents, school administrators, and local politicians believed it as well—even your teacher believed he was in charge of your learning since he may have been held accountable if his students did not perform well. However, there is no way he could have been totally in charge of learning. To paraphrase an old adage: you can lead students to knowledge but you can't make them think!

Students who believe their minds are "empty" and that someone else is responsible for filling them up with new learning find it easy to let themselves off the hook when things aren't going well. They will often blame their lack of success on the teacher, saying things like "he was a really bad lecturer" or "she taught chemistry in a way I could not understand." Now don't get us wrong. We're not saying that all professors do everything right and that when students don't do well it's always their own fault. What we are saying is that it is important to do your part. Learning is a shared experience, an experience where both you and your professor bring important ideas to the experience.

GET IT TOGETHER

We have seen students give up in a class because they don't care for the professor—maybe she lectures in monotone—or they find the subject to be a real snoozer. Whatever the specific situation, it seems that the relationship with the professor plays a huge role in some students' ability to learn in class. Part of this is probably based upon a belief that the professor is responsible for student learning. However, if you decide not to do the work, who will suffer? Hint: not the professor. Some of our students have said they can sometimes find the will to finish the work by making it a competition with themselves by saying, "I don't like this professor, but, darn it, I will try to do well in this course *despite* her!" Creating competition helps them through the class. Try it—it is far better than failing.

Are You Math-Brained or English-Brained?

Some people hold the belief that knowledge is innate—either you are born with an ability to learn something or you are not. We often hear students say they can learn in some subjects but are totally hopeless in others. Other people believe everyone can learn everything. Again, most people hold a middle-of-the-road belief.

This component of beliefs about knowledge is a bit tricky because there are some things that people are just good at and it appears to be innate. Think about your own experience—is there something you do well? Maybe you can play any instrument or sport and be pretty good right from the start. Maybe you can draw, fix cars, learn languages, or write. There are lots of abilities that just seem to be natural talents. The question is, how much is inborn and how much is developed? Although this is an interesting idea to pursue, we are going to discuss this component in the way we see it impacting most college students—believing that knowledge is innate cuts one off from learning.

When students tell us they are history-brained and not science-brained (or any of the other something-brained versions we hear), what students are saying is that they believe they *can't* learn in these other disciplines. Chances are, they give up at the slightest difficulty (remember the speed-of-learning belief?) and don't give themselves a chance to learn. One of the authors of this book held a very strong belief in innate ability as an undergrad. She thought she was math-impaired. She jokes that she registered for Math for Idiots I and II to fulfill her math requirements. When she entered graduate school, she was sure she was going to flunk out because there was a statistics requirement for the degree. However, she had developed more mature beliefs about knowledge since undergrad school and was able to give the task the time and attention it deserved. She may have worked longer than some other students, but she eventually got it. (She even took an extra stat class in the end.) She probably wasn't ready to do that as a freshman.

When we talk with our students about their own personal beliefs about knowledge, they often find they are able to make some needed changes simply because they understand a little more about the role their beliefs play in learning. So the next time you find you are cutting yourself off from knowledge, think about your own beliefs.

Transforming Your Beliefs

After reading about the different categories of beliefs, you may find that your own beliefs need some modification. So how can you make a change? There are several things to keep in mind:

- **Think about what your professors expect from you and then select the most appropriate strategies.** Even if you've always used flash cards to learn history, take the time to reassess and make sure your strategy will help you achieve the level of thinking required. Sometimes making little changes to how you study can have a big impact on what you learn and how you think about learning.

- **Be in charge.** It is easy to sit back and let the professor's words wash over you in lecture. But once you make a mental shift to consider yourself the key to learning and knowledge, you will be more apt to pay attention. You might even find yourself more interested in the topic—really.

- **Learn to live with ambiguity.** There will be plenty of things you will learn that are not certain and have no definite answer. And that's okay. It's what makes life interesting. Repeat as needed: "I can live with ambiguity."

- **Give yourself more time.** You might want to set a timer (or just watch the time on a clock) to see how long you can persist at a given task before giving up. Then, the next time you do that task, try to go a little longer—make it a competition with yourself to see how long you can concentrate.

- **Don't worry about what others are doing.** We all know someone who seems to breeze through college—a natural in every subject. Forget about them and focus on doing the best you can.

Research has indicated that in order for people to make changes to a belief, they must first be dissatisfied with their current belief. So if you have read one of the sections above and thought, "Oh no! That's me. I need to do something about this," then you have already taken the first step. In addition, to change a belief people need to be aware of the alternatives. Again, you are covered once you have read the different types of beliefs in this chapter. In our own research on this topic, we have found that students begin to make needed changes to their beliefs about knowledge just by hearing about the theory and thinking about their own situation.

If You Read Nothing Else, Read This

○ Everyone holds personal beliefs about knowledge. These beliefs affect how one learns.

○ Sometimes students give up too quickly because they believe learning should happen quickly.

○ Knowledge consists of more than simple facts.

○ Students can give up too easily if they believe they cannot learn in a particular subject.

CHAPTER 12

A MOMENT OF SILENCE, PLEASE: CONCENTRATING WHILE YOU STUDY

- Worried that you can't concentrate on your schoolwork because there are just too many distractions?
- Concerned about finding a good place to study?
- Think that you could use some strategies to improve concentration in general?

If so, read on . . .

earning and studying are not the same thing. In chapter 10 we talked about how sometimes learning can happen unconsciously (for example, that song on your iPod that you hate yet somehow know every word to), but studying should never be unconscious. If it is, you have probably fallen asleep. Zzzzzzz. Remove the textbook from your face and read on.

Sometimes students tell us that studying makes them tired. It's true that studying can make you tired; if you are doing it right, studying takes an enormous amount of energy and concentration. But has the following ever happened to you? You are reading your biology (or history or accounting) text and you look up after a few pages—and have absolutely no idea what you've just read. If so, you weren't really concentrating and that time you spent looking at those pages was, well, wasted. Finding ways to concentrate is one of the toughest challenges facing many college students. The first step toward achieving better concentration is setting up an environment that is favorable for learning.

Creating a First-Rate Learning Environment

Take a look at the place where you do your studying. Are you somewhere that allows you to really focus on your work? Would you recommend this type of learning environment to your friends? Or are you in a place that may actually detract from your ability to concentrate, such as on your bed or, worse yet, on your bed with the TV on? Sometimes students don't give much thought to where they are studying, but if you can't focus, you probably are not getting much real studying done.

Learning without thought is labor lost.

—Confucius

Use the following chart to help you think about and assess your current learning environment. Check all that apply.

THE INSIDE SCOOP

Research has shown that students who study in an environment similar to where they will take their exam tend to do better on the exam. This phenomenon is called state-dependent memory, which means that you will do better on a test if you take the test in the same "state"—the same mental state, that is—you were in when you did the learning. This is because your environment gives your mind cues that help it more easily access the information. So try to create an atmosphere like that in your classroom: make the lighting, temperature, and comfort level similar to those you will experience during testing. You may even want to find an empty classroom to use, if possible. What state are you in?

My studying location	My concentration level in this location rated from 1 (poor) to 10 (excellent)
Bedroom	1 2 3 (4) 5 6 7 8 9 10
Living room	1 2 3 4 5 6 (7) 8 9 10
Kitchen	1 2 3 4 (5) 6 7 8 9 10
Library	1 2 3 4 5 6 7 8 (9) 10
At work	(1) 2 3 4 5 6 7 8 9 10
Other_____	1 2 3 4 5 6 7 8 9 10

My studying area	My concentration level in this location rated from 1 (poor) to 10 (excellent)
On my bed	1 2 (3) 4 5 6 7 8 9 10
At a desk	1 2 3 4 5 6 (7) 8 9 10
On my sofa	1 2 3 4 (5) 6 7 8 9 10
At a table	1 2 3 4 5 6 7 8 (9) 10
Outside	1 2 3 4 (5) 6 7 8 9 10
Other_____	1 2 3 4 5 6 7 8 9 10

My environment	My concentration level in this location rated from 1 (poor) to 10 (excellent)
Quiet	1 2 3 4 5 6 7 8 9 (10)
Music playing	1 2 3 4 5 (6) 7 8 9 10
TV playing	1 2 3 4 (5) 6 7 8 9 10
Roommates/others talking	1 2 (3) 4 5 6 7 8 9 10
Other_____	1 2 3 4 5 6 7 8 9 10

Some students believe they should make themselves as comfortable as possible while studying and choose to study on their bed or on a cushiony sofa. However, it turns out that people concentrate better when they are not entirely comfy and relaxed. You will find you are able to focus better if you choose a straight-backed chair, such as a desk chair or kitchen chair.

If you found that your studying location, area, and environment were all good to excellent (at least 7s or above) in terms of concentration, then congratulations! You are well on your way to success. If, on the other hand, you have found that you are not currently in a good situation for learning (less than a 5), then your homework for tonight is to try out some different locations until you find one or two that work for you.

Getting Rid of Distractions

Think about a time when you were really engaged in whatever you were doing. In fact, you were so into it you lost all sense of time and space. Perhaps you were lost in a good book, or maybe you were in the zone in your basketball game. There is a term for this type of engagement—you were "in flow." That is, you were able to rid yourself of all distractions and focus completely on the task at hand.

Now picture yourself studying. What image do you have? Are you in flow, or are you sitting with your books and notes open but your mind is a million miles away? Think about the noises you hear. Is there someone talking? Music playing? Clocks ticking? Phones ringing? Visualize what you are focusing on. Is it the chapter you are

Many students find they concentrate better with a little noise in the background (like a radio playing softly or the white noise of a fan humming), but you can't concentrate with the television on, because you will quickly find yourself engrossed in whatever is on the tube. In fact, the entire purpose of TV is to try to get you to pay attention to it. Studying is hard enough without having to compete with the draw of the television. So if you are having trouble concentrating while studying, turn off the TV—please. Oh, and while you're at it, turn off your cell phone too.

Adam, a sophomore English major, lived in a house with two roommates. Unfortunately for Adam, one of the roommates found the need to practice his electric guitar every time Adam sat down to study. To add to Adam's troubles, his other roommate continually had friends over at all times of the day or night. Adam found it hard to concentrate if there was any noise while he was studying. Needless to say, he didn't do so well on his first round of exams and—shock—he blamed his roommates for his failure because they were always making so much noise. Adam failed to realize that it was his responsibility to fix these problems. Rather than becoming angry with his roommates, he needed to work out the problems. In fact, the roommates didn't even realize there was a problem until Adam brought it up. The point is that you need to take responsibility for your own learning, and if something or someone is getting in the way of your ability to concentrate on your studies, you need to do something about it.

reading? A noisy roommate? A sudden urge to clean your room? A growling stomach? About a hundred things you are currently worried about? Whatever things you picture hearing or seeing are the distractions you need to get rid of before you study. We know this is sometimes easier said than done.

When you sit down to study we want you to be able to focus on what you are doing (sometimes it is hard enough to just get started, right?). So let's identify those things that can distract you while studying.

The distractions students face while they study come in two flavors: external distractions and internal distractions.

The finest words in the world are only vain sounds, if you cannot comprehend them.

−Anatole France

A man can fail many times, but he isn't a failure until he begins to blame somebody else.

−John Burroughs

If you are returning to college after hav-ing a family, then you know it is not always easy to "get rid of distractions." Our best advice is to carve out some study times in the evenings when you are off-duty or to plan to study when your family is sleeping (either early in the morning or at night). This strategy has worked for both of us.

EXTERNAL DISTRACTIONS

External distractions include noise, other people, light, TV, snacks, phone calls, IM, and so on. Some of these dis-tractions are fairly easy to fix because you can simply move to a better loca-tion. Go to the library or another quiet place to get some serious studying done. Other distractions can be a little more difficult to deal with. You may have noticed there are a lot of fun things to do on your campus, and there is always someone around to talk to or do something with. So if you are not studying because a friend offers something better to do, then you can quickly find yourself in some trouble, because there is always something more fun to do than study. But part of being a college student is learning to priori-tize. And because you are a student, studying should always be close to the top of your list of priorities. Besides, you will be able to (1) have a better time when you play and (2) concentrate better on your schoolwork if you get it out of the way first.

⚡ GET WIRED

Technology can be quite distracting, right? The cell phone is ringing, IM chiming, TV playing. Oh, and of course we can't forget about checking Facebook at least three times a day. Concentrating in the face of all of this technology can be tough—especially when you are required to use your computer to complete an assign-ment. Our best advice is to use the technology as a reward; for example, "I won't turn on IM or check MySpace until I write the outline for my paper." In addition, we suggest that if your assignment does not need technology (such as reading your textbook), and if technology distracts you, plan to read with your computer and phone turned off.

INTERNAL DISTRACTIONS

Internal distractions are more complex than the external ones because they can take so many different forms and sometimes happen unpredictably. There are several dif-ferent types:

Physical distractions. These include feelings of hunger, sleepiness, or illness. If you find you are always tired or hungry when you plan to study, you may have to move your studying sessions to a different time of day. Or try taking a quick walk or eating a light snack before you study. If you find you always feel ill when you study (for example, you get a headache every time you read), you may want to get a physical to make sure nothing is medically wrong or an eye exam to see if you need to wear glasses while reading.

> **THE INSIDE SCOOP**
>
> Eye doctors have found that students who have trouble concentrating in school often can be cured of this problem by wearing glasses (or contact lenses) while reading. Some students just need a reading lens that will help their eyes relax even though they can see just fine. If you have always had trouble concentrating or if you get sleepy every time you read, you may find the solution through a simple eye exam.

Internal anxieties. These can include worrying about test performance, personal problems, or other responsibilities you have. If these concerns are keeping you from getting your work done, try to put the problems that are worrying you into perspective. Is it something that can wait or something you need to deal with before you can study? If you find you are never able to concentrate because of your anxieties, you may want to talk to a friend or a counselor and come up with a plan of action.

Boredom. You may be feeling bored or uninterested in some of your classes, or you may even have an intense dislike for certain courses. However, you need to be able to make it through all your courses. So how do you concentrate on courses you don't really like? One way is to tell yourself that the semester lasts only fifteen weeks (give or take a week or so). You can do anything for fifteen weeks, right? A better approach is to find something about the course that interests you. Anything, no matter how small, may make it easier for

> I took a speed-reading course and read War and Peace in twenty minutes. It involves Russia.
>
> —Woody Allen

Janet thought she would have more fun in college. She loved her new friends but found all her courses boring, really boring. In fact, there wasn't one she liked at all in her first term. It seemed to her that she hardly had time to think about anything before the class moved on to another topic. So she found herself tuning out during lectures. She didn't read her texts too often because they were also pretty dull. Janet came to us after her first round of exams (after cramming to get through five weeks' worth of material in all her classes) to learn some better time-management skills. Although this was a concern and we did talk to Janet about time-management strategies, we focused more on addressing the boredom issue. We asked Janet to interview her professors to find out what they liked about their fields (surely there must be something, otherwise why would they spend their time on it?) and to talk to students majoring in the subjects she was studying. The hope was that she would find something of interest in each course that she could latch on to (we also sent her for some tutoring and met with her several times). Janet needed to overcome a mindset that she was learning for someone else (the teacher); she needed to believe that she was learning for herself. This is a process that takes some time, but it can be done.

you to get through the course. You might also try studying with others. Sometimes this can give you just the push you need to make it through the course.

Daydreaming. Daydreaming while studying can become a habit for some students. And some may not even be aware they are daydreaming until they close their books and realize they don't remember squat about what they've just read. The first thing you need to do if you're a daydreamer is learn to recognize when you are beginning to drift off. Then you need to be able to separate studying from daydreaming. When you find yourself dreaming, stop studying and allow the thoughts to come, then regain focus and start studying again. Another good suggestion is to simply stand up, turn away from what you were studying, and clear your mind. This only takes about thirty seconds, and then you can get back to work. Or push the daydreams out of your mind by writing them down and then resume studying. Your goal is to be able to separate the dreaming from the studying.

Perfectionism. Sometimes students find themselves paralyzed by perfectionism or the need for everything to be done exactly right. Although this may sound good in theory, spending a lot of time perfecting things unnecessarily can actually hamper your ability to concentrate. Try to make the distinction between the things that need to be letter-perfect and those that just need to be good enough. (Hint: your room doesn't have to be spotless before you can study—trust us. For most students, this is a good thing.)

Identifying the things that keep you from concentrating is not always easy, and you may find that they vary from day to day. Our best advice is to monitor yourself, and when you find your motivation for studying is slipping, ask yourself what is getting in the way of your ability to focus. Once you can recognize the problem, you can begin to use strategies to fix it.

Six Ways to Improve Concentration

When you get down to studying, do you find yourself thinking about everything in the world except the task at hand? Here are some strategies that will help you focus—they may actually cut down on the time you need to study because you will get so much more accomplished.

Keep a jot list. Have a pad of paper where you can write down your "worry list"—all those thoughts you have (about calling home, checking email, doing laundry, or cleaning your room) that keep you from concentrating on your studying. Some students find it helpful to jot this kind of information into their daily planners so it becomes their to-do list. Or it can become your reward for getting your work done—"I will check my email once I finish reviewing my notes."

Set a purpose. Before you study, know what you want to accomplish in the session. Be as specific as possible—"studying science" is not really a purpose, but "understanding the concepts in chapter 7" would be a good studying purpose. It is also a good idea to set a purpose for reading. Think about what you already know about the topic and ask yourself questions that you will answer while reading. This is a great way to keep focused.

Take an active role. If you have ever read a chapter in your text and then realized that you have no idea what in the world you just read, then you know how important it is to really concentrate while studying. Otherwise, you are simply wasting time. One way to take an active role in your studying (instead of passively turning pages) is to take notes while you read. We will talk about this in more depth later, but for now, note taking simply involves writing down all the key information in your own words as you read.

Study in the same place and approximately at the same times. Some students are very easily distracted by a change of scenery. If they study outside, they end up playing with the grass or watching people walking by. If they study in the library, they end up browsing the stacks or watching other people trying to study instead of getting their work done. If this is you, then plan to study in the same place—preferably a place you know well (such as your room) so you are not distracted by new things. However, some get bored quickly when studying in the same place and find their concentration improves when they have a few places to choose from. So figure out whether you do better in the same place every time or whether you should plan to have several places where you can get studying done. You should also plan your study sessions for the same time each day. This helps you work when you can concentrate best and it helps make studying a habit—if it's 7:00 P.M., then it's time to study.

Have a set start and end time. Many students tell us they just set aside two or three evenings per week for studying. They plan to study for as long as it takes to get the work done. However, these students often find that without a start and end time for studying, they end up wasting a good deal of the evening without getting too much accomplished. They say things like "I studied for five hours last night." But when you talk to them about how much of that time was really spent studying, it is often more like an hour and a half. If you set a time limit for your studying, you tend to get more work done because you have imposed a deadline for yourself. The trick is to plan enough time in your schedule to get everything done.

Be here now. If you find your attention is a million miles away from your studies, you need to pull yourself back. Every time you find your mind wandering, repeat this phrase until you find yourself focusing again: "Be here now." Try it—it really works!

GET IT TOGETHER

Some students have a terrible time just getting started. We always have students in our classes who get way behind, and before they know it, they have tons of anxiety. The scenario goes something like this: Jenna sits down to study. She has good intentions, mind you, but ten minutes into her study session, her friend Lila comes in and wants her to go to a movie. Jenna doesn't think twice. She closes her books, combs her hair, grabs her purse, and she's out the door. "I'll catch up tomorrow" is her last thought. The next day, the same scene happens—different person, different invite—but Jenna gets further behind. Then guilt and panic set in and the Jennas of the world say, "Tonight's the night. I'm going to stick with it and get caught up. I'm serious." Sure you are. If you are Jenna in disguise, try sticking with it. Just once, say no. If you do this once, it will give you the confidence to know you can discipline yourself if you want to.

If You Read Nothing Else, Read This

○ Create a study space where you can focus. We suggest sitting in a straight-backed chair in a room with good lighting. Try playing some quiet background music if it helps you concentrate.

○ Get rid of distractions. Remember to consider both external (noise, roommates, room temperature) and internal (hunger, test anxiety, daydreaming) influences on your concentration.

○ Have a plan for getting your concentration back. Set studying hours and studying goals to keep yourself on track.

CHAPTER 13

YOUR COURSE SYLLABUS IS YOUR FRIEND

- Worried that you don't really know what your professors expect from you?
- Concerned about keeping track of and understanding the special policies in all your courses?
- Think that the role of a course syllabus is just for your professor to waste paper and make you believe the course is harder than it is?

If so, read on . . .

In high school, you probably showed up to class each day with little or no idea where the course was heading, what topics you'd be covering, or when all the exams were going to happen. Only the teacher had this knowledge. In college, however, professors provide you with a lot of this information in the course syllabus, which is usually distributed at the beginning of each term in class or on a course-support program such as WebCT. A syllabus can be as simple as one sheet of paper listing reading assignments and test dates. Or it can be as thick as the Sunday newspaper, chock full of detailed course information. Some professors consider the syllabus to be a contract with their students: if you successfully complete the tasks described in the contract, you will pass the course. Other professors consider their syllabus to be a work in progress. These professors tend to make minor changes to the syllabus throughout the course (though major tasks like exams and paper assignments usually don't change).

One of the steps to becoming a successful college student is to know how to read your syllabus for important information about the course—information that other students might miss. For example, your history professor may tell you in the syllabus that he believes that history is not made up of "facts" but that it is a story that is continually changing as new information is discovered. This simple statement tells you an awful lot about the type of test questions you can expect from this professor. We'd bet that you wouldn't be asked many questions about names and dates. Instead, you probably will be asked questions that require you to make interpretations of and think critically about events.

DO YOUR HOMEWORK

After the first day of classes, go through your syllabi (the plural of syllabus) and highlight all the important information such as exam dates, due dates of papers or projects, and key information about what is expected of you in class. Then put them somewhere safe and don't lose them! We suggest you keep the syllabus for each class in your notebook or binder for that class so you can refer to it often. This is one way to monitor your learning.

> Knowledge is of two kinds; we know a subject ourselves, or we know where we can find information upon it.
>
> —Samuel Johnson

Anatomy of a Syllabus

Here are the first few pages of a typical syllabus. Read over the sections; then we'll discuss the sorts of things you can expect to find in a syllabus.

This section tells you what to call your professor, where to find her, and how to contact her.

This section also tells you what you need to buy for class. Note that this class requires more than just a textbook.

In this section you find information about the professor's philosophy of the course as well as what is expected of students.

After reading this section, you will know not to ask Dr. Smith if you can turn in work late. She simply won't accept it.

LEARNING TO LEARN

Professor: Dr. Smith
Office: 225 Land-Grant Hall
Office Hours: M 10–1, W 12–4 and by appointment
Phone: 555-0000
Email: smith@bigu.edu
Text: Nist, S. L., & Holschuh, J. P. 2000. *Active Learning: Strategies for College Success.* Allyn & Bacon.
Supplies: Schedule book
Email account
Folder with pockets
(These supplies are not optional; purchase them when you purchase your books.)

GENERAL INFORMATION

The purpose of Learning to Learn is to teach students how to become better learners by developing efficient and effective studying behaviors. Learning to Learn helps students learn and apply more mature study strategies and select strategies based on the text, the task, and their own characteristics as learners.

It is important for students taking Learning to Learn to understand that successful completion of the course demands practice. As strategies are taught, students are expected to apply them to college-level materials presented in class as well as to other courses in which they are enrolled.

EXPECTATIONS REGARDING ASSIGNMENTS

You are responsible for assignments whether or not you are in class the day they are assigned or the day they are due. If you are going to miss class for any reason and wish to receive credit for the assignment due that day, you must get the assignment to me at the beginning of class on the day it is due.

GRADING

As with other courses, grades depend primarily on how well students perform on exams and other course requirements. Exams will consist of objective questions, essay questions, and scenarios based on problem-solving activities. Grades will be determined using a point system and will be weighted as follows:

Exam 1	20%
Exam 2	20%
Project	10%
Practice and quizzes	20%
Final exam	30%

> This section explains how grades are computed and weighted.

TENTATIVE COURSE SCHEDULE

(Note: Reading assignments are due on the day they appear in the syllabus. This means that on August 21 you should have read chapter 1 before you come to class.)

8/16 Syllabus; introduction to the course
Differences between high school and college

8/21 What is an active reader?
Starting out on the right foot
Reading assignment: chapter 1

8/23 Active learning
Four factors that influence learning
Reading assignment: chapters 2 & 3

8/28 Motivation
Studying cycle
Gearing up for class
Reading assignment: chapters 5 & 12

> By using the word *tentative,* Dr. Smith is telling you to expect changes to the schedule. It also tells you that she will be somewhat flexible about covering the topics.

> In this section you also find daily discussion topics, daily assignments, and important dates for exams and projects.

8/30	Figuring out the task
	Annotation
	Reading assignment: chapters 10 & 13
9/4	Time management
	Assessing your learning
	Reading assignment: chapter 4
9/6	Exam 1

LISTEN UP

It is always a good idea to let your instructors know when you are coming to office hours so they can be sure to be there. Most professors try to keep their schedules free during office-hour time, but take it from us—things crop up all the time. If you do not let your professor know you are coming, you may find an empty office. And nothing is more frustrating than actually hiking across campus to see your professor and not finding him there.

Although syllabi differ depending on the course content and instructor, the following features are present in most. Check out your syllabi and make a mental note of which of these elements you find. Spending a little time getting to know your syllabi can help you a great deal in the long run.

How to reach your instructor. This information is very important to know. Generally, the syllabus will tell you the instructor's office hours, office phone number, and email address. Sometimes your instructor will tell you her preferred mode of communication: "Students may find it difficult to reach me in my office because I am usually working in the lab, so my advice is to contact me by email."

The grading policy. You will find several pieces of information about how you are being graded that should answer the following questions: What counts as an A— 90 percent or above? What happens if you get 89.55 percent? Are grades calculated using a point system? Are exam scores curved? If you are writing papers, is there a grading rubric or some set of criteria that the instructor follows? Are your assignments graded by the professor or by a teaching assistant? All this information should be found somewhere in the syllabus.

Texts and materials. Your syllabus will let you know what you need to purchase for the course. Most courses require you to purchase at least one textbook, but many also require other supplies, such as calculators, art supplies, lab equipment, or computer software. In addition, the syllabus will tell you about supplementary materials you may need to find in the library, on a website, or elsewhere on campus.

SAD BUT TRUE

Craig was taking intro to chemistry. He was very relieved when the professor announced that all grades would be curved for each exam because he'd always heard that curving helps student grades. After each test, students were given an answer sheet so they could figure out their score, and grades were posted about a week after each test (the curved grades, however, were not calculated until the end of the term). Craig figured that he was making a low A based on his point scores for each exam. He was pretty angry when he found out that the curve actually dropped his grade to a high B. His professor was using a traditional curving method, which means that some high scores needed to be curved downward in addition to some low scores being curved upward. We are not sure if curving is the fairest system, but many professors continue to use it.

Special policies. Some instructors have attendance policies wherein you lose points for each absence (or gain points for perfect attendance). Others have participation policies wherein you earn course points for becoming involved in class discussions. Your instructor may even offer extra credit for participating in a research study or doing some extra work. You might find it helpful to note these policies by highlighting them in your syllabus.

Course requirements. Your syllabus will contain information about what you will need to do to demonstrate your learning in the course. This includes schedules and descriptions of tests, papers, reports, projects, presentations, homework assignments, or

GET WIRED

Most textbooks have a resource page on the publisher's website. Even if your instructor does not require you to use these resources (or even tell you that they are available), it is a good idea to check out the webpage to find more information about the text, other links, and even a bank of test questions about the material.

anything else you will need to do. The course requirements section should also tell you if there are any prerequisites for the course (for example, you must successfully complete Math 101 before taking this course).

Instructor's philosophy. Contained within most syllabi is some insight into how your professor views the content she is teaching. Consider this statement from Dr. David Zehr's History of Psychology course at Plymouth State College: "This course is not designed to merely teach you the 'facts' of psychology's history. Anyone can memorize names and dates. And if that's all we did, then even I'd be tempted to cut class on a regular basis! To the contrary, it is my hope that this course will provide a framework that will help you better understand the complexity and diversity of contemporary psychology; understanding the present is inherently easier if one possesses a perspective on what has come before." This professor spells out his view of what history is and why he thinks it is important to learn history. If you were a student in this class, you would know from reading the syllabus that memorizing names and dates would not be anywhere near enough for preparing for the professor's exams.

> ### 🏛 DO YOUR HOMEWORK
>
> Most professors do not offer any type of extra credit work (and get irritated with students who request extra credit work), so if extra credit options are not stated in the syllabus, don't even bother asking. Instead, focus on doing well on the assigned tasks.

> ### ☹ SAD BUT TRUE
>
> Sara was taking an intro to music course and knew that she would be graded over three exams. She did fairly well on the exams and was sure there was an error when she received her grade at the end of the term. She had earned a C for the course. When she contacted the professor, he told her that she did not complete all of the course requirements. Sara told the professor that she had saved her old exams and that, according to her calculations, she was making an 83 percent. The professor agreed with these calculations, but said she had lost points because in addition to the exams, students were required to attend three music concerts, and Sara did not turn in tickets to prove her attendance. Sara did not even know this was a requirement, but when she looked at the syllabus, there it was in black and white.

Course objectives. Your syllabus should contain several statements about what the instructor hopes you will learn as a result of the course. For example, Dr. Deborah Martin of Clark University's School of Geography states the following objectives in her American Cities course:

- To provide a historical context of North American urbanization and the contemporary patterns of urban growth and suburbanization
- To inform your knowledge of the economic and social roles of cities
- To encourage a geographic approach to understanding urban processes
- To help you to observe the landscape analytically

After reading these objectives, you would know you would be expected to gain knowledge about North American urbanization and to think critically about it by applying the geographic theories you learn and by making your own observations.

Other professors give you more of an integrated view of their philosophy and goals. Dr. Ian Lukas, from the University of Georgia, writes the following statement in his American History syllabus:

> William Faulkner wrote that, "History isn't dead. It isn't even history." Doing history often involves a kind of contradictory double consciousness: the attempt to understand and interpret the past on its own terms, as those who lived it made sense of their lives and the worlds around them, and to grapple with history's profound impact on the present, guided by questions invariably drawn from our own times.
>
> Given this, the goals of this course are to introduce you to key themes and events in American history from Reconstruction to the post-Cold War era, and in the process, to familiarize you with what it means to read, write, and analyze like a historian. The course is designed to provide you with the skills to articulate basic historical questions, identify the primary and secondary sources you need to answer those questions, and interpret the necessary evidence both on its own terms and from our contemporary perspectives. This will not only give you a sense of how historians think, but also

The absent are always in the wrong.

—English proverb

introduce you to ongoing historical debates—both those that take place in the halls of academia and those waged in the broader public arena.

Having this kind of information can be incredibly informative as you plan out how to prepare for the course.

Study tips. Your syllabus will often contain helpful hints, such as "be sure to read the text before coming to class" or "previous classes have noted that it is much easier to study this material in a group setting." Explore your syllabus for this type of information; it will really help you know how to prepare for the course requirements.

Course calendar. The course calendar provides information about the order of the topics to be covered and also about exam dates and other deadlines. Note these important dates by highlighting them in the syllabus and by putting the dates into your schedule book. If you have homework requirements in the course, other smaller assignments, or special events such as a field trip or a visiting speaker, note them as well so you don't forget about them. In addition, if your professor revises the original calendar, note that information as well.

GET IT TOGETHER

Once you get your syllabus, go buy your books. We have noticed a disturbing trend where some students wait to buy books until right before the first exam. Unfortunately, by this time in the term, bookstores are typically out of stock of the current semester's book or they have already sent the "extra" stock back! However, if you have not been reading your book all along, you may find yourself in deep trouble just trying to catch up. Our advice: keep up with your reading by following the reading schedule in your syllabus outline.

What Can Your Syllabus Do for You?

We don't think we can stress enough the importance of your syllabus. When you start any new class, you should carefully read the syllabus. Then you should put it in a place where you can easily access it and won't lose it (like in your class notebook). After you have been in the course for a week or two, you should read your syllabus again. It is amazing how much more you will get out of the second reading once you are familiar with the professor and the expectations of the course.

Your syllabus will help you study for your class. Check the syllabus for the topics you need to cover for each exam, but look at more than just the chapter numbers. Often your professor will list discussion topics for each class meeting. These are the most important ones to cover in your studying. In addition, reading over your professor's course philosophy can give you an idea of the kinds of questions that will be asked. For example, if your biology professor states that "there are no truths in science," then you know that when your book presents several theories for a science concept, your professor will ask you to evaluate all of them rather than memorize just one.

Your syllabus can help you organize and think about course material. Use it to help plan your weekly schedule. Check out your assignments for each week and plan accordingly. Suppose you find that you have three history chapters, two biology chapters, and thirty precalculus problems to work this week. You can use this information to help plan out your studying sessions. In fact, information in your syllabi is one of the most important resources at your disposal. So get the most out of each syllabus by referring to it at least once a week.

> I fear explanations explanatory of things explained.
>
> –Abraham Lincoln

If You Read Nothing Else, Read This

○ **Syllabi contain a wealth of information.** Use them to find information about how to reach your instructor, grading, and special policies, texts, and requirements for the course.

○ **Examine your syllabi for information about preparing for the course.** Take a look at statements about your professor's philosophy, course objectives, and information regarding studying for course exams.

○ **Keep your syllabi handy.** Use the information you find to help plan your weekly studying schedule.

CHAPTER 14

WHAT'S UP, DOC? UNDERSTANDING YOUR PROF'S EXPECTATIONS

- Worried that you will be clueless about how your professor will test you?
- Concerned that even if you can figure out your professor's expectations, you still won't know how to study for the exams?
- Think you should try to study for every course in the same way?

If so, read on . . .

One of the keys to being successful in college is the ability to get inside your professor's head and try to understand the way he thinks. No way, you say. Don't even want to go there, you think. All those "stories" inside your history professor's head. The excitement your botany professor gets from explaining why some flowers are white and others are lilac, even though they come from two purple parents. Two purple parents? Whatever. The fact remains, however, that if you can figure out how your professors think about their disciplines, you'll understand how they want you to think about that content. When you know how you're supposed to think about the information, then you can also anticipate how your professors will test you. Actually, it's not too hard once you get the hang of it.

Professors have you do stuff in their courses. We call this stuff "tasks." Tasks can be things like knowing what kind of tests you'll have and the level of thinking that is required on these tests. Tasks can be in-class essays or out-of-class papers. They can be multiple-choice tests that ask you to memorize a bunch of facts or critical reviews that make you think till it hurts. Tasks can be carried out on the computer, in class, or in the privacy of your own room. You may think this all sounds pretty simple. You go to class; your professor tells you that you will have a multiple-choice test on Friday. Bingo. Task known. Sometimes, however, it's not that easy.

Have you ever studied for a test really hard but then couldn't figure out where your professor's questions came from? Mars maybe? If that's happened to you, chances are you didn't understand the task. So knowing how to prepare for exams is one reason it's important to know what a course's tasks are. Why else is it important to know the tasks? How do you figure it all out? And what if you can't figure it out? What do you do then? Read on.

Why Bother Figuring Out the Tasks?

Part of being successful in college (and in life) is figuring out what others expect of you, especially your professors. When you were in high school, you had your teachers for a longer period of time, often for the entire school year. You were taught in smaller groups and, therefore, you got to know your teachers fairly well. You were evaluated through homework, quizzes, and frequent tests. Chances are you earned a gazillion points in any one grading period. In addition, your teachers may have given you lots of supports—study guides, terms to know, questions to think about—before each major test. All these things helped you to figure out the type of questions and information your teachers might ask you. You knew what you had to do, perhaps without having to think much about it. You made good grades on your tests

> Don't play what's there, play what's not there.
>
> —Miles Davis

and report cards. And you probably were able to earn extra credit to boot. Life was easy then. In college, figuring out what you have to do—the tasks, that is—can be more of a challenge, but it is a key skill to have if you want to be successful. Why, you ask?

1. If you can figure out the task, you'll know how your professor wants you to think about the material. Some professors may ask you to think about information in a superficial way. They may simply want you to memorize information rather than apply it. But most want you to think beyond what is in the book and lectures. They expect you to think deeply and to make connections between ideas. Once you understand how to think about course material, half the battle is over. Okay, only a quarter of the battle is over.

URBAN LEGEND

A university professor gave an examination question in which he asked, "What is the difference between ignorance and apathy?" The professor had to give an A+ to a student who answered, "I don't know and I don't care." (Trust us—it's not quite that easy to earn an A+.)

2. If you can figure out the task, you can select the appropriate learning strategies. If you use the wrong kind of strategies when you study, you're just spinning your wheels. Wasting time. Getting nowhere. In situations where you put lots of time into studying for a test and still did poorly, your strategies probably didn't match the task.

3. If you can figure out the task, you can earn good grades on the exam. And (following this line of thinking), if you score high on the tests, you'll make a good grade in the course and even learn something in the process. It's important to think about what you are supposed to do in each of your college classes. Once you know the task, you should be able to choose the right strategies.

Figuring It Out

A moment's insight is sometimes worth a life's experience.

—Oliver Wendell Holmes

Occasionally, you will have a professor who is easy to figure out. That's not saying you'll earn an A. We simply mean that she's straight up about what she expects from you. She may even say things

Kevin was enrolled in Introduction to Anthropology. There were so many bold-faced words in the text that he was sure he knew what he had to do to prepare for the multiple-choice exams—in a word, memorize. For the first test, Kevin made about 150 flash cards to learn all the new terms. He'd flip through them waiting for the bus, before class started, any time he found a few free minutes. He also put in a good deal of study time at home and felt prepared because he had every card memorized, front and back, before the exam. Sounds good, huh? Kevin put in the time and made some strategies, so he should ace the test. Imagine his surprise when he couldn't answer the majority of the questions because they focused on synthesizing and applying all the terms he had dutifully memorized. He realized that although he knew definitions, he really did not understand what they meant in the big picture. He began to get a handle on the fact that he needed to make a change in his study approach before the next test.

such as, "This is what you have to do to be successful in here" or "I want you to think about the material in this way" or "Here are some studying tips for this class. Do these things and you'll do well." But most of the time, it takes a little more maneuvering. More often than not, figuring out the task is like putting together the pieces of a puzzle where each piece comes from a different place. If you're having problems figuring out what it is your professor expects, you have several sources to tap. Remember that you may have to get bits and pieces from most or all of these sources in order to have a complete picture of the task.

READ YOUR SYLLABUS

As we discussed in the last chapter, your syllabus should outline your professor's expectations. It should tell you if you will have multiple-choice or essay tests. You should also find information on how many tests you will have, how many papers you will have to write, and the approximate dates they will be given. There also may be hints in the

There's a link between figuring out the task and being successful in college. It has been shown on several occasions that students who can figure out what their instructors expect from them do better in college. In fact, even if you start out not understanding the task but figure it out after the first exam and make adjustments in your studying, you will end up doing well.

syllabus about the type of thinking your professor expects. For example, if your syllabus states something to this effect, "In this course, you will be expected to read your text, take detailed notes both in lecture and in your discussion group, and then make connections between what you read and what you hear," you can be fairly certain that you will have to synthesize the information and think about ideas at deeper levels.

> Results! Why, man, I have gotten a lot of results. I know several thousand things that won't work.
>
> —Thomas A. Edison

THINK ABOUT HOW YOUR PROFESSOR LECTURES

After a while, you'll catch on to the idea that professors have different lecture styles. Some profs will make a general statement first ("All dogs have fleas") and then fill in the details ("Some dogs have more fleas than others. Indoor dogs have fewer fleas than outdoor dogs . . . yadda, yadda, yadda"). This is an *inductive* style of lecturing: the key point is given, followed by details. Other professors will provide the details first ("Some dogs have more fleas than others. Indoor dogs have fewer fleas than outdoor dogs . . . yadda, yadda, yadda") and then finally get to the big picture statement ("In sum, all dogs have fleas"). This is a *deductive* style of lecturing: details are given first and followed by the key point. Most students prefer the inductive style because they at least are aware of the big picture and can get that in their notes. Sometimes, when a professor is throwing lots of details out there first, it becomes harder to figure out the main point. Professors can also lecture in a storylike fashion, something that is very common in the humanities, particularly history. Or there may be little lecture and more discussion or demonstration or problem solving.

Besides the lecture style, we suggest you pay attention to the type of information the professor stresses from the textbook. History profs will often stress the order in which things happened (chronology), political science profs will stress charts and flowcharts, and science profs will stress diagrams. The point we want to make is that sometimes students aren't aware that thinking about how their professor lectures gives them some important insights into the way questions will be asked on the exam.

TALK WITH PAST STUDENTS

It really doesn't matter if they made an A or an F in the course. The purpose of talking to former students is to get as much information as possible about how the professor tests. And we don't mean the exact questions she asked, because the same items usually aren't used from term to term (and that kind of knowledge would count as academic dishonesty). If the tests you will take are multiple-choice, try to find out if the questions on past tests focused on facts (who, what, when, where questions) or on higher levels of thinking, asking you to recognize examples or apply information to new situations. If you will have essay exams or other kinds of exams that require you to write, ask former students how the exams were graded and what kinds of information you would need to include in order to maximize your score.

TALK WITH CLASSMATES IN THE KNOW

There will always be students in your class who seem to hang on every word the professor says, ask thought-provoking questions, take notes that look as though they

SAD BUT TRUE

Sonja was enrolled in a botany class that she enjoyed very much because she was thinking of majoring in landscape architecture. She had taken advanced biology in high school along with other life sciences, so she felt very comfortable and confident about doing well in the course. But her professor taught quite differently from her high school teachers. Both lectured and had students work through computer modules, but her college prof used loads of diagrams during his lectures. Sometimes they were similar to those that were in the textbook, but other times Professor Wilson seemed to produce them out of thin air. Not only did he know botany, he could also draw! Because Sonja could hardly draw a stick figure, she never put any of the diagrams in her notes. Few students did. Instead, they just wrote down the lecture material—that is, until after the first test. Sonja couldn't believe it. She studied long and hard for the test, but because she had never been tested over diagrams in the past, she ignored them. And the test was full of them. Almost every question referred in some way to one of the diagrams. By using diagrams as a big part of his lectures, Professor Wilson was sending a message about the task, a message that Sonja and many others in the class didn't even recognize.

As you are working on figuring out the task, it's important to make sure you are very clear what you will be expected to include when you're answering identification questions. On our campus, for example, most history professors give tests that require students to answer identification questions in addition to essay questions. In order to get full credit on the identification items, students must first define the item and then explain the significance of it. Students who give only the definition receive only half credit. So ask rather than lose half the points.

were professionally done, and, in general, have it together. (Note: these are probably not the students on Facebook who look as though they haven't slept in days or appear to be in a 24/7 party mode.) If you don't have much of a clue about what you're supposed to be doing, chat with those who do. Ask them how they are studying and the types of strategies they are using in order to prepare for the exams. Be honest and tell them you're having a hard time figuring out what the professor expects, but don't give them the idea that you are trying to get out of doing the work on your own. For example, saying something like, "Hey dude. Can I copy your notes?" after you have slept through class will probably not endear you to the student who has taken some time to figure out the task and then does what he needs to do.

DO YOUR HOMEWORK

If your task involves writing—essays, short answers, or identification items— be sure to find out if your professor subtracts points for spelling, grammar, and usage errors. A few professors we know do, because they see it as their task not only to help you learn their discipline, but also to encourage you to improve your writing skills. Actually, it is a trend now on college campuses for courses to have goals beyond teaching basic content. Improving writing skills and developing critical thinking skills are two popular targets.

LOOK AT RETIRED EXAMS

Depending on your campus, you may or may not have access to old, "retired" exams. Some campuses keep test files in the library where students can check them out. Some professors will let you look at retired tests—or at the very least provide you with examples of questions that they have used on previous exams. Another resource for old exams is students who have taken the course in previous terms. Sometimes even campus groups, such as Greek organizations and student governments, keep test files. If you have access to retired exams, don't make the mistake of trying to memorize answers to the questions or just studying the information required to answer questions on this particular test. The purpose of looking at old exams is to give you an idea of how the professor tests. A word to the wise deserves mentioning: don't ever, ever "buy" an old exam. If you do, chances are you are engaging in some form of academic dishonesty. Students who sell old exams certainly didn't come by them honestly.

LISTEN FOR "IN YOUR FACE" COMMENTS

We are continually amazed at the kinds of information students don't attend to or put in their notes. We have been in classes where professors give students very clear signals about the task, in some cases almost hitting them over the head with information that they will have to know. All too often such signals go unheeded by students, particularly if these pearls of wisdom are thrown out right at the beginning of class when students are settling in or in the last couple of minutes when the prof is winding down his lecture and students are already putting away their notebooks and thinking about something else. So be smart. When your professor makes a really profound statement like "Gee, that would make an interesting essay question," write it down in your notes with a big TQ (for "test question") in the margin. Such statements are another piece of the puzzle of determining the task.

TALK TO A TUTOR

Because campus tutors work with and talk to lots of students, they often have insight into what is expected of you in the courses you are taking. Even if you are not having trouble with the content, you can make an appointment to run your studying approach by the tutor. If you are memorizing when you should be synthesizing, the tutor can usually set you straight.

GET IT TOGETHER

Students who fall behind in their work often don't realize that they might need any additional help until it's too late. These students sometimes will seek out a tutor, and when that doesn't help, they blame their weak performance on the tutor. It gives them an out (for example, "It wasn't my fault. I had an awful tutor or I would have done better."). The message here is simple—tutoring doesn't help much if you're not keeping up by going to class, taking decent notes, and doing the reading.

Computer Tasks in Your Classes

Believe it or not, when we were undergraduates in college we didn't own computers (and it really wasn't even the dark ages). Today, however, having a computer is even more important than having a cell phone or a credit card on campus. Even if you don't have your own computer, professors will expect you to have an email account that you check regularly. And gone are the days of turning in a handwritten paper— you may be expected to turn in your finished paper via email attachment and in the proper style, to boot. In addition, you will need to use a computer for some course assignments (especially in literature, business, engineering, and mathematics classes) and may even take some exams on computer. If you want to find a book in the library, chances are you will need to get on a computer to locate it.

Most college campuses have computer labs that students can use free of charge (although many campuses now charge a "tech fee" for use of computers and other technological services). If you need them, there are often courses you can take to familiarize yourself with how to use computers in general or how to use the computer services offered by the school (check your college's bulletin or website to find out where you can get this kind of training).

Although your college professor may look as old as the hills, he's probably pretty knowledgeable about computers, and part of your task will be to figure out how to use the required technology. Like all educators and researchers, college profs have had to stay somewhat current, and many are integrating technology (specifically computers and the Internet) into their classroom teaching in a wide variety of ways. You may encounter one or more of the following:

- Computerized course-management systems (such as WebCT). These systems allow professors to put syllabi, quizzes, homework assignments, and other course materials online. Students can often check their grades or meet in virtual study groups on these sites.

- Course notes. Some professors put lecture notes or other content online. These supports can help you evaluate your own notes or learn more about a topic you found especially interesting.

- CD-ROM supplements. Sometimes you will need to purchase a CD-ROM or other software supplement when you buy your textbook. They are becoming more popular in several content areas but especially in the sciences, where the CDs present slides, videos, or demonstrations that could not be represented in a traditional textbook.

- Exam modules or tutorials. Many professors (and most textbook publishers' webpages) offer exam modules. These sites provide practice questions so you can get a sense of what the exam will be like. They can also be used to help you monitor your learning of the material. If you take a computer module after you have finished studying for an exam and you do well, you know you've learned the material. If, on the other hand, you miss a lot of the items, you know what you will need to rehearse and review some more before taking the test.

- Email assignments. You can expect that some of your assignments will need to be turned in online. It may be just a one-page email journal, a lab report, or a full-scale paper that you will need to send via an email attachment, so be prepared. Your professors will expect you to know how to turn in these assignments.

- Podcasts. This teaching supplement is becoming so popular that some campuses require students to have the technology available to download podcasts. Most supplement what goes on in the classroom, but we foresee the day when entire courses will be taught this way.

- Computerized exams. This format is becoming more widely used on college campuses. You may take all your exams in this format or, more commonly, only the final exam. In fact, many freshman English courses now require all students to write and edit their papers and their exams on the computer.

FOR ADULTS ONLY ⊗

We have found that sometimes returning students don't use technology as they should. Perhaps they are afraid of it or perhaps they just don't know how to use it. Our advice: seek some help—either from your professor, a tech-savvy friend, or even the student worker in the campus computer lab. Usually, when the professor requires some type of additional technology for the course, it is to *aid* the student. So by all means, use every resource you can get.

Find out as much as you can about the role of computers and technology in your classes. Listen to what your instructor says about the subject and read over your syllabus. The more you know about what's expected in this arena, the better prepared you will be to do what's needed.

But What If You Still Don't Get It?

If you have exhausted all your sources and resources and still can't figure out what your professor wants, don't give up. There are still a couple of things you can do.

Most students who have difficulty figuring out the task don't realize it until after the first test. They think they know what they are doing, and they put time into studying, but they earn a disappointing score on the first test. Now is not the time to throw in the towel. Now is the time for regrouping and action. Rather than shoving your exam or paper inside your backpack (a denial tactic we have seen over and over again), spend some time going over it to see if you can figure out the kinds of things you did wrong. If you took a multiple-choice test, what types of items did you miss? If you took an essay exam, why did you have points taken off? If you did poorly on a paper, why? Take some time to see what you did right and what you did wrong. Look for patterns. Ask yourself: How does Professor Smith want me to think about this information? Just what is the task? How can I change my test preparation behaviors to match what she wants? We have found that most students who spend time evaluating their test performance end up improving their grade significantly on the next exam, paper, speech, and so forth.

Another alternative is to make an appointment to talk with the professor, often a scary thought, we know. Take your test or paper along (unless your prof keeps them) and ask him to go over it with you. Make notes about what he says; these comments may help you as you continue through the course. Students tell us that having a conference

GET WIRED

As strange as it sounds, there are profs who ban the use of laptops in their classes. Why, you ask? It seems with the integration of wireless Internet on many college campuses, some professors are finding that students are tuning out rather than taking notes. Find out your professor's policy on laptops (usually in the syllabus), and if you decide to bring one to class, please, pay attention to the lecture.

with their professor after a poor performance may be a bit intimidating at first, but they gain information that will help them do better. As we have said earlier, most professors want their students to succeed, and they are willing to meet with them if they are having problems. Sometimes it's enough just to say to your professor something like "I thought I was on the right track. These are the things that I did. . . . What am I doing wrong? How should I be thinking about this material?" Questions such as these show her that you are serious about learning in her course.

If you realize right from the start that you're lost and clueless about what direction to take in learning the material, don't wait until after the first test. Go—run—to see your professor as soon as you realize you don't know what the heck is going on. If you are hesitant or really nervous about talking with your professor face-to-face, see if it's possible to use email. A word of caution, however. No matter how lost and confused you are, try to articulate your difficulties. Telling your professor that you don't know what your problems are—or worse yet, blaming your lack of understanding on him—will not get you anywhere. Recognize that even if you are having trouble figuring out what you're supposed to be doing, there are alternatives to doing nothing. Talking with your prof is the best place to start.

> **URBAN LEGEND**
>
> After learning about conditioning, a psychology class decided to train their professor using positive reinforcement. In order to pull this off, the class only paid attention when the professor stood in one specific corner of the room. When he wandered from that spot students started shuffling papers, talking to each other, and generally looking disinterested. The story goes that eventually the professor was "trained" to stand in that one corner for the entire lecture. Yeah. Right. This one has been around for a while. "Training" your profs really isn't this easy.

Smart Strategy Selection

Although we will discuss specific test-taking strategies later in this book, it's important to understand that the strategies you use to study should match the task. Remember, you can't choose the most efficient and effective strategies if you don't know what it is you're supposed to do. Here are just some of the tasks that professors may expect from you:

- A multiple-choice test that mostly asks you to memorize information

- A multiple-choice test that asks for "higher-level" thinking, perhaps including questions focusing on examples or the applications of ideas

- An essay test that asks you to analyze, synthesize, or critique theories, events, and so forth

- A paper that asks you to provide support for your stance

- Identification questions that ask you to define a term and also give examples of the item or explain its significance

- Problems where you have to show your work, even though it's a multiple-choice test

- A speech or presentation

- A group project

Although this is a rather short list of different tasks (there are lots and lots of other alternatives), how you would approach each of them would differ, in some cases pretty dramatically. For example, if you have a multiple-choice test that just asks you to memorize, making a bunch of flash cards with the terms and definitions would probably get the job done. But if the multiple-choice test has questions that ask you to provide examples or link ideas, you will definitely want to ask yourself how and why questions, use strategies that help you visualize how the ideas are connected, and maybe even work with a study group.

We have found that a good number of students tend to categorize tasks too broadly to be of much help. They can tell you if the task is a test or a paper and, if it is a test, whether it has multiple-choice, matching, essay, or short-answer questions. But that's about it. If you can only identify the task in the broadest sense, you're probably going to have some difficulty deciding on the right strategies and approaches for studying.

If You Read Nothing Else, Read This

○ When you have defined the task, you have figured out what it is your professor expects from you. Defining the task involves knowing both the type of test or other activity you will be facing AND the level of thinking necessary to complete the task.

○ It's important to figure out the task so you can think about the material in the way your prof wants you to, so you can select the best strategies to use, and so you earn good grades on tests and papers.

○ To figure out the task, use your syllabus, think about your professor's lecture style, talk with students who have taken the class before and with current classmates, look at old exams, listen carefully for hints, and meet with a tutor.

○ If you still don't get it, meet with your prof or regroup after the first test.

CHAPTER 15

TAKE NOTE!

- Concerned about your ability to keep up with taking notes when your prof is talking a million miles an hour?
- Worried that you don't know how to study effectively using your lecture notes?
- Think that writing down only what the professor writes on the board is the best way?

If so, read on . . .

"What do I want for lunch?" "What's going to happen today on my favorite soap?" "This guy (girl) sitting next to me is kind of cute. Should I talk to him (her)?" These are some of the burning questions that may run through your mind as you sit in yet another lecture. Because taking lecture notes seems like such a passive activity (you just have to sit there, after all), many college students find it difficult to pay attention for the entire period, especially if the professor is, well, dry, dull, and boring.

Taking notes is an everyday occurrence in college, so it's something you need to do well. As a matter of fact, you need to do it extremely well. Students who take good lecture notes and know how to use them to their advantage usually do better on tests, plain and simple. And we all know that doing better on tests leads to good grades, an excellent GPA, a great job, . . . the presidency. Good lecture notes are the meat and potatoes of learning.

Write On: Some Terrific Note-Taking Tips

No matter how you take lecture notes, there are some general tips that cut across all formats. Your goal here is to get to the point where these behaviors become routine, no matter what class you're in.

BE THERE—ON TIME

Nothing is worse than plopping down in your seat, out of breath from rushing up five flights of stairs, right when the professor is beginning to lecture (or worse yet, after she has started), and finding that your pen has fallen somewhere into the bottomless pit of your backpack. By the time you've found your pen and are ready to take notes, the professor is already wound up and going full steam ahead—and you, my friend, have missed some really important stuff. So move it. Get your butt in gear. Try your best to get to class a few minutes before it starts so you can be ready to go when your professor starts lecturing.

SIT IN FRONT

Don't be shy. Let the prof see your smiling face—especially in large lecture classes. Students who sit in the front of the classroom and those who are in the professor's line of vision tend to listen better, ask questions, take better notes, and even perform better on tests than students who hide in the back. It's especially important to sit in the front if the visuals the professor uses are of poor quality (things like overheads, PowerPoint presentations, or material written on the board) or if the acoustics are bad. On our campus, even some of the smaller lecture rooms in major

Third Law of Applied Terror: eighty percent of the final exam will be based on the one lecture you missed and the one book you didn't read.

—Author unknown

Students who sit near the front of the classroom perform better than those who sit in the back. In fact, the closer to the front you sit, the better you'll tend to do. Those who sit closest to the front tend to make more grades of A and B; those in the middle, more Cs; and those near the back . . . well, you figure it out. The message here: the nearer to the front the better, especially in large lecture classes.

classroom buildings have such poor acoustics that students in the back of the room have to strain to understand what we are saying.

BE PREPARED

Have everything out and ready to go when the lecture begins. As soon as you get to class, get out everything you think you will need. Take out your notebook and pen and have clean sheets of paper ready to go. If you're taking notes on your laptop, be sure the battery is charged, turn it on, and be ready when the lecture begins. Once you're set, if you still have time, take a few minutes to read over your notes from the last lecture. It will get your mind ready for the lecture to come and will help you keep up your attention better.

DO YOUR OWN THING

Outlines or other visuals provided by your professor are a great way to help you organize your notes, but think of them only as a place to begin. It has been our observation that when professors provide students with an outline to frame their lecture or when they put terms and definitions on the board, students will copy the professor's notes and then drift off . . . zzzzz. Keep in mind that most outlines are just that—something brief meant to help you organize your notes and give you the key points. As your professor lectures on each point, include the additional explanations in your notes. We can guarantee you that your prof will expect you to be able to fill in the details on test day.

USE A BINDER, PLEASE

We're not sure why binders fell out of favor with college students. Perhaps it's because they are a bit more bulky to carry around. Whatever the reason, binders are much better for holding your notes than spiral-bound notebooks (and they're cheaper in the long run since you can reuse them). Using a binder makes it easier to organize your notes. If you miss class, you can easily insert notes you copy from someone else;

class handouts are also easily inserted. Gone is the worry that you'll lose important handouts because they might fall out of your notebook. And if someone wants to borrow your notes for a particular class day, you don't have to give her your entire notebook, just the pages she needs.

If you take notes on a laptop, you will still need a binder or a section of a binder for each class. You can put in your syllabus, course handouts, and, for courses where you may need to know diagrams (like biology), the visuals the prof displays in class. It's hard to draw a diagram of meiosis on your computer!

WRITE LEGIBLY

Because you'll have to use your notes to study from, write as legibly as you can while still taking notes at one hundred miles per hour. You'll be upset with yourself if you can't even decipher your own handwriting. No scribbling allowed. Make your notes nice enough in appearance that you will want to spend time with them—neatness counts! Of course, this is not a problem if you're taking notes on your computer.

KEEP AT IT

Write or type for the entire period. It's much better to get too much information in your notes than too little. Because listening to a lecture is a relatively passive task, you need to do something to keep active. If you're not writing, your mind will wander or, worse yet, you'll nod off and drop your pen, which will clatter loudly on the floor. But if you are actively listening and writing, the chances are you will attend better.

HEADS UP

Listen for cues during the lecture. Some professors lecture in an organized manner. Their lectures tend to flow, and they provide you with cues as they talk. If you are fortunate enough to have professors like this, listen for words or voice changes that alert you to important information. For example, professors may cue you to important lists ("There are three explanations of why people forget information. First . . . "), definitions ("Psychologists define repression as . . . "), examples ("Examples of schizophrenic behaviors include . . . "), or rhetor-

Nothing is a waste of time if you use the experience wisely.

—Auguste Rodin

Brian hated history. And so when he had no choice but to register for an introductory history course to round out his schedule the first term, he was not a happy camper. To add insult to injury, his professor talked a mile a minute and, in Brian's mind, lectured in a really bizarre way. He started every lecture with a bunch of facts, facts that were hard to connect. Brian was certain he wouldn't be tested on these facts so he never wrote them down. He always used this part of class to zone out or to work on some of his math problems. He figured he would wait until the important material came and then just write that down. No use wasting paper and cluttering up his notes. But by the time his history professor got to the "good stuff," Brian was off in la-la land. If he did catch anything, he had a hard time making sense of it since he had effectively tuned out a big part of the lecture.

By the time the first exam came around, about four weeks into the term, Brian had about ten pages of notes—total—and most of them weren't in any shape he could use to study from. After he failed that test, he decided he'd better rethink his approach to note taking. Even though it was like torture, he began to listen more attentively and write down all those facts that the prof spouted out. Pretty quickly he realized that when his prof did discuss the important stuff—the big picture—those facts served a purpose: they outlined the key points of the professor's forthcoming lecture. Brian still hated history and still found it difficult to stay focused during the lectures, but he discovered he could take notes from professors who lectured this way. Brian didn't exactly ace the class, but even after his awful performance on the first test, he managed to get a C+ in the course.

ical questions that they then proceed to answer ("Why are there several explanations of how memory works?"). They may also throw out very obvious cues ("This is really important for you to know, so be sure to get it in your notes"). Also listen for vocal changes. The more important the information, the greater the tendency for professors to talk louder and slower. Finally, don't forget about visuals. When a professor presents visuals, especially diagrams, this can be a cue that you will be expected to know that material at test time. Some students even keep their text open while taking notes so they can make notes on the diagrams in the book as the instructor is explaining them.

LISTEN, THINK (FAST), AND THEN WRITE OR TYPE (FAST)

Accept the fact that you are not going to be able get down every word the professor utters. Students who try to get down everything that is said in lecture usually wind up getting half thoughts. If you have ever found yourself trying to take notes and getting half a phrase written before the teacher is on to another idea (which you have already missed), then you know how frustrating taking notes can be. But actually, it is not that important to get down every single word. Instead, try listening to the entire thought, quickly paraphrasing what was said, and then writing that information in your own words. Remember, ideas that simply go in your ears and out your pen, without going through your brain, are not going to be well remembered later. This advice works as well for writing lecture notes as it does for typing them.

REVIEW YOUR NOTES REGULARLY

You don't want to wait until a day or two before a test to start reviewing your notes. We suggest that you go through the notes as soon as possible after class. Do it whenever you have small pockets of time. In addition, try reviewing your notes from the previous day while you are waiting for class to begin.

COMPARE NOTES WITH A CLASSMATE

One of the best strategies for making sure your notes are complete is to set aside some time to compare your notes with someone else's. We suggest you choose someone from each of your classes who seems on the ball—it can really help you clear up confusing points or missing ideas.

Taking a good set of lecture notes that can stand the test of time takes more than just showing up. You need to come to class prepared to take notes for the full period, and you need to review your notes on a daily basis.

Be Creative: Use the Split-Page Method of Note Taking

The best method of note taking we have found is called the split-page method. It's called this because you divide (or split) your paper into two columns, as shown in the figure on page 176. You take notes on the wider right-hand side and then use the left-hand side (which will have a two- or three-inch margin) to write questions or annotations once the lecture is over. You can buy special notebook paper, usually called law paper, which has the wider margins already set for you, but this paper often costs three times more than the regular stuff. So we suggest splitting your own paper. To split your page, you can either draw lines on several sheets of paper before you go to lecture, or you can simply fold the narrower margin back.

Once you have your paper ready, keep these tips in mind:

⚡ GET WIRED

If you use your laptop to take notes in class, check out Microsoft OneNote. It gives you the flexibility to take notes in a variety of ways and can help you organize your notes throughout the semester. It also has a search feature where you can type in keywords and find exactly the page of notes you are looking for.

- Date your notes in case you need to refer to notes given on a specific day.

- Number each page so if you take pages out of your notebook to study or to lend to a classmate, you'll be able to get them back in the right place.

- Take notes in the larger right-hand space. (You'll write in the left-hand margin later.)

- Write in pen rather than pencil. Pencil fades, smudges, and smears. This can be a big problem if you have cumulative exams and you can't read your notes from two months ago.

- If you are using your laptop, there is software available that will let you type in a split-page method. Be sure you follow some of the same procedures as you would if you were taking notes in longhand—date your notes, number the pages, and take your notes in the larger right-hand column.

At last you are ready to take some notes. Here are some guidelines to taking notes in an organized way. These guidelines apply for handwritten and laptop notes.

- Write in simple paragraph form. Don't try to make detailed outlines. Students who outline tend to leave out lots of important information and often concentrate more on the outline itself than on the material that should be included.

- Indent or underline key points. This will help you distinguish main ideas from details.

- Skip a line or two between those key points. This way you will know at a glance when there is a shift in ideas.

- Identify examples. Marking them with an "X" or in some other way alerts you that the info is important to study.

- Number lists. Often tests will ask for "three causes of acne" or "four reasons why you shouldn't squeeze pimples." If you know how many reasons or causes there are to study right from the start, you will do better.

- Write in phrases. Don't attempt to write in complete sentences, but be sure to get enough information so you understand the point.

- Use abbreviations. It saves a considerable amount of time. For example, if your professor is lecturing on President John Fitzgerald Kennedy, it's much quicker to abbreviate it as "JFK" than to write it out each time. See page 202 in chapter 17 for more on using abbreviations.

Examine what is said, not him who speaks.

—Arabian proverb

SPLIT-PAGE NOTES IN ACTION

To see how your split-page notes should look, consider the example below. You've taken notes in the larger right-hand side of your notebook paper but you're not quite finished yet. (We warned you that there was a lot to this note-taking business.) Now it's time to do something with that smaller left-hand side. As soon as possible after

11/10/07	Memory Lecture Notes	title of lecture
types of memory—3	MEMORY—3 TYPES OF MEMORIES	

annotations or questions

What is sensory store? — 1. Sensory Store (SS) — key point
  —lots of info comes in that we don't pay attention to

What function does STM serve? —sometimes called a "gatekeeper"
  —only info that's processed (gets attention) can go into

How does info get into STM?

supporting information indented and organized

2. Short-term Memory (STM)
  —limited capacity (7 + or - 2)

Define and give an ex. of chunking
  BUT
  —can be expanded by
  → chunking
  [def] grouping things together into units in order to remember more

What are the characteristics of STM?

2- or 3-inch margin

  (ex) Soc. Sec # is remembered as 3 "chunks" rather than 9 indiv. pieces of info
  —is short
  —only lasts ~30 sec unless info is rehearsed

the lecture, take ten or fifteen minutes to read through your notes (it's a great way to review while the information is relatively fresh in your memory). As you read your notes, you can do one of two things. You can either

1. Write questions in the margins you can ask yourself as you study

2. Annotate key words, then verbally rephrase them into questions as you study

The important thing is to think about information that your professor will ask and the way you think she will ask it. Think back to what we said earlier about understanding the task. We said it then, but hey, it never hurts to repeat the good stuff: the key to doing well on exams is to figure out what your professor wants you to know. As you are writing your questions or annotations in the margins of your lecture notes, what your prof wants becomes crucial. If there is not a match between the types of questions you pose in your notes and those that your professor asks, you're sunk.

LISTEN UP

There is a small business in our town, strategically located near campus, which sells notes from a variety of core courses offered on campus. They hire students who are taking the classes to be their note-takers. Then, before exams, students can purchase packets of notes (they are generally pretty expensive). The notes are typed and printed on a dark red paper that cannot be copied. Hordes of students buy these notes, and often they get shortchanged. Some of the note-takers are hardly stellar students themselves (we know of one instance where the note-taker got a C in the course). Information in the notes is at best incomplete and at worst incorrect. Although this business is certainly enterprising and we are sure the owners make buckets of money, we think it's important for students to learn to take good notes themselves. The message here is buyer beware.

You're Almost There: Self-Testing Using the Split-Page Method

One of the key advantages of taking notes using the split-page method is that it allows you to do what we call "blind" self-testing. Think about the way you normally study from your notes. The scenario may go something like this: You open your notes and study by "reading through" them for a period of time. And you probably spend equal amounts of time on everything—things you know well are given the same amount of time as things you are struggling with. When you "feel pretty good" about what you know or you simply run out of time, you quit studying. Does any of this sound familiar? Although this procedure may have worked fairly well for you in high school, it may not be so successful in college. So we offer you a better way, a way that will help you use your studying time a bit more wisely. Try this approach:

1. Begin by doing what you perhaps have always done: read through your notes a couple of times to review and familiarize yourself with the major topics. Focus and concentrate. Read them out loud if you have to. But don't stop there.

2. Fold your notes back so all you can see is the narrower left-hand margin where you have your questions or annotations. If you have typed your notes during class, you will need to print them in order to study from them effectively. Ask yourself the question or turn your annotation into a question.

3. Try to answer the question without looking at your notes. Say everything you know about the concept, providing explanation and examples when appropriate. Be concise and accurate but thorough.

4. Now look at your notes. How much of the information did you remember? Was what you said earthshakingly brilliant and accurate, or do you still have a way to go?

5. Continue asking yourself questions as you plow through your notes. Find some way to distinguish the questions you know from those you need to spend more time on. For example, you might check off those you know or highlight those you need to study more. Then you will put in additional time only on those questions you have not checked off.

Self-testing is not only a more efficient way to study your notes, but it will also make you feel more self-confident going into your exams. If you are self-testing correctly, when exam day rolls around, you should know the material and feel confident that you will ace the test.

Different Strokes for Different Folks: Modifying the Split-Page Method

There may be times when you want to modify the split-page method somewhat depending on the types of tests you will have and the type of course you are in. Every course is not a lecture course, after all. In addition, there may be parts of this method that you simply want to modify and personalize. We encourage that! In fact, good students are flexible in the way they use strategies; they change strategies to suit themselves as learners. The one element we strongly suggest you keep, however, is the left-hand margin of your paper for your questions or annotations. This feature allows you to self-test. Here are some ways our students have modified the split-page method to suit their needs.

CONSOLIDATING TEXT WITH LECTURE

In courses where there's lots of overlap between lecture and text, some students like to use the back of their paper to add material that is related to the lecture but is found only in the text. If you are in a course that is taught in this manner, take your notes in the split-page method as described above, but take them on the front of the paper only. Then, as you read your text, write notes on the related material on the back of the page. As you study, you will have everything in one place and won't have to bounce from lecture notes to textbook.

DISCUSSION CLASSES

Some classes have discussion sessions once a week and some rely heavily on discussion all the time. Our students often tell us that it is difficult to take notes during discussion because it's hard to figure out which ideas to include. For discussion classes, we suggest a three-column approach to note taking. In the narrower left-hand column, write the question that is posed by the professor or discussion group leader. Divide the larger space into two columns. In one, jot down student responses. You can jot them all down and sift through them later or just write down those you think are worthy—ideas you think would be good to include on an essay exam, for example. In the last column, write any additional comments your professor makes. Be sure to get down (in brief paragraph form, of course) all your prof's important points.

179

VISUALS GALORE

It's common for some professors to lecture using diagrams, particularly in the sciences. The prof will put up a cross section of a root or a diagram of a cell and wax eloquent about it for thirty minutes. If you have a professor who teaches using diagrams, get reasonable replicas into your notes. It is also important that you get down the lecture notes that go with that diagram. If you have both, you can better determine what your professor wants you to learn and why he has used a diagram to make his point. You might want to draw each diagram on the top of the page and describe it below or divide the larger side of your paper into two columns—one for the diagram and the other for the explanation. When you go back to review your notes for the day, check your textbook for a similar diagram. If one is present, make a note of the page number in your notes so when you study, you can refer to a visual that may be clearer than yours. This step is particularly important if you're artistically challenged, like we are. (Also remember to write questions or annotations in the margins of your lecture notes to use for self-testing.)

> **🔊 LISTEN UP**
>
> In many discussion classes, professors create their exam questions based on class discussion. By taking notes during such a class, you are creating a study guide that many of your classmates (those who are not taking notes) will lack. So rather than tuning out during discussions, tune in. There could be lots of good stuff here to use come test time.

LECTURE NOTES ON THE WEB

With more and more professors using Web-based components as part of their courses, notes on the Web are becoming common. We know several professors who have student workers scan in their notes after each class. Although we believe this actually may encourage some students to take the easy way out—you know, skip class and then download the prof's notes—they can be very helpful if you compare your notes with your professor's as a way to make sure your notes cover all the important points. If you have access to notes on the Web, go to class everyday and take the best possible notes you can.

If Your Professor Posts the Notes Before Class . . .

Try the parallel notes method. To use parallel notes, you print out you professor's notes using only one side of the page and place them in a three-ring binder. Then, as your professor lectures, keep your binder open to the appropriate page, but take your own notes (expanding key ideas, jotting down examples, and so on) on the facing blank binder page. You can then go back and add the self-testing questions just like you do using the split-page method.

If Your Professor Posts the Notes After Class . . .

Take notes in class using the split-page method. Once your prof's notes are posted on the Web, download them and compare yours with his. Insert important information you may have missed into your own notes, then read through the expanded notes to review. Remember, though, that having access to your professor's notes (or anyone else's) does not take the place of taking notes yourself.

Taking good notes and being able to use them efficiently and effectively is one of the keys to being a successful student. It's a skill you should develop early in your college career.

GET WIRED

Throughout this chapter, we have mentioned how to modify your lecture note taking if you have a laptop. If you know how to type and if you can afford it (two big ifs), a laptop computer can be a very efficient and effective tool for note taking. The advantages: (1) you can organize your notes as you type; (2) it's easy to reduce or add to the notes you have taken; (3) your notes are always legible; and (4) it helps you concentrate and pay closer attention to what is said. An important reminder: when you take your laptop to class, use it for taking notes, not for checking email or surfing the Web.

GET IT TOGETHER

We have seen a number of capable students crash and burn because they did not see the importance of taking good notes until it was too late. Sure, taking notes requires some effort, but since you are in class anyway, assuming you followed our advice in chapter 3, you might as well get something out of it. Your notes are your only record of what happened in class. If you find yourself falling asleep, try to sit up and take some big, deep breaths. That should help you get enough oxygen to your brain to stay awake and write. Another alternative (ahem, we realize this sounds a bit odd) is to put a fairly thick rubber band around your wrist. When you find yourself going off into some faraway place, snap the rubber band. It will bring you back and help you focus. Some students swear by this method.

If You Read Nothing Else, Read This

○ Some note-taking behaviors should be routine. For every class, you should be ready to take notes when the prof begins lecturing, write legibly, keep at it for the entire period, listen carefully, write in simple paragraph form, and review your notes regularly.

○ In order to take notes in an organized way, use the split-page method, annotating or writing questions based on the information in your notes.

○ Self-test as a way of reviewing for your exams.

○ Know how to modify your note taking for situations other than straight lecture classes.

CHAPTER 16

GETTING IN GEAR: PREPARING TO READ YOUR TEXTS

- Concerned that you won't be able to concentrate when you have to read your textbooks, especially in a subject you hate?
- Worried that your textbooks are huge and just seem to have too much information to cover in one semester?
- Think that just opening the chapter to the first page and jumping in is the best way to read your texts?

If so, read on . . .

Preparing to read is really good for students, yet for some reason we have a hard time convincing most to do it. However, we are not going to let our prior failures prevent us from telling you about the amazing benefits of warming up for reading. And we're not asking you to do anything subversive. So . . . read on.

For most things in life, you warm up in some way. You stretch before you work out, run your car for a few minutes before driving it on cold days, and tune your guitar before you play. But students rarely think about warming up before learning—they just go into it cold. Really, this is how you were taught to do it during your entire school career. You were expected to go from literature class to math class to Spanish class without doing anything to help you switch gears from one subject to another. No wonder it was often hard to get focused. But you will find that you are a much more effective learner when you take the time to warm up before you start to read—or before you go into a lecture, for that matter.

Preparing to read your texts doesn't have to take long. All we are asking for is a few minutes of your time—five to ten minutes in most cases. Basically, you just want to get a sense of what the text will cover. You also want to think about what you already know about that topic. That's it. We know it sounds pretty basic, but it is a crucial step that many students skip.

Get to Know Your Textbooks

Before you begin to read anything in your texts, take a few minutes to familiarize yourself with their contents. Why? Your textbooks are one of the key components of learning. Yep. Even in this technological age, about 85 percent of all the learning you do in college involves text of some sort, so becoming familiar with the contents of each book helps you better use one of the most important tools for learning. Each textbook is written with some overarching plan in mind, but this organizational design is not immediately noticeable to most students, who usually just open up to the first chapter and start reading. By previewing a few chapters before you start to read, you can get a sense of the author's purpose as well as the format, structure, and design of the book.

Q THE INSIDE SCOOP

Students who take the time to warm up before reading remember considerably more of what they've read. As an added bonus, these students are also able to concentrate better and make stronger connections between ideas—which can really come in handy at exam time.

HOW DO YOU PREVIEW THE TEXT?

Previewing your text is simply a matter of examining the contents of each chapter and thinking about what you know about the topics. Follow these suggestions to get started.

Marcus, a first-semester freshman, was having some trouble. The college did not receive his student-loan check. After many, many phone calls, he thought he had finally straightened things out. But he also didn't get the money he needed to buy books. He was getting way behind, but there was nothing he could do about it, or so he thought. During the third week of class, one of his instructors noticed he didn't have the text and told him about a service offered by the university that would allow him to borrow up to $200 interest free for buying books, paying bills, and so on. This was just what he needed until his loan came through. The moral to Marcus's story: find out about the services offered by your college—no one wants to see you going without your books.

1. **Start with the table of contents.** The questions below will help you identify the organization of the material. They will also get you thinking about what you already know about the topic, because we're sure you know something.
   - How many chapters are there?
   - Are the chapters grouped by idea or unit? If so, what are these ideas or units?
   - Does the table of contents contain detailed information about the headings and subheadings in each chapter?
   - What do you already know about the ideas contained in the text?

2. **Read the preface or introduction.** It's amazing how much helpful advice is contained in these sections. The following questions will help you pull out hints for reading and thinking about the content.
   - What is the author's philosophy on the topic?
   - What advice does the author have about reading or studying this material?
   - What motivated the author to write this book?

3. **Examine the material at the end of the book.** There are usually several aids contained at the end of a textbook. These questions will help you identify what is available for you there.
   - Is there a glossary of terms? If so, skim some of the words. How many are somewhat familiar to you?
   - How is the book indexed? Are there both general and specialized indexes?

- Are there appendices or activities?
- Are there answers to problems or questions?
- What other features appear at the end of the text?

4. **As torturous as this may sound, preview a couple of text chapters.** Previewing will allow you to become familiar with the structure and format of each chapter. The information you will find in response to these questions will help you see the "big picture."

   - How difficult to read does the writing in the book appear to be?
   - How are the chapters organized?
   - Are there headings and subheadings?
   - Are there bold-faced and italicized words? If there are both, on what occasions is each of these styles used?
   - Do the chapters begin with objective questions or statements?
   - Are there introductions to each chapter or text section? If there are, what do these introductions tell you about the units or chapters you will be reading?
   - Do the chapters contain figures, diagrams, pictures, or other graphics? If so, what kind of information is depicted (is it key information or supporting information)?
   - Do the chapters end with summary paragraphs, thought questions, problems, or exercises?

Warming Up

Think about the last time you studied. Did it take you a good five or ten minutes to begin to focus on your reading? If so, you were getting yourself ready to read in that time. You were getting rid of distractions and getting your mind ready to learn. But if you did not warm up and you were trying to really read or study during this time, those five to ten minutes were wasted because you were not really concentrating.

One of the best reading warm-ups that can actually help you learn more during your

As knowledge increases, wonder deepens.

—Charles Morgan

reading is called prereading. When you preread, you go over the text chapter before you actually read it. We know this sounds like extra work, but stick with us. We would never suggest anything that would waste your time, and we guarantee you that it will be a good thing in the long run. There are several benefits to warming up, or prereading, before you start studying.

LISTEN UP

Many students buy used books to save some money. We suggest you skim through the text and select a book that has not been written in or highlighted. We've heard that some students actually look for highlighted books, figuring that someone has already done the work of selecting key information for them. But what if the previous owner failed the course?

- **It gets you psyched up.** Many students tell us that the way they prepare for reading is by looking through the book, not to see what the chapter is going to be about, but to see how many pages they have to trudge through (and how many pages are made shorter by pictures or figures). But knowing what you are about to read actually makes you more interested in learning the topic. Honest. You should find yourself much more motivated to learn about the topic at the end of your warm-up.

- **It makes your mind ready to learn.** By prereading the chapter, you are giving yourself the time you need to be ready to focus on what you are about to learn. This means you will be able to concentrate on your reading and get more out of

SAD BUT TRUE

Meg could never get herself to study her sociology book. All those bold-faced words. Ugh. Every time she tried to read, her mind would wander to the point where she just decided that she was not good at sociology and never would be. She even started to question her ability to finish her college degree. But the problem was much simpler. When Meg studied sociology, she would just sit down, open her text, and attempt to start reading. If she couldn't focus after ten minutes, she would get up, take a break, and plan to come back to it at a later time (a tip she learned at her freshman orientation). What Meg didn't realize is that without warming up in some way, it can take much longer than the ten minutes she gave herself just to get going. Adding a five-minute prereading time could really get her ready to focus.

it. No more wasting time at the beginning of studying; now you have a purpose the minute you sit down at your desk. Having a purpose is a good thing.

- **It helps you organize.** Prereading the text gives you clues to how the author thinks about and organizes the material. As you go through the chapter, you may make an observation such as, "Oh, I see. This political science book is set up by decade, but within each decade the author discusses domestic policy, then foreign policy, economic policy, and social policy." During your prereading you are creating a mental outline that you can follow when you read the chapter.

- **It creates better comprehension.** When you preread, you are figuring out the key ideas in the reading. This will help you understand what you are reading—it sets the groundwork for efficient studying.

We think you'll find these benefits to be worth the little bit of effort required in prereading.

GET IT TOGETHER

We know. You don't have to tell us. "Warming up" seems like a waste of time. Why would anyone want to do more work? But if studying isn't your thing at all and you actually have to force yourself to even open the book every time you sit down to study, it might be a strategy for you. Remember that half the battle (okay, 20 percent) is just getting started, so give the warm-up thing a try. It just might start you on the path where you can stay on track better than you currently do.

Ready . . . Set . . . Read!

You have gotten the big picture of your text and you know how the book is organized. And come on now, it really hasn't taken you *that* long. Now it's time to preview the chapter you are about to read to learn more about the ideas contained within it. There are several steps involved in this stage of prereading, though they should not take you more than a few minutes.

1. **Look at the chapter title and think about what you already know about the topic.** This activity helps you set your purpose for reading and gets your mind clear of other thoughts and ready to focus on the topic at hand. This will also help you

set your reading purpose when you start to read. For example, in a psychology course you might encounter the chapter title "Aging." Just this one word can get your mind ready to think about the process of growing older. Is it really about wrinkles and poor memory?

2. **Read the chapter headings and subheadings.** This information can tell you a lot about the subject. The headings and subheadings point out key concepts and ideas presented in the chapter. They also help you determine the overall organization of those concepts, which makes it easier to see how these ideas relate to one another—the big picture. In our "Aging" chapter, perhaps there is a heading "Sex after Sixty," something you don't even want to picture, but helpful in understanding some of the concepts the chapter will cover.

3. **Look at the figures, charts, pictures, and graphs.** Graphical aids often tell you about the key points of the chapter, so don't just skip over them. Be sure to read the captions below each graphic during your prereading. We have found that some texts (especially in the sciences) discuss the most crucial points in figures, and by previewing the figures before you read the chapter, you will be better able to connect the text information to the information contained in the figure. Our "Aging" chapter may have a table listing the number of times, on average, that couples have sex from ages twenty to eighty. This information can help spark your interest and personalize the material. (Ugh. My grandparents still have sex?)

THE INSIDE SCOOP

Thinking about what you know about the topic, or activating your prior knowledge about that topic, helps you to be able to connect new information to what you already know. According to research on learning, the ability to relate new information to previous knowledge will help you remember that new information at test time.

4. **Scan the bold-faced or italicized words.** In most classes, you will find a lot of new content-specific vocabulary, that is, words that are specific to the subject matter. Usually, knowing the meaning of these content-specific words is key to understanding the material you are about to read. Reading the definitions during your previewing will help you remember their meaning as you read. One word you might learn in our "Aging" chapter would be *geriatric*.

5. **Check out the end-of-chapter materials.** A summary or some reading questions may appear at the end of the chapter. Knowing what type of information is contained in these materials can help you focus your attention on the key points when you read the chapter.

6. **Make a plan for reading the chapter.** Think about these questions as you plan your approach:
   - Will it be helpful to read the chapter before you attend the lecture? The vote is still out on this one, but it is usually best to read before the lecture for most classes. However, in some courses (especially mathematics), students get more out of the reading by just previewing before the lecture and reading after class.
   - When and where will you read the chapter? It is best to read as soon as possible after previewing.
   - Will you need any special materials, such as a calculator or dictionary?
   - What kind of information will you be looking for? Are there cause and effect or compare and contrast relationships? Are there a lot of new terms? Is a chronology of events described? Are a variety of viewpoints represented? Are several theories discussed?
   - How long do you estimate it will take you to read and understand the chapter material?

Try to make prereading a part of your studying routine. The more you practice this strategy, the more you will come to value its usefulness.

Reading on the Computer

Reading from a computer screen is physically and mentally more demanding than reading from paper. Some current research has indicated that people tend to read more slowly and with less accuracy when reading from the screen. However, there are some advantages to reading information on your computer: you have access to a wide range of information through the Internet; computerized texts can make use of hypertext or other features that allow you to quickly compare different materials; and online texts can also include video or audio clips.

Most professors have not yet made the switch to having all text materials online. Even if you are taking a distance-learning course, you will probably have to buy and read a traditional textbook. However, should you be asked to read a lot of material on your computer, there are some things you should keep in mind. Some research has suggested there is a decline in reading comprehension that can reach 40 percent when a person reads online. One factor that affects comprehension is the monitor's display: its flicker, glare, image quality, color, and text size. Some of this can be fixed by making sure you have a good monitor and it is at the optimal settings for picture quality and color.

But if you find you are having trouble reading on the computer, our best advice is to print out what you need to read (if you can). If printing just won't work for you, another way to overcome any dips in speed or comprehension is to practice. Read as much information on the computer as you can. Maybe read the morning paper online, or read online movie reviews instead of watching them on TV. Basically, you want to gear up for computer reading if you know you will need to be doing a lot of it.

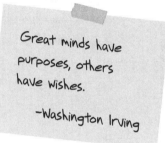

Great minds have purposes, others have wishes.

—Washington Irving

If You Read Nothing Else, Read This

○ **Familiarize yourself with your textbooks. Look at how the information is organized and how the chapters are set up. This type of information will help you see the big picture that the author had in mind while writing the text.**

○ **Prereading helps you warm up for reading. Warming up for a few minutes before reading will help you concentrate better. The big benefit for you is that you will actually remember what you've read.**

○ **Preread by reading headings, subheadings, bold-faced and italicized words, diagrams or charts, introductions, and conclusions. It should not take more than a few minutes, and then you will be ready to read.**

CHAPTER 17

ACTIVE READING

- Concerned that you won't be able to remember anything you have read?
- Worried that if you write in your textbooks, it will take too much time and you won't be able to sell them back to the bookstore?
- Think that highlighting is the best way to mark your books for later studying?

If so, read on . . .

Okay, so some people hate to read, but in college you have to. And you're trying to make the best of it. You sit down to read your anthropology text. You are in a comfy chair dutifully highlighting the pages of the chapter. Armed with a handful of colorful markers, you highlight everything that seems important. How about pink for today? Once you have made it through, you close your book, pat yourself on the back for completing your reading, and breathe a sigh of relief. But wait. . . . What do you remember? Anything? Aghast, you realize that you just wasted another forty-five minutes. What's the deal?

The deal is this: you're not reading actively. Active reading requires more than just letting your eyes run aimlessly across the page, highlighting as you go. Yet some students consider any time they spend with their book open to be reading. What you want to do is read in a way that will help you remember the information. When you highlight, you tend to read passively. You probably won't remember much of what you have read five minutes later because instead of learning from what you've read, what you did was mark the information that you wanted to come back to learn later. However, in college you can average over 250 pages of reading per week if you are taking a full course load. This means you will barely have time to get through the material once, much less go back and reread everything. Now you are thinking, "I just bought a whole bunch of highlighters—one in every color they make. Are you saying that I need to throw them out?" No. You can use them for other things that we'll talk about later. But there are more effective ways to handle the tons of reading you will be faced with.

Active reading feels different than passive reading. Your mind is engaged and you are clicking with the material. To get a sense of what it means to read actively, try this activity:

1. Choose something to read from either a textbook or a magazine (but make it a nonfiction piece). It should be something you are somewhat interested in but also something you don't know a whole lot about. Try to pick a piece that will take you at least five minutes to read.

2. Brainstorm and write down everything you know (or think you know) about the topic. You don't have to be sure of your facts at this point. You are just trying to remember all you know about it.

3. Now, read the article. As you read, check your knowledge. Make some mental notes, or use these marks in the margin of the text:

    + This is information I knew already.

    − This is information I thought I knew, but it turns out I did not.

    o This information is new to me.

    ? This information is confusing to me.

    ! I'd like to know more about this piece of information.

4. Check your comprehension. What new information did you learn from this reading? How much information did you already know? Was there some information that you had misconceptions about (you thought you knew something, but the text said otherwise)?

If I had a choice between sleeping with seven boa constrictors or reading, I would most definitely pick the former.... [But] there could be nothing more boring than sitting down and reading ten chapters on who made love to what brother. Reading for education is not exactly a Terminator movie.

—Anonymous College Student

You probably noticed that you read this piece of text differently than you normally read your textbooks. But keep in mind that this was only an activity to help you read actively. We really don't want you to mark your books in this way (though if you have siblings or children in middle school, it would be a great strategy to show them). Why did it feel different to read this way? Because you had a task—a purpose for reading. You were checking your knowledge as you read. This is a process that good readers use all the time. In fact, when you are reading something in which you have a lot of interest (a novel, an article about a hobby), you probably already use this process without even thinking about it. Basically, you are continually checking the new information with what you already know about the topic and making modifications to your knowledge as you learn new ideas. So how do you create this atmosphere of active reading while you are reading your textbooks? Read on.

😟 SAD BUT TRUE

Grace dutifully read her textbooks every night. She was very careful to keep up with assignments because she didn't want to fall behind. So, armed with a pile of highlighters, she would read and mark. Blue for definitions, yellow for examples, green for details—you get the picture. When she was finished, she would note with satisfaction that she had made quite a few marks. In fact, Grace marked just about everything. Grace was in for a big shock when she started studying for her exams and realized that she didn't remember one thing from her reading. Horrified, she began to read over her highlights (which covered almost all the text) and found much of the information to be downright confusing. She had the right attitude toward getting her work done, but what Grace needed was a new strategy to help her read for learning.

Reading for Learning

How many times have you sat down to read with your only goal to get the mind-numbing assignment finished? You really had no intention of learning anything from your reading (though that might have been nice). Rather, you were focused on getting it done: "I have to read these twenty boring pages of biology tonight. Can I plow through ten pages before I fall asleep or give up?" If this describes you, then you were not really reading for learning. To read for learning you must set a reading purpose, just as you did in the activity on page 193.

Reading for learning from your texts is a three-step process:

1. Ask questions about the headings and figures.

2. Read actively by staying engaged in what you are reading by answering the questions you posed and by taking notes as you read.

3. Review and rehearse the information so you remember it. (This will be discussed in the next few chapters.)

We know this sounds demanding and it is, but once you get the hang of it, it's not so bad.

LISTEN UP

Did you ever notice how your textbooks have those blue (or gray) text boxes? The publisher and author who created that text box are saying, "This information is so important that we will pull it out of the text and highlight it in another color so all the readers will be sure to see it." What do most students do when they come across a text box in their reading? You guessed it. They skip over that section—even though it may contain the key to all the important information presented in the text. Professors know that students tend to skip text boxes and will often ask questions about that material. Our advice? Read the text boxes, of course.

Strategies for Active Reading

The best strategy we have found to help you set and keep your reading purpose is annotating, that is, taking notes in your text. Unlike in high school, where writing in your books was punishable by death, you own your textbooks in college. You have spent a lot of money on your books, and they are yours for better or worse, so make the most out your reading by writing in them.

Annotation is a strategy for active reading wherein you write the key information (such as major points, definitions, and examples) in the margins of your text. You are looking for and marking all the information you will need to remember from each chapter. Because it gives you a purpose, you'll find that annotation helps you concentrate while reading, and it actually helps you learn from the text.

Text annotation works because it

- Gives you a purpose for reading

- Improves your comprehension

- Provides an immediate test of your understanding

- Increases your concentration

- Keeps you from having to reread the chapters over again

- Creates a study tool that will help you prepare for exams

DO YOUR HOMEWORK

Some students use underlining or highlighting as a shortcut to learning. They read and highlight what they will come back to later when they are studying for the test. But this method is much less effective than reading to learn the first time because, in reality, highlighting is a passive activity. Annotation, on the other hand, helps you think about and learn the information as you are reading. Then, when you go back to study, you have done a lot of the hard work already.

THE INSIDE SCOOP

Students who annotate their texts perform better on exams than students who did not. (We know. We've done some of this research ourselves.) In addition, students who annotate actually spend less time studying because they have been learning the material as they annotated rather than leaving it until right before the exam.

The Nuts and Bolts of Annotation

Before you annotate, you need to get a sense of what the chapter or section is about. That's why we suggest you read brief portions of text—at least a paragraph or two— before you annotate it. If you try to read and annotate at the same time, you will end up writing way too much information because you think everything is important. Of course, you also might annotate too little because you don't yet know what is important, nor do you have a sense of the big picture.

READ BEFORE YOU WRITE

Read at least one paragraph before you write anything down. The amount you need to read ahead will vary. In some texts, you may be able to read an entire section before annotating; in others, only a paragraph. For example, you can probably read more about "television violence in popular culture" than you can about "the lifespan of the nematode worm" (though we have some good friends who would argue that nematodes make for a fascinating read). It depends on the difficulty of the material and on how much you already know about the topic. So use your best judgment and try reading varying amounts of text to see what works best for you. Remember, everyone is different and what works for your roommate may not work for you.

THINK ABOUT THE IDEAS YOU'VE READ

If you were going to talk to someone else about the information, what would be important to tell them? This is the material you will annotate. In fact, some of our students take this idea one step further by imagining that they will need to tutor someone on the material. They tell us their goal is to annotate enough information to be able to teach the topic.

WRITE KEY IDEAS IN THE MARGINS

Try to be brief. Your annotations shouldn't be longer than the text itself. Be on the lookout for:

- **Definitions.** These are usually the bold-faced or italicized words in your text.

- **Examples of the main ideas.** Examples often find their way onto your exams. But

197

don't get caught up in using only the text examples. If you can think of an example from your own experience, write it down—you'll be more likely to remember it.

- **Details or characteristics of the main ideas.** You need to annotate this information to get the full picture of each concept. If you just annotate the key ideas, but leave out the details, you won't have enough information to use for studying and will find you need to resort to rereading everything (a big waste of time).

- **Lists.** If your book states, "Scientists have discovered five types of . . . ," be sure to note that information. In fact, even if your text does not explicitly state that the information you are reading is a list, but you notice that it can be summed up in a list, annotate it in this way. For example, if you were reading about procrastination and noticed this list of information, you would annotate it like this:

> **3 CAUSES OF PROCRAST.**
> 1. lack of time mgmt skills
> 2. lack of topic interest
> 3. habit

Making your own list will help you organize the information in your memory.

- **Names, dates, and events.** It is not enough, however, just to note the dates; instead, focus on why the dates or events are important. Why do we care about this event? Use dates to provide a chronology of events, but don't use them to memorize facts.

- **Cause and effect or comparison and contrast.** This kind of information is not always obvious in your texts, but it is frequently what professors ask about (especially on essay exams). Whenever you see these kinds of relationships in your texts, you can mark them with a C/E or C/C in the margin.

- **Possible test questions.** Put a big TQ in the margin whenever you see something that strikes you as a point you will be tested on.

- **Confusing information.** If there is information you don't understand while you are reading, mark it with a question mark. Then be sure to ask about it in class the next day.

REVIEW YOUR WORK

Check your annotations to be sure they make sense. If you had only your annotations to study from, would you have enough information marked? If not, go back and fill in any gaps.

A Sample Annotation

We include this sample for two reasons. First, we want to show you how annotations are organized—to give you a sense of what kind of information to note and how to note it. Second, we actually want you to read about how people remember things. So in addition to examining it for information on how to annotate, read the passage to learn a little bit about how memory works. We will be referring to this information as we show you other strategies later in *College Rules!*

Do you know the difference between education and experience? Education is when you read the fine print. Experience is what you get when you don't.

—Pete Seeger

GET IT TOGETHER

Okay. We can see your brain working overtime here, thinking about reasons why you can't annotate. Small margins. My book has small margins so that lets me off the hook, right? Of course not. If you meet a text with really small margins, invest in some larger-size sticky notes to write on, or cut strips of notebook paper and insert them in the binding of each page. We do not suggest taking notes in a separate notebook. It is important to keep the annotations with the original text so you can refer to the text if there is something you do not understand and so you can review important diagrams and figures as you study your notes. Most students find that the sticky notes work really well and use them not only in texts with small margins but also when they have to read periodicals or information they printed from the Web.

Human Memory System

Though every person thinks and remembers information, scientists do not fully understand how the human memory works. Many of the ideas and theories about memory are quite controversial, but most scientists agree that memory involves three different types of storage: sensory store, short-term memory, and long-term memory. In addition, there are three processes that enable memory storage: encoding (getting information into memory), storage (keeping the information in memory), and retrieval (getting the information back out).

According to this theory of memory, information enters through the **sensory store** where it is either acted upon or forgotten. An individual is bombarded with information nearly all the time, much of which is not attended to. Right now as you are reading this passage, you might not be aware of the clock ticking or the hum of a fan or the people talking quietly around you because you are paying attention to your reading. The sensory store can be considered a gatekeeper for the mind. You would become quickly overloaded if you had to attend to all the stimuli around you. The information that is ignored by the sensory store is not processed or is "forgotten." The information that is processed by the sensory store can be encoded into short-term memory.

Short-term memory (STM) cannot handle much information at one time. In fact, research has indicated that the capacity for short-term (or working) memory is seven plus or minus two items. This means that you can keep anywhere from five to nine ideas in your working memory. The Bell Telephone company conducted a good deal of this research; thus, it is no wonder that your phone number is seven digits long. One can expand the capacity of STM through a process called chunking. **Chunking** is a type of organization in which letters, digits, or words are grouped into some psychologically meaningful or familiar sequence. Consider your social security number. At ten digits it is beyond the capacity of STM. However, when the information is chunked into three groups of number, one can easily remember them: 186-888-0000.

Besides having a limited capacity, short-term memory also suffers from decay after about thirty seconds. That is, information becomes inaccessible after a relatively short period of time. However, information can be renewed in STM through maintenance rehearsal. **Maintenance rehearsal** is the act of mentally repeating the information to be recalled. An example would be looking up a phone number in the phone book, then repeating that number to

Margin notes

3 types of storage: SS, STM, LTM

3 MEMORY PROCESSES:
1. Encoding –getting info in
2. Storage –keeping info
3. Retrieval –getting info out

Info enters thru SS
–acted on or lost
–filters info
–info process in SS moves to STM

STM: Limited capacity 5–9 items

Bell phone co. research –phone # 7 digits

def chunking – grouping ideas meaningfully to expand capacity of STM
ex soc. sec #

Info lost from STM after 30 sec.

def maintenance rehearsal–renews info in STM by repeating info.
ex. looking up phone #

yourself several times as you walk over to the phone to dial the number. Although this process works well for keeping information alive in short-term memory, **elaborative rehearsal,** or adding meaning to the information you are trying to remember is necessary for storage in long-term memory. For example, if you were introduced to a new person, let's call her Joan, you could say to yourself, "I have an aunt named Joan and this person has blue eyes like my Aunt." By connecting meaning with this information rather than merely repeating the name several times, you are more likely to recall it.

Long-term memory (LTM) stores an unlimited amount of information for an unlimited amount of time. LTM holds many different types of information such as factual knowledge, events, motor skills, perceptual information, beliefs about ourselves and others, and familiar environments. To use the information contained in LTM, it must be retrieved, but unlike in STM where all information can be scanned, information must be recalled using cues. This process is similar to using a call number to find a book in the library. LTM also differs from STM in the way information is stored. Information is usually stored in STM in terms of the qualities of the experience (what was seen, heard, touched, smelled, or tasted) and is often remembered through sound. Information in LTM is stored primarily in terms of meaning (we associate the great taste of grandma's apple pie with the smell of her house and the wealth of experiences we shared with her) rather than sensory images. Although memory does not decay from LTM there are many theories on why it is often difficult to recall. When we say we can't remember something, we are actually saying that we can't access the information from our long-term memory.

Annotations:
def elaborative reh. –adding meaning to info to store in LTM
ex remembering Joan by my Aunt Joan

LTM–unlimited storage of info for unlimited time –many types of info–facts, events, beliefs, etc. –info must be retrieved using cues (unlike STM where info is scanned)

LTM–info stored by meaning
ex grandma's pie

C/C STM & LTM T.Q.!!!
STM–info stored by qualities or senses
Many theories on why we can't access info in LTM–not really forgotten

ABBREVIATION EXAMPLES

w/	with
b/c	because
b/4	before
w/in	within
△	change
↑↓	increase or decrease
h'er	however
ex	for example
*	most importantly
b/t	between

Notice how the information is organized in the example text. Definitions and examples are labeled, as are key ideas. Text questions are noted, as are comparison and contrast relationships. In addition, notice how the information in the annotations is abbreviated as much as possible. When you annotate, use any abbreviations you would normally use when taking notes in class. Here are some common abbreviations used by students, but don't feel you need to stick to these. Be creative and come up with some of your own.

Remember to create and use abbreviations for content-specific terms, such as "STM" for "short-term memory" in the passage above. But be careful not to overabbreviate.

😣 SAD BUT TRUE

Scott, a sophomore management major, learned annotation in our course and thought he could do it and save time by using abbreviations. So Scott abbreviated every term in his history text: IR for industrial revolution; MP for the Marshall Plan; 3CoVW for three causes of the Vietnam War. Though this was a great idea in theory, he abbreviated to the point that he couldn't understand what he had written and ended up needing to reread his entire text before his cumulative final. The moral of Scott's story is to read over your annotations to make sure they will make sense the next time you read them. Good annotations stand the test of time.

Studying Your Annotations

When you annotate, you create a study guide you can come back to again and again, which is really useful if you have cumulative finals. Gone is the need to reread your texts. You have already pulled out all the information you will need to study and (most importantly) you have written it in a way that you understand. And if you find you have to reread something, you can do it selectively.

To study your annotations, use the following steps as a guide:

1. **Cover up the text.** You don't want to reread entire pages, just your annotations.

2. **Read your annotations and rehearse the material.** Ask yourself questions. Do you understand all the key ideas? Do you understand how all these concepts relate to each other and how they relate to the larger concepts?

3. **Reread selectively.** If you find a section that is not entirely clear to you, uncover the text and reread only that section.

4. **Test yourself.** Once you are comfortable with the material in the text, try to self-test. Look at chapter headings and subheadings. Cover up the text and the annotations; then try to say the information to yourself.

Once you have tested yourself several times on the information, you may want to compare what you've read with the information in your lecture notes. This will help you start to pull the ideas together.

LISTEN UP

Many students believe rereading is the best way to remember information from their texts. In fact, rereading is the number-one strategy reported by college students. But as you probably learned by reading the memory passage, simple rereading is less effective than using a strategy that helps you elaborate on the information in a way that makes it meaningful for you.

THE INSIDE SCOOP

If you have a mild case of test anxiety, there is no better cure than feeling confident that you know the information. Self-testing is one of the best strategies to determine what you do and do not know.

The man who does not read good books has no advantage over the man who can't read them.

—Mark Twain

If You Read Nothing Else, Read This

○ Good readers are active. Active reading means you are focused on the text and learning as you go. Highlighting your books does not usually lead to reading actively.

○ Annotation encourages active reading. Gone are the days of reading and not learning. To annotate, you summarize the key ideas of the text in the margins using your own words (a good test of your understanding).

○ Use your annotations to study. Annotations provide a way to test yourself on the information you'll need to remember for the exam.

CHAPTER 18

THREE RS AND AN M: REMEMBERING WHAT YOU HAVE READ AND HEARD

- Worried that you won't be able to remember all the important information you'll need to know at test time?
- Concerned that you don't know how to select the right strategies for what your professor expects you to do?
- Think you'll be able to recognize when you've studied enough?

If so, read on . . .

Warning! Warning! If you don't read and reflect on any other chapter in this book, do so with this one. There are piles of important stuff in here, some of which is hard to make exciting or fun to read (though we have tried our very best). So here's the point where you need to suck it up, read on, and learn the real secrets of academic success in college. Trust us; you'll be glad you did.

Have you ever spent a substantial amount of time reading a textbook or "studying" your notes only to find that you remember little of what you have read? Have

An education isn't how much you have committed to memory, or even how much you know. It's being able to differentiate between what you know and what you don't.

—Anatole France

you ever looked up a number in the telephone book to make a call, been briefly interrupted (even for a few seconds), and then found you couldn't remember the number? Do you find yourself thinking, "My grandma has a better memory than I do"? If any or all of these things have happened to you, you may feel frustrated or even stupid. Get over it! It happens to everyone, or at least everyone who doesn't know about the three Rs and an M. No, that's not readin', 'ritin', and 'rithmetic. Our three Rs stand for reflect, rehearse, and review, and the M stands for monitor. Got that?

We've found that many students skip the 3RM step when trying to study and learn information. In fact, when we ask students how they studied for an exam, they often say (with pride), "I read the text." We respond (with encouragement), "That's a good start, and then what did you do to study?" They reply, "What do you mean? I read the book." We shake our heads, saying, "But reading and studying are not the same thing!" "Huh?" they say (feeling confused). We assure then that a student who only reads the text but doesn't reflect, rehearse, review, and monitor will have trouble remembering information later. No wonder so many students chalk it up to a bad memory!

THE INSIDE SCOOP

Students who rehearse and review information remember up to three times more than students who just read. Three times! That means there's a big payoff in reviewing, especially in courses where cumulative final exams include material from the entire term. So we suggest that you plan a portion of your study time each day to rehearse and review—even when you don't have an exam that week.

Reflecting: Thinking about Information

You have probably already figured out that successful college students are active readers and critical thinkers. They become involved in their work as students by reflecting on the information they come in contact with. Rather than reading just to get

Carl had always done well in chemistry in high school, so he decided to take Introduction to Chemistry to meet his lab science requirement. He figured that since he never had to spend much time studying it in high school and he always aced the tests, the same would hold true in college. The first week or so of class reviewed material he'd already learned, so he didn't read much of his text nor did he take very good lecture notes. What little he did read and hear didn't sink in, because he really didn't think about it. As a matter of fact, Carl continued to tune out and lag behind even after the material got more difficult to follow. Before he knew it, the first test was upon him, and he was totally lost. But Carl still had confidence that he could pull it out. After all, he had done it in high school without too much effort. He decided to devote the weekend to studying for the test, which was on Monday. He got up early Saturday morning, got out his textbook and his notes, and set to work . . . for about forty-five minutes. He skimmed through a chapter without really thinking much about the material and was stunned that he could not work the problems at the end of each section. Rather than reflecting on the information and trying to make sense of it, he simply slammed the book shut and decided it was a lost cause. He spent the rest of the weekend trying to get his friend, who was also in the class, to explain things to him. But that didn't go very well either because, although his friend understood the material, he couldn't explain it very well. Carl learned the hard way that there is no shortcut to learning difficult material.

the job done or attending class just to be there, they engage in activities that keep them connected to the tasks, and they think about the material as they go along. That's what reflection is. It's making sense of what you are trying to learn rather than simply skimming over it.

Earlier you learned about annotation, you know, writing all that important stuff in the margins of your texts. Annotation requires a considerable amount of reflection because you have to think about what you've just read before you annotate it. If you simply copied the exact words in your textbooks, you wouldn't be reflecting. Reflecting requires that you put the material in your own words as a way of making sense of what you are reading or hearing.

If you don't take time to try to make sense of information by putting it in your own words or by talking about it with other students—in other words, by reflecting—

you may have a difficult time making it through your classes, particularly classes in which you have to work a little harder in order to be successful. And you're certainly not going to learn very much if you use Carl as a role model, slamming your book shut and giving up.

Rehearsing: Getting Information into Your Memory

You've reflected on a chapter that you have been assigned to read, so you pretty much understand it. Now you're ready to learn it in such a way that you can store it in your memory and get it back out again when you need to. In order to do this, you need a crash course on memory. Think for a minute about how memory works. Why can you remember some information fairly easily and other information seems not to "stick" no matter what you do? Since you've already read something about memory, let's do the very brief version of the memory crash course, just to give you some time to reflect.

Basically, you have two different memory systems: short-term memory, or STM, and long-term memory, or LTM. Both are important. STM holds information for a short period of time, up to about thirty seconds. And it holds only a small amount of information—seven plus or minus two pieces of information, to be exact. This means that STM can hold somewhere between five and nine pieces of information at one time. STM is the part of your memory you use when you look up a phone number, close the phone book, and immediately call the number. STM holds information when there is no need to remember it for very long. In addition, phone numbers (without the area code) consist of seven digits, well within the range of the number of pieces of information that can be held at one time.

The mind is like the stomach. It is not how much you put into it that counts, but how much it digests.

—Albert Jay Nock

Your long-term memory (as its name implies) holds information for a longer period of time, up to a lifetime, even. That's why you can remember stuff that you learned years ago: the alphabet, the multiplication tables, the name of the puppy you had when you were three. LTM also allows you to drive your car to the mall without getting lost and to remember stories that your grandparents told you when you were young.

Think how difficult learning would be without an LTM. But how does information get from your STM to your LTM, and how do memories in LTM become "permanent"? Why does some information get into LTM while other information doesn't? Let's go back to the phone-book example we used earlier. You look up the number, close the phone book, dial . . . and the line is busy. You hang up the phone and start to dial again only a minute later, but you can't remember the number. Why? The answer is simple: you haven't rehearsed. Simply defined, rehearsal is acting on information, doing something to it in some way so it moves from STM to LTM so you can remember it later. If you wanted to remember that phone number in case the line was still busy when you tried again, you could have said it several times or you could have written it down. (Actually, in this particular example, you could simply have used the redial function on your phone, but you get the point.)

Knowing a little bit about how memory works makes it easier to understand why reading alone, or simply listening to a lecture, isn't enough. After all, if you can't remember a seven-digit phone number after a minute without rehearsing it, how can you expect to remember the information contained in several textbook chapters and three weeks' worth of lectures? It's not that you have a poor memory; it's simply that you need to learn some ways to rehearse information so it gets into your LTM where you can use it later.

There are two basic ways you can rehearse: repeat it aloud or to yourself several times, or write it down.

SAY IT AGAIN, MAN

You can say it to yourself or out loud. Just like actors rehearse their lines by saying them over and over again, you can learn information by repeating it

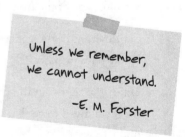

Unless we remember, we cannot understand.

–E. M. Forster

GET IT TOGETHER

We have met many students who make no attempt to remember anything they learn in their classes. Instead, they memorize the information but never really think about it at all. They might do okay on the exam but then forget the material within a few days. Should they have a cumulative final, they would need to learn it all over again. Even though you might not see the point in some of the stuff you are learning, if you make an effort to learn it at deeper levels, you will remember it longer—and you just never know when you will need to use it.

until it's fixed in LTM. The problem with simply saying information, however, is that there is no record for you to study from later on. In addition, this type of rehearsal sometimes leads to rote memorization, so you may have trouble remembering the information after a short period of time. Rote memorization really works only when learning tasks that you will do automatically (such as driving a car) but does not help you make connections that will allow you to get back to the information once it is no longer fresh in your mind.

GET IT IN WRITING

Writing gives you a more permanent record from which to study, so we suggest writing information first and then saying it as the better way to rehearse. There are lots of different ways to organize information when you use writing as a way of rehearsing. Some alternatives include the following.

Concept Cards

You probably have made and used concept cards without knowing it. You may have called them "flash cards" and used them to learn vocabulary words or in courses where you had to learn definitions. Although our concept cards may look a little different than those you have made, the purpose is the same. Look at the example on the opposite page of the front and back of a concept card for STM.

1. On the front of the concept card, put the term you want to learn (in this case, "short-term memory").

2. Under the term, put the page in the text where more information can be found (so if you need to get back to the information in the book, you know where to find it).

3. In the upper-right-hand corner, put a word (or phrase) that helps you organize the information by providing a larger concept (in this case, "short-term memory" would be subsumed under the general concept of "memory"). This will help you organize the concepts so you can learn them together.

4. On the back of the card, write all the important information you need to remember about STM. This would include both a definition and an example.

5. You can make your cards as you read rather than annotating—but use this technique only in courses where learning terms is the main focus—or you can use your annotations to make your cards. Either way, you have a written record from which you can now rehearse.

6. When you rehearse, look at the front of the card, say the term and all the information you should know about it (here's where the talking part comes in). Then flip the card over to see how much you remembered. Concept cards are good to use in classes where you have to learn lots of definitions or formulas. Students also find them useful for studying a foreign language.

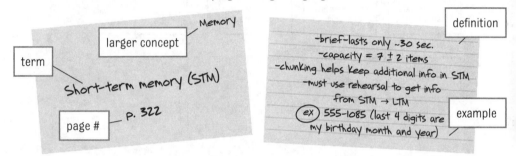

Concept Maps

Concept maps are actually outlines that are constructed in such a way that you can see how information is related. If you have ever read your textbook and thought, "How will I ever remember all this stuff?" you were in need of a concept map. When you make traditional outlines, it's often difficult to see how all the information connects, so we rarely recommend outlining as an effective strategy. However, when you make concept maps, the relationships among ideas become clearer. There is no one best way to map, and it may take you a bit of time to figure out what will work best for you. It would only be on a rare occasion that you would map an entire chapter. Rather, mapping works well for concepts where it's important to see relationships. Look at the two concept maps on page 212. This gives you an idea about the variety of forms that mapping the same information can take.

Charts

Charts are a good rehearsal strategy to use when you know you will have to compare and/or contrast information. If you have ever said to yourself, "All this stuff seems

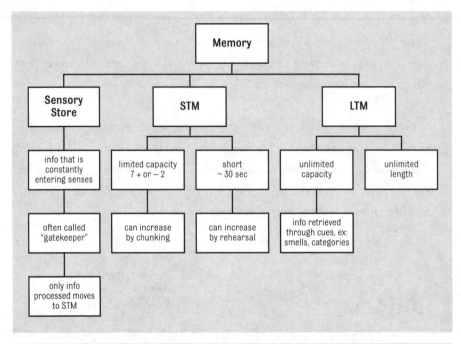

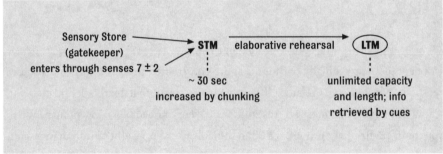

the same, so how will I ever be able to tell them apart?" you were in need of a chart. The hardest thing about constructing charts is coming up with descriptors to compare and contrast with. For example, in the chart on the opposite page, we contrast STM with LTM. Note that our descriptors are purpose, length, capacity, and role of rehearsal. It's important that the descriptors are terms that can apply to all concepts you wish to compare or contrast. The best way to figure out the descriptors for a chart is to read over your annotations of the sections in your text that you want to use for a chart and think about the information contained in all sections—did you read definitions, examples, theories, characteristics, research, formulas? This information would become your descriptors.

One of our favorite computer programs is called Inspiration. This software allows you to map out ideas in very creative ways. It can help you see relationships between ideas, integrate new knowledge, and expand your understanding of the material. You can use it to create concept maps or to brainstorm and organize ideas for a writing assignment. At the website, inspiration.com, you can download a free trial. Try it out.

	STM	LTM
Purpose	Stores info for brief periods	Stores info for long periods—a lifetime, even
Length	~30 sec.	Unlimited
Capacity	7 ± 2 items	Unlimited, never fills up
Role of rehearsal	Maintenance reh.— "refreshes" info in STM	Elaborative reh.—necessary to get info to LTM

Time Lines

Time lines are used only when you have information you need to know in chronological order. You might use time lines in history, art history, political science, geology, or any other course where you need to know things over time. You may have made time lines in the past where you had only a date and an event or person. We suggest using your time lines to include more information—not just the event, but why the event was important to know. In this way, a time line can help you see how one event led to or influenced another. See the example of the events in the Nixon Watergate hearings on page 214.

Many students tell us they are visual learners. If this describes you, then concept mapping just might end up becoming your favorite strategy because it allows you to be creative in visually depicting how the concepts are related. The format a map can take is limited only by your imagination. Or if you like the idea of outlining, mapping nets the same results, only in a more organized way.

Date	Events and Impacts
1971	Nixon installs secret tape recorder in White House. Wants to stop information leaks out of WH (Plumbers). *Washington Post* begins publishing "Pentagon Papers" on Vietnam.
1972	Five burglars arrested in Democrat's national office at Watergate hotel trying to place "bugs." GOP aide among those arrested. Nixon reelected with large majority of vote.
1973	Former Nixon aides Liddy and McCord are convicted. Senate hearings on Watergate begin. VP Agnew resigns due to charges of tax evasion. Nixon ordered to turn over WH tapes—missing 18.5 minutes go unexplained.
1974	Nixon loses public support. Aides indicted for obstruction of justice. House adopts three articles for impeaching the president, but Nixon resigns from office (first president to do so). Ford becomes president—eventually pardons Nixon.
1976	Jimmy Carter elected.

Questions and Answers

Questions and answers are sort of like the study guides your high school teachers may have given to help you prepare for a big test. Our version asks you to create your own study guide by writing questions and answering them in a way that allows you to test yourself. The secret is to make up good questions—questions that match the task—and then to write out concise yet complete answers. Because objective questions are generally narrower in focus, questions and answers work best for objective-type tests.

- Begin with the traditional question words. If you know your test will focus mostly on memorizing information, concentrate on questions that begin with who, what, where, and when.

- If the test questions will be more thinking and synthesis questions (as is more common), write quite a few "why" and "how" questions (and not too many "what" questions).

- Use the right format. Put your questions on the left-hand side of your paper and the answers on the right.

- When you study, cover up the answer to the question and talk through the information.

- Uncover the answer and check to see how accurate and complete your talk-through was.

- Use a highlighter to mark questions that you need to spend more time on. (Now's the time to use your highlighters. Yea!) Your questions and answers should look something like this.

Questions	Answers
1. Define and give an example of chunking.	Chunking is the grouping of items together so that you can increase the capacity of STM. Ex. Telephone number (706) 555-1212 Soc sec # 111-11-1111
2. Why would you have trouble remembering this sequence of letters in your STM: imagoodstudent?	Because 14 pieces of info exceeds the capacity of STM. It only holds 7 ± 2 pieces of info.
3. How could you move the string of letters above from STM to LTM?	You could chunk the letters into words and then use some elaboration to remember it. Notice that it spells "I'm a good student." Now if you connect that to your own knowledge ("Hey, I *am* a good student") then you will remember that information.

DO YOUR HOMEWORK

If you find yourself writing questions you can answer in a word or two, you probably need to put a bit more thought into your questions. Rule of thumb: if it takes more words to write the question than it does to answer it, you need to ask a tougher question. Remember, this strategy works best when the questions you pose really make you think about the concepts. In almost all cases, you will need to write questions beginning with "how" and "why" rather than all "what" questions.

Reviewing: Keeping Information in Memory

Now that you have gotten information from your STM to your LTM, you want to keep it there. Unless you engage in activities that help you keep the ideas you have learned in your LTM, you are likely to forget them. Reviewing helps you hold onto what you've learned.

When we talk with students about how they review, a common answer is that they read over the material, either from their text or from their notes, a couple of times. Although this is a good start, it's not enough. It's important to do more than simply read over things. Each time you review, you should reduce information down to its essentials, both so you have a reasonable amount of information to remember and so you can focus on the most important information. About two-thirds of what you read in texts and at least some of what you hear in lecture is filler—material that is there but that is not particularly important for you to remember. Your first task when you review is to figure out what is most important to learn and then to concentrate your reviewing on that.

TALK-THROUGH CARDS

One of the best ways to review is to make talk-through cards, like the one below. Here's how to make and use one.

- Use an index card (a piece of paper will do in a pinch) and list the key pieces of information you need to remember in an organized way. How much information you will put on your card depends on the topic. For a very difficult concept, you might just talk through one or two pieces of information per card. But in some courses, you may be able to talk through an entire chapter (or more) with one talk-through card. Notice that on our card you can tell which bits of information are the key ideas and which information supports each key idea. Cues are also provided to help you remember when you need to know examples.

- After you have read through your rehearsal strategies (concept cards, concept maps, and the like), annotations, and lecture notes, use your talk-through cards to cue you to important information. This is one of the last things you will do before you take the exam. Start with the first major idea on your card and then say (aloud) what you know about it without looking at any other materials. Make connections between this idea and other key ideas. Be precise.

- Say the information out loud because when you don't (or if you just say it to yourself), you can fool yourself into thinking you know stuff when you really don't.

- If you get stuck on something you have written on your card, go back to the source—text, lecture notes, or written rehearsal pieces—and read through the rocky part again. Be sure you understand the material before you go back to your talk-through card and proceed.

Once you make your talk-through card, reviewing will be easy. Remember, the information should already be in long-term memory. The goal of reviewing is to keep it there. Here's an example of a talk-through card.

STUDY GROUPS

Another good way to review is to join or form a study group. The best study groups meet for weekly review sessions, perhaps more frequently as test dates get closer. Productive study groups tend to have these characteristics:

- They include classmates, but not necessarily your good friends (this way you are less likely to chat).

- They are relatively small. Five members is about the maximum any group should have.

- All members pull their weight. When you become part of a study group, you should make a commitment to come to each session prepared. If you organize a study group, try to invite classmates you know are interested in staying on task.

- The groups don't take the place of reflecting and rehearsing on your own. You need to do much of the work on your own and use your study groups as confirmation that you know and understand the material.

- Study groups are best used for reviewing information, for troubleshooting difficult material, and for testing each other.

- If you have a regular study group, meet at the same time and place each week. This tends to lessen the confusion about where and when to meet and encourages you to stay on task from week to week.

It's important that you understand the purpose of reviewing. You have reflected and rehearsed; for the most part, you know the material. You're reviewing to keep that information in long-term memory so you can retrieve it accurately on test day or for future courses (or even after you enter the workforce). Reviewing can be done for ten or fifteen minutes here and there, at points in your day when you might otherwise get nothing done. Our students are always amazed at how much difference it makes to use small pockets of time for reviewing. Even ten minutes a day every day yields big rewards.

LISTEN UP

All of this reflecting, rehearsing, and reviewing stuff sounds like loads of work, doesn't it? It does take time but it doesn't have to be an overwhelming task, and the payoffs are huge. If you create a studying cycle wherein you are reading and annotating for one course and rehearsing and reviewing for another, it's much easier to stay on top of things. The only people who think college is a cakewalk are those who have already graduated, and they may have forgotten just how much work it was.

Monitoring Your Learning

Have you ever thought you did really well on a test, only to get it back with a big, fat D (or worse) on it? Or have you thought you understood a theory or how to solve a problem only to get an item on a test you swore you had never even heard about? If you have been in this situation (and most students have been), you may be having difficulty monitoring your learning. We think monitoring is one of the greatest difficulties college students face, right after time management and staying motivated.

Monitoring is sometimes a problem for college freshmen because they haven't had to do much monitoring in high school. Your high school teachers may have explained everything from your textbooks clearly enough that you never really had to figure things out on your own. They may also have given you study guides (or even told you the exact information you would be tested on). As a result, you really didn't need to monitor your learning. They did it for you. What a deal.

In most college classrooms, however, things operate a bit differently. Your college profs expect you to know when you're having problems understanding something and to ask for help when you need it. That's another reason why it's so important to keep up with your reading and studying. If you put it off until right before the exam and then find that you are totally confused about some of the material, you won't have time to get the help you need and you won't feel confident going into the exam.

To monitor your understanding during reading, make notes about ideas that confuse you as you read your textbook. During lecture, do the same. If your professor's explanation isn't clear, ask her to rephrase it or articulate what you don't understand. If you are in a very large classroom setting where it's impossible (or intimidating) for you to ask questions during class, see the prof after class, send your question by email, see a tutor, or talk it over with classmates. Whatever method you choose, monitor your learning as you go along. It should be part of a continuous cycle: reflecting, rehearsing, reviewing, monitoring.

Monitoring is also very important as you ramp up your studying as test time nears. We might go so far as to say that if you leave monitoring out of the studying formula, you will not have an accurate perception of how well you will perform. Before you take a test, you should have a pretty good idea of the concepts you know very well, those you know fairly well, and those that may pose problems. Certainly after the test you should be able to predict with a high degree of accuracy how well you did. If you leave with a feeling that you aced the test only to discover that you made a low C, or if you feel as though you didn't do well at all when, in fact, you end up earning a B, you need to work on monitoring your learning. Students who consistently overpredict their performance tend not to change how they study and are likely to be disappointed when they receive their grades at the end of the semester.

Students who consistently underpredict never muster the confidence they need in testing situations and tend to feel a lot of test anxiety. Here are a few tips to help you monitor your learning:

- Keep up with your reading and other assignments.

- Think about your understanding of the concepts as you complete each assignment and hear each lecture.

- Evaluate your learning at the end of each studying period by quickly talking through or summarizing what you have learned.

- Be honest with yourself. If you don't understand something, don't ignore it. Get your questions answered as they occur.

The secret to monitoring is to do it as you go along. Monitor as you read and annotate, during lectures, and as you are making concept cards or using other rehearsal strategies. If you realize your understanding is breaking down, reflect on the information some more or ask your professor or students in your study group. Monitoring during test preparation is also important, but if you haven't monitored all along, it may be too late to do it well when it comes time to prep for an exam.

If You Read Nothing Else, Read This

- When you reflect, you think about the information, making an effort to make sense of it.

- When you rehearse, you use strategies that help get information into your long-term memory. Strategies such as concept cards, concept maps, charts, and questions and answers, which involve writing, are good ways to set information in your memory.

- When you review, you work to keep information in your memory. Talking through the information in a planned and organized way lets you review it.

- When you monitor, you stay on top of what you know and what you don't know. Monitoring should be an ongoing part of your studying routine.

CHAPTER 19

STUDYING SMARTER

- Worried that you don't really know the best ways to study?
- Concerned that you can study "hard" yet still not earn good grades?
- Think that you should study biology the same way you study history?

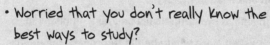

If so, read on . . .

As a general rule, your profs do care about you. They want you to be successful and will work with you to make that success a reality. But frankly, most professors really don't know how to tell you the most effective ways to study for their courses. They might just tell you to study harder or study longer. And, as you have probably realized by now, it's not necessarily studying harder or even longer that makes the difference. (We don't even know what "studying harder" means, but it sounds painful!) The key is studying smarter.

Studying smarter means knowing and using the most appropriate strategies for each particular learning situation. It means having a pocketful of approaches that you can use depending on the course you are taking, the kind of test you are studying for, and how you learn best. Studying smarter means being flexible. It means knowing that you study for chemistry differently than you study for history or French. That's why having lots of strategies to choose from makes learning in college easier. Sometimes it even makes learning fun (really!).

☹ SAD BUT TRUE

Mara made an appointment to see her statistics professor after totally failing the first exam. This was a positive move on her part, but unfortunately, the meeting didn't go particularly well. The chain of events went something like this:

- Mara arrived at Professor Olson's office on time.
- Mara sat down and wove a tale of woe about studying really hard, harder than she had ever studied in her life.
- Mara also lamented the number of hours she put into studying for the course.
- Mara teared up and tried not to cry.
- Professor Olson smiled sympathetically and nodded his head.
- Professor Olson asked Mara what she did to prepare for the first exam.
- Mara said, "I studied really hard. I put in a lot of time."
- Professor Olson smiled and nodded his head.
- Professor Olson said, "Study harder. Study longer."
- Mara nodded her head and left feeling very frustrated.

Being Flexible: Selecting and Modifying Strategies

Throughout *College Rules!* you have read about a variety of strategies. If you use them, you can learn and remember information better. But not all of these strategies will work in every class, for every student, or for every professor.

Not every strategy will end up being carried out in the exact way we have presented it. In fact, one of the most important ideas you should learn about using strategies is that you need to be flexible and modify your strategies to fit both the task your prof gives you and your own personal preferences as a learner. Try things out. Make strategies your own. Don't be afraid to experiment. Students we know who do well in college consciously consider their approaches to

If someone had told me I would be Pope one day, I would have studied harder.

—Pope John Paul I

studying and have a variety of tricks up their sleeves to make learning easier, less painful, and more successful.

One of the misconceptions that students often bring with them to college is the idea that, if they put time into studying, they should gain big rewards in terms of good grades. But that is not always the case. Think of Mara. She said, "I'm putting in a lot of time," but she was still doing poorly in the course. Although it's important to put time into studying—you'll never be a member of Phi Beta Kappa by putting in only enough hours to get by—what you do during that time is equally important. Time alone ≠ success.

FOR ADULTS ONLY

If you are a nontraditional student, you really have to study smart. Because you may have a family and job to deal with beyond your college responsibilities, it's particularly important for you to study as efficiently as possible. Use small pockets of time to study with concept cards, maps, charts, or other portable strategies—on the bus, while you're cooking dinner, during a break at work. If you have kids, get them to quiz you. You'll be spending some quality time with them, they'll feel grown-up, and you'll be reviewing. Everyone wins!

Students who put in what they consider to be "a lot of time" but still aren't reaping the rewards of good grades are probably making one of two mistakes:

1. They're not being honest with themselves about the actual amount of time they are investing (that hour break does not count toward study time, nor does the time "getting ready" to study by surfing the Web or checking out Facebook).

2. They are actually spending a lot of time in course-related activities,

LISTEN UP

Recently, one of our students realized that making to-do lists helped her remember things she had to get done. But the problem was that she kept losing her lists. To solve this problem, she started writing her lists on her bathroom mirror using washable markers. Every time she went into the bathroom, she saw what she still needed to get accomplished and could mark off what she had done. We think this is what strategy modification is all about. She solved her problem by creating an effective technique that worked for her.

but they are not using the most appropriate or efficient study strategies (like memorizing definitions when they need to be applying the concepts).

Now let's get down to the nitty-gritty and talk about ways to study in a variety of disciplines. Our goal is to help you realize that one size does not fit all. Different courses require different approaches because they have different types of content, exams, requirements, and lecturing styles. Different students use different approaches since no two students are alike. What we present are guidelines to think about as you decide which strategies you will select. We'll talk a little about each discipline, the kinds of tests that are generally given, and which strategies students in the discipline often see as good matches for studying smarter. Although courses are traditionally divided into three groupings—sciences, social sciences, and humanities—we have taken the liberty of further dividing them so we can be a bit more specific about studying foreign languages and mathematics.

Acting Like Einstein: Studying in the Sciences

The sciences can be broken down into many subcategories, each with several courses as part of that subcategory. These subcategories and examples of the different disciplines that fall under them include

- Exact sciences: chemistry, physics

- Biological sciences: biology, medicine, forestry, botany, zoology, agriculture

- Physical sciences: geology, astronomy

- Engineering and computer sciences: electrical engineering, industrial engineering, information technology, information science

WHAT'S THE FOCUS?

Science courses tend to focus on basic principles and well-researched, but not necessarily proven, theories. (By the way, when scientists say that theories aren't "proven," that statement reflects their views about the discipline. Scientists continually seek new information and revise theories based on new information. "Not proven" means there is more to know, but the theory still has merit.) They stress the relationships among ideas and are usually taught in a sequential or hierarchical manner. For example, in biology you would learn about the structure of cells before you'd learn how cells group to form organs and systems.

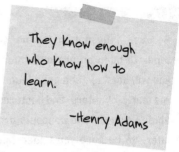

They know enough who know how to learn.

—Henry Adams

Science courses usually involve a "hands-on" element in the form of a lab. In the lab, you'll probably engage in discovery learning. You might examine different types of cells under a microscope so you can better learn to differentiate plant from animal cells (in a biology lab), or you might examine different types of rocks and soil (in a geology lab).

Science textbooks and lectures are loaded with new terms and definitions, which are usually introduced at warp speed. In fact, a term that is defined in one paragraph may be used to define another new term in the next paragraph. These terms often represent key concepts and are also interrelated. In science, most professors rely heavily on diagrams for teaching purposes. Diagrams will be everywhere—in your textbooks, lectures, and computer modules.

WHAT SHOULD YOU ALREADY KNOW?

At the very least, your professors will expect you to have some knowledge of the scientific method—how basic laws and principles are discovered and researched. They also assume you can understand the relationship between scientific principles and the proofs that support them.

FOR ADULTS ONLY X

Students who have been out of school for a while may need to bone up a bit on scientific concepts and problem solving before returning to college. Basic principles and laws of science may be long gone from memory. Science courses that require you to use math, such as chemistry and physics, may also require some additional work. If you fall into this category, think about joining a study group or getting a tutor right from the beginning to help you fill in the gaps.

WHAT CAN YOU EXPECT?

Tests in science courses tend to be objective—multiple choice, true or false, matching, and some diagram labeling or interpretation. In the exact sciences, you will be

🎧 LISTEN UP

Because information in the sciences tends to build on previous information, you will need to get a good foundation in the early chapters and lectures to be able to understand concepts presented later. So be sure you understand each concept as it is presented before you move on.

required to solve problems as well. Additionally, at least some of what you do in the lab part of the course will also be tested, although on some campuses course and lab testing are separate.

WHAT SHOULD YOU DO?

Because there are lots of terms to learn in science courses, concept cards are a good starting point. But don't make the mistake of thinking that's all you should do, unless, of course, your prof just expects you to memorize. You'll need to use other strategies to help you see how ideas connect. If you're a visual learner, concept maps are great tools for learning science. You will also need to study diagrams. Some students like to copy them from their texts or notes and then talk through the important information. If you are in a science course that requires problem solving, such as chemistry or physics, talking through the information, doing practice problems, and studying with others are all constructive ways of approaching these courses. With some modification, concept cards also work well for learning formulas. In science courses, it's also helpful to read before you go to class, since some of the same terms that are introduced in your textbook will also be used in the lecture.

🧩 GET IT TOGETHER

Once students start along a studying path, they are reluctant to change strategies—even when they are not working. We have done some research where we found that students who were struggling in biology and who failed the first three (of four) exams continued to use the same study strategies, which clearly were not effective. We are not sure exactly why this phenomenon occurs, but if you are not doing well in a course, consider changing your studying plan. Read this chapter extra carefully to help you make the most effective strategy selections for each of your courses.

Beyond Freud and Mead:
Studying in the Social Sciences

Like the sciences, social sciences can be clustered into different categories. These categories include

- Social orientation: psychology, sociology, education

- Study of cultures: anthropology, archaeology, human geography

- Political orientation: political science, pre-law (some include history in the social sciences, but we think it's a better fit under humanities)

- Business: economics, accounting, marketing

WHAT'S THE FOCUS?

Because it is difficult to prove much about people and social institutions, such as the legal and educational systems, social scientists rely on theories about what generally happens in society. The major problem students have in learning the social sciences is that they often confuse fact and opinion. Social science texts are usually arranged around particular topics. These texts tend to use an abundance of organizational aids—headings, subheadings, italicized words—to help you follow a chapter's organization. They also use lots of visual aids, usually in the form of tables, charts, and time lines that summarize information. Photographs are also often present, primarily to create interest.

Unlike science, there are not lots of new terms in social science, but there are terms that are used in ways you may not be familiar with. In other words, terms like "family" or "class" take on new, specialized meanings that could require additional attention.

WHAT SHOULD YOU ALREADY KNOW?

Social science professors will expect you to know something about people and how people and societies function. For example, they would expect that you would be able to understand their lecture on "social class" with only a brief definition of the term because you have lived and functioned in society. They also assume you can distinguish fact from opinion and understand that in the social sciences an interpretation rather than an objective recounting is prevalent.

WHAT CAN YOU EXPECT?

Tests in the social sciences tend to require you to do more writing. This writing can take the form of papers, essay or short-answer tests, or group projects. You may have some objective questions on exams, but usually they are combined with some form of writing.

The reverse side also has a reverse side.

—Japanese proverb

WHAT SHOULD YOU DO?

It's especially important in the social sciences to have a good grasp of the task, because there are a variety of ways that social science professors can test you. If the task is more heavily focused on writing, you will need to predict questions, talk through the information you would include in your answer, and even practice writing out the answer to a question or two. In the big scheme of things, concept cards won't help much in social science courses, particularly if you use them in traditional ways, because there aren't many new terms to learn.

The Art of the Dance: Studying in the Humanities

The humanities include a wide range of disciplines, including

- Literature: classics, English and foreign literature, writing

- Philosophy and theology

- Fine arts: art, music, theater, drama

- History

WHAT'S THE FOCUS?

The humanities are perhaps the most difficult to generalize since they include a broader variety of courses and disciplines. For example, literature stresses points like the author's purpose, character development, tone, and mood, requiring you to think critically about and interpret what you are reading. Other types of humanities courses focus on historical events and are often organized chronologically or, in the case of the fine arts, by different movements or periods. Humanities texts vary in the amount of new terms that are included, from few in history to lots in philosophy and even in the fine arts. They also vary in the amount and types of visual aids used. Art and history courses rely heavily on photographs; other humanities courses may include time lines and occasional graphs or diagrams.

WHAT SHOULD YOU ALREADY KNOW?

Literature professors assume you know something about the structure of stories, plays, poetry, and so forth. They also assume you know how to interpret literature, that you can detect symbolism, extract themes, and recognize figurative language. Other humanities professors expect that you have some knowledge of historical chronology (World War II came after World War I, which came after the Civil War) or general movements in art (impressionism, Dadaism). In most of the humanities, you will be expected to do a fair amount of writing, so your profs will expect you to have acquired decent writing skills and a working knowledge of grammar and spelling.

WHAT CAN YOU EXPECT?

In courses that focus on literature, history, and philosophy, there will be a heavy emphasis on writing. In literature, you may have to write essays that ask you to compare and contrast the works of different authors or interpret symbolism. In history, you may be asked to analyze and interpret the influence of historical events. In the fine arts, you may have to write papers or do projects about different movements or analyze how historical events influenced art, music, or the theater. You may even have tests that ask you to identify pieces of music and works of art as well as their creators. But few humanities courses offer a steady stream of objective testing.

WHAT SHOULD YOU DO?

Because humanities courses are quite varied, you'll need a number of strategies to meet their wide-ranging demands. In general, however, annotation is a strategy that can be used effectively, with some modification, in most humanities courses. In history, for example, students often fall into the trap of annotating every little fact and lose sight of the big picture. But when you are annotating and reflecting on your history text and when you listen to lectures, you should concentrate on the key conclusions that are drawn. Then annotate only the most important supporting information.

In addition, because most of the humanities have a heavy historical focus, creating time lines is a good strategy to help you put events or movements in historical perspective. These time lines can then be used to predict essay questions and to be sure you understand the course material's chronology. Questions and answers would work well for courses in which you have to answer identification questions.

In literature, it's very important to carefully read your assignments with a critical eye. Make brief notes in the margins of your books that will enable you to think about the issues your professor discusses in class. Mark crucial passages with sticky notes so you can refer to them as you review for tests or prepare to write papers.

Parlez-vous Français? Studying Foreign Languages

Studying a foreign language is often considered part of the humanities, but because it offers different challenges, we will deal with it separately. Many students believe studying a foreign language means learning vocabulary, grammar rules, and sentence construction. Although that is the main part of learning a language, there is also an emphasis on learning about the culture and the people.

One of the interesting aspects of foreign language courses is that the first course is generally fairly easy, especially if you have had a couple years of a language in high school. Initially, you learn words with high usage, regular verbs, and general grammatical sentence structure. Chapters are usually arranged by topics, such as going to a restaurant, planning a trip, or meeting new people. Each chapter offers dialogues for you to practice and activities where you can apply a particular skill you have learned. Most language courses also include the often dreaded language lab, where you listen and respond to conversations by native speakers.

But foreign language courses tend to get difficult quickly, often without students even noticing it until they have fallen way behind. Let's face it, learning a language requires lots of memorization: grammar rules, verb tenses, vocabulary, and on and on.

And very quickly, all that memorization must be applied to reading, understanding, speaking, and perhaps even writing about longer and longer pieces of text.

That's why it's important to commit some time each day to studying a language. Here are a few suggestions to help make learning a language a bit easier.

- Do all of the practice activities, even if they aren't all assigned.

- Have a "language hour" with classmates (or native speakers, if possible) to discuss problems and practice speaking.

- Modify the traditional concept card by putting the foreign word on one side and the English word on the other. Cards can also be used to learn grammar rules and irregular verbs.

- Never miss a lab. We know you would rather do just about anything else, but listening to a native speak the language helps you develop an ear for the language and improves your speaking skills. Also, if your campus has an international coffee hour (or something similar), as ours does, attend whenever possible. You'll make new friends and be able to practice not only speaking the language but also developing an ear for it.

- Get into the culture. Nothing makes learning a language more fun than understanding cultural traditions. Check out local festivals or campus organizations.

- Plan a trip (even if it's for graduation) to the country whose language you are learning. If that's not possible, try visiting cities that have thriving enclaves of people from the country whose language you are studying. Planning a trip gives you a real purpose for studying because in your travels you will be able to actually use your language skills (in fact, you might even have to).

X + Y = What? Studying Mathematics

Like foreign languages, studying math requires some different approaches and a different mindset than studying other disciplines. Some students have the attitude that they just can't do math, which, in turn, can end up being an excuse for not putting in much effort. The problem isn't so much that students don't have an aptitude for math as that they simply lack the background. And if you get to college and still don't have the background, you're going to have to work extra hard to be successful in math and math-related courses. But we are confident you can do it.

Another problem that gets in the way of learning math for many students is the idea that there are no practical applications of math. "When am I ever gonna need calculus?" you ask. Perhaps you won't ever use calculus per se, but you probably use the skills that underlie calculus more frequently than you realize. That's because math is about problem solving, and we all know that life throws us one problem after another.

☹ SAD BUT TRUE

Larry absolutely hated math. It had been a source of frustration for him since elementary school. He could almost pinpoint the day it began: when his class started on percentages and fractions. He didn't get it in fourth grade and he did not get it now that he was headed off to college. Now he had to do fractions with letters in them (all that x and y stuff). What was that about? Larry was glad that at least there was now a term for his affliction: "mathematically challenged." That described him perfectly. During summer orientation, Larry met with his advisor, Ms. Mason, to discuss his course schedule for fall. Her suggested schedule included the first-level math course, freshman English, political science, and introduction to ecology. Everything sounded fine to Larry except the math. He informed Ms. Mason that he was going to put off taking his math requirement as long as possible. Then maybe his math anxiety would go away and he might be able to do enough to eke out a C. Although Ms. Mason tried to convince Larry that he needed to take math sooner rather than later, he would not budge. She even suggested he enroll in a preparatory class if he didn't feel he was ready to tackle the credit course: "You have nothing to lose and everything to gain by having some success. Get in at a level you'll feel comfortable with." Larry held firm and took a geography course rather than the math. And Larry held firm the next semester as well, and the next, and the next. In fact, he let it go so long that he had not only forgotten just about all he had learned in high school math, but he was also at the point in his coursework where his lack of math credit was keeping him from taking some other courses he thought he would enjoy. The last we heard of Larry, he was still trying to find some way around the math requirement.

Because college math courses build on what you have learned in your previous schooling, it's important to begin at the right level. If you find yourself overwhelmed during the first week of class, you're probably in over your head. When this happens, you have choices to make. Are you going to withdraw from the course and take a lower-level one, even if it means sitting in on something you won't get graduation credit for? Or do you feel confident enough in your ability to do the work if you get

> Always remember that people will think you're smarter if you flunk a test because you didn't study rather than flunking it when you did study.
>
> – Anonymous

tutoring or other assistance? Either choice requires you to put in some extra effort to do well in the course.

For those who are at the right level of mathematics and will be successful with some effort, try these tips:

- **Stay current.** Because math concepts build on one another, it's important to stay on top of things. Although you may be able to catch up with your reading in other courses, it's very difficult to play catch-up in math once you get behind.

- **Read your textbook and annotate in the margins.** Math textbooks have become more reader-friendly in the last couple of years (hooray!) and offer understandable explanations and study aids. Although we generally don't recommend reading your texts more than once, we do in certain situations, and this is one of them. If math is particularly difficult for you, you might try reading your text before the lecture and then again after the lecture. It helps your understanding to read it, listen to it, read it again, and then work on the problems.

- **Review daily.** Don't wait until a day or two before an exam to review all the concepts you will be tested on. This point is so important we will say it again— review daily.

- **Take good lecture notes.** Be sure to pay close attention to detail when your professor explains a problem. Mathematics requires attention to detail.

- **Ask questions—lots of them.** Failure to understand even a minor point can have grave consequences later on, so clear up problems as they come up.

- **Talk things through by putting words to formulas.** If you can talk about a problem, it shows you understand it. It is not unheard of to have "math essays" that ask you to write out the mathematical processes.

- **Practice, practice, practice.** Do application problems even if they aren't assigned; and do a variety of problems.

- **Use concept cards to learn formulas and important mathematical principles.** A good approach is to put the formula on one side of the card and a brief explanation of the formula on the other side. For math principles, put the principle on one side and an example problem using that principle on the other side.

- **Always ask yourself: Does my answer or solution make sense?** Professors tell us that if students would check to see if their answers made sense, fewer test items would be missed. One chemistry professor told us that students tend to confuse units of measure and, if they would just think through their answer to see if it made sense, they would be able to catch their mistakes.

- **If appropriate, draw diagrams, especially for word problems.** Diagrams can help you see relationships and information that may not be apparent from reading the problem alone.

- **Study smarter.** It's about being flexible and knowing which strategies to use in which situation. Those who study smart put time into learning (everything takes time, remember, usually longer than you thought it would). But they also learn efficiently and effectively by knowing and using a variety of strategies.

DO YOUR HOMEWORK

One of the major problems students have is that, although they do fine when they work on the problems at the end of each section of the book, they don't know what to do when problems involving different concepts from several sections are put together on a test (which is often what you'll see on math tests). Make sure when you do your homework that you mix it up and practice different types of problems. Try combining some problems to come up with larger ones. By doing this, you'll be able to recognize when confusion sets in, and you can get help for it early on.

If You Read Nothing Else, Read This

○ Strategies are not set in stone. Be flexible and modify strategies depending on the task and your own preferences as a learner. What works for one student won't work for another.

○ It's important to know how to adjust and modify from discipline to discipline. You study humanities differently than the sciences, which in turn, are approached differently than the social sciences.

○ Studying foreign languages and mathematics requires a unique use of strategies.

CHAPTER 20

EVERYTHING YOU WANTED TO KNOW ABOUT RESEARCH AND PRESENTATIONS BUT WERE AFRAID TO ASK

- Worried that you'll be assigned research papers and you won't have a clue where to start?
- Concerned that you don't know what plagiarism is and isn't?
- Think that you know how to do effective library and Web searches?

If so, read on . . .

I f you have made it to this point in *College Rules!*, you have probably picked up a few tips along the way and feel pretty good about your knowledge of what it takes to be academically successful in college. But we're not finished yet. Although college demands that you spend a good deal of time studying in more traditional ways, you also need to have some tools to carry out research projects and to do class presentations. That's what this chapter is all about—guiding you through the research process. Although our goal is not to teach you how to write a paper (that's for your composition prof to handle), we want to guide you through how to do your research project from A to Z. Because research tasks come in many forms, most sections of this chapter should stand on their own, so you can pick and choose which ones fit your particular assignment. We start with a discussion of how to find the resources you need to do your research.

Finding Resources in the Library and on the Web

It is probably more common now for students to do research on the Web than to traipse to the "bricks and mortar" library that looms over most campuses. However, at some point in your college career, your professor will require you to use both resources. So we're going to start with the library, an often intimidating place at first glance, and then move on to talking a little about finding information on the Web.

FEAR NOT YOUR LIBRARY

Many undergraduates are reluctant to use the library because it appears to be too big and not user friendly—scary even. We have known students who have wandered aimlessly through the stacks looking for a book or article when a simple question to one of the librarians would have saved considerable time and energy. We have also known students who avoid the library, even when library resources are needed. With a little general advice, you should be able to figure out how your library works and how to use it efficiently and effectively. Keep in mind that lots of the information housed in libraries—books, periodicals, newspapers, scholarly articles, government documents, and so forth—is not available online. And this is what you should think about as you decide what sources are best to pull from the library and which are better left to the Web. For example, if you must use original sources from the 1950s, say, you'll have a much better chance of finding them in the library than by going online. But if

> The outcome of any serious research can only be to make two questions grow where only one grew before.
>
> —Thorstein Veblen

For students returning to college, it is especially important to find out if your library has scheduled orientation sessions. If so, be sure to sign up or show up. Attending an hour-long session can save you tons of time down the line and can familiarize you with the most efficient and effective ways of doing library research (they don't have a card catalogue anymore—gasp!). It will be well worth your time.

you need original sources from last week, check online first. So to fully investigate your research idea, think about the specifics of your topic. And remember, several trips to the library may be in order. Although policies and procedures differ from campus to campus, here are some general guidelines to follow as you head to the library.

What's your question? When you set out for the library, have a clear notion of what you want to know. Take some time before you go to form your question (or questions) so you don't waste time trying to figure out what you're there for. Narrowing your question is particularly important because it's really easy to get overwhelmed with all the information that's there. If your question is too broad, it's very easy to get hundreds of results from your library search. And all of a sudden, every remotely related subject can seem essential. No student, no matter how dedicated, has the time to go through each and every source that pops up. The narrower your search, the more likely you are to come up with sources you might be able to use.

What's your position? Once you know your question, then it's time to take a stance so you can find the materials most closely related to your approach. Because most initial research questions are very broad, it's important to take a position so you can

DO YOUR HOMEWORK

How easy it is to do research, whether at the library or online, may depend on the degree to which you have thought about what you want to write about. Students who have only a vague and generalized topic find themselves overwhelmed with all that is out there and have a hard time sifting though everything. When this happens, progress is often slow and frustrating. So, use some brain power and think about your topic before you run to the library. You will save yourself both time and stress in the long run.

narrow your search. So if your topic is U.S. tax policy (a very broad topic indeed), your stance might be about the need to simplify the tax code to make it more accessible for taxpayers to understand (still broad, but a good starting point).

How do you search? College libraries generally allow you to conduct computerized searches of what's available in the stacks. Although libraries differ, look for three key pieces of information as you begin your search:

1. **The call number.** This number tells you exactly where the resource is located and is probably similar to what you used in high school. Although it may not make sense to you, there is a logical numbering system that actually makes it easy to find what you're looking for, once you know the set up, that is.

2. **Location.** On large campuses, it's particularly important to know which library houses the resource. We have seen many students get frustrated on our own campus when they go to the main library only to find that what they need is way on the other side of campus in the science library. It is also important to know the location within the library. Our main library has eight floors filled with good stuff (it's a huge place!), so you need to know which floor your source is on.

3. **Status.** When you look up an article or a book, you will get information about its availability. Is it checked out? Is it on reserve? Is it available at all? There is nothing more frustrating than dragging yourself to the library only to find your book has been checked out.

What if I run into trouble? First of all, don't despair. Your first line of defense is to ask the research librarians, who should be able to help you. They can help you refine your search and locate materials. They may even be able to point you in the direction of other resources that you didn't know existed. The best advice we can give you when you are doing research in the library is to ask for help. Don't just spin your wheels. Librarians enjoy helping students with their research and possess lots of knowledge about the library's resources.

If you are doing your searches in your dorm or from anywhere other than the library, sometimes you can help yourself sort through your massive search results. Think about the following:

- **Publication title.** Does the title of the book or article seem to be a match with your topic? Does it sound interesting or does it seem to be somewhat off topic? Although you can't judge a book by its cover, sometimes you can judge quite a bit from its title.

- **Author.** Are a lot of the results written by the same author? If so, he or she is probably an expert and therefore a pretty good source.

- **Date.** If you are writing on a topic where current ideas are essential, think about the date of publication when evaluating your search results. For example, you wouldn't want a source from the 1980s if your topic was "the role of technology in warfare."

URBAN LEGEND

Several different people have claimed that their alma mater (or someone else's) built a new library but did not factor in the weight of the books. After the building was completed and the books were added, the building began to sink. Now the university can only put books on every other floor. There has also been a joke floating around the Internet about this, saying that with budget cuts, the campus library is housing fewer and fewer books each year and so the building is beginning to rise.

HOW TO EVALUATE WEB RESOURCES

Many students turn to the Internet to do research because they think it's easier—they can do it from the comfort of their room, print out the information they need, and then take a nap. The problem with the Web is that anyone can put up anything—even make it look good and sound credible—and call it their version of the truth. We want you to be able to evaluate what you find on the Web on the basis of its credibility, not on what it looks or sounds like. Think about the following:

- **Who is writing this stuff?** Is it a noted expert in the field, a high school student who has a bone to pick, a business that has something to gain, an organization that supports a certain cause? Your answer to this question should tell you a lot about the quality of the information. If, for example, you were doing research on the link between tobacco use and cancer, you would get very different information from the American Tobacco Corporation than you would get from the American Medical Association.

- **Why does the site exist in the first place?** What's its purpose? Is it trying to educate you on an issue or is it trying to sell a product or convince you of a very limited point of view? Although commercial websites can sound convincing, if they are obviously trying to sell you something, whether it's a product or a viewpoint, you should have your antenna up.

- **How does the information you have found compare to that on other websites?** Usually there is a good deal of overlap, even on very controversial ideas, so if you find sites where someone is making claims

LISTEN UP

It is human nature for people to gravitate to websites that support their own views. But be careful about basing your arguments solely on a one-sided viewpoint. Always consider who is responsible for putting the information out there and think about whether this individual or group has a reason to be biased. Remember that there are two sides to every story, and a good researcher investigates his problem to the point that he understands what he is up against. For example, even if you believe the drinking age should be lowered to eighteen, you should still be able to argue that it needs to remain at twenty-one.

that no one else is discussing, that should send up a red flag. You should also try to evaluate the extent to which the site is biased. For example, most of the tobacco companies probably have similar viewpoints on the issue of secondhand smoke, so you might think, "Gee, there's quite a bit of overlap here." But you also have to consider why their views might be similar and think about how credible this makes the information.

Forget the Five-Paragraph Essay

Okay, you're on a roll. You've gathered credible and high-quality information and you feel you have a good grasp of the issue. Now you're ready to write. Unfortunately, the writing phase involves a bit more than just sitting down at your computer and producing a final product in one sitting. That would be too easy. And because writing for your stodgy college professor may be a bit different than writing for your high school English teacher, there are several factors you need to keep in mind.

YOUR AUDIENCE HAS CHANGED

For many students, much of the writing they did in high school focused on personal experiences, a five-paragraph essay, or the absolutely dreaded "research paper." These types of writing are generally very different than the kinds of research you will be asked to do now. After all, you're in college. More is expected of you. In high school, "research" involved selecting a topic and simply writing about it. For example, you may have written about immigration or the civil rights movement. For these papers, you most likely collected information and reported what you found.

In college, you will find the tasks have changed and the expectations are greater. Your professor will expect you to take a stance, form a thesis statement, and argue a position. Your thesis statement lets your professor know the main crux of your argument and briefly explains what you will write about. The research paper on immigration becomes one of arguing for or against punishing companies that hire illegal aliens or whether amnesty should be permitted for people who have lived and worked in the country for many years. In other words, you use what facts you find about immigration in the United States to support your argument for or against punishing the businesses that hire illegal aliens. From your thesis statement, your audience knows right from the beginning what stance you will take. Your job then is to provide support for that stance. You are certainly expected to do more than summarize the issue. You are expected to pull together ideas from credible sources and critically think about what they mean.

START SOONER RATHER THAN LATER

When you have to do research and produce a paper as a result, procrastination can be the kiss of death. Think back to when we talked about time- management issues and remember what we tried to make clear then: everything takes longer than you think it will. Gathering the research will take longer and the writing will take longer too. And because a research project is often worth a large percentage of your grade, you will need to start early in order to turn in your best work. In addition, if you start early and need help, you will have the

> When something can be read without effort, great effort has gone into its writing.
>
> —Enrique Jardiel Poncela

time to get it. Most professors are willing to give you feedback on a work in progress, especially if you ask for it well in advance of the due date. Most also get bent out of shape if you wait until the day before the paper is due to discuss the problems you are having finding information or developing your idea.

The writing process involves four main stages: you organize, draft, revise, and assess. (Stay with us now. It's not as hard as you think . . . if you start early, that is.)

You organize. After you have gathered all your resources and you are satisfied that you have the most appropriate information to support your argument, you are ready to organize. You can organize in lots of ways—note cards, outlines, color-coding (yeah: another use for those highlighters), or maps—any way that works for you. The way you organize is really not that important; it's selecting the key points and then organizing your support that makes the difference.

GET WIRED ⚡

There are lots of great websites and software programs devoted to helping you organize information. Check out http://del.icio.us to keep track of websites, books, music, or anything else you want to organize. Backpackit.com will help you organize files, to-do lists, notes, webpage bookmarks, and so forth. It will even let you send yourself email reminders to get stuff done. Devonthink.com will let you store, classify, and integrate documents, pdfs, email, video, or audio files. It is a database for stuff that doesn't easily fit into regular databases. These are just a few examples—there are many, many more out there.

You draft. Once you have everything organized, you can begin writing your first draft. Be sure you have a solid thesis and each of the points you want to make is appropriate to your argument. At this stage, don't worry about getting it perfect. Get your thoughts down, making sure your support relates to your thesis. Once you have a working draft (realize that this can take some time and does not magically happen), read what you have written, making some notes in the margins about what you should concentrate on when you come back to the paper. The notes should focus on information you need to clarify, support you need to add, or connections you need to make.

You revise. After you have a respectable draft, put your paper aside for a day or two. What seemed like a stroke of genius at 2:00 A.M. on Monday may cause a "what the heck was I thinking?" response on Wednesday. (This even happens to seasoned writers like the authors of this book!) When you return to your draft fresh and alert, concentrate first on your notes in the margins. Clean up your content, making sure you haven't left out important information. Check to see if your content is sound and that you are sticking to the points you want to make. In other words, make sure that you're not rambling. If you have done a good job in organizing and drafting, the revising process shouldn't be too difficult.

A couple of other things deserve mentioning regarding the revision process. Once you're satisfied with the content, don't forget about cleaning up the grammar and mechanics of your paper. This can make a huge difference in your final grade. In some classes, professors will take off points for grammar; in others, poor mechanics may just make your paper seem weaker to the prof. Keep in mind that you are writing for an academic audience, one that is probably a stickler for following the conventional rules. You will also want to make sure you have cited your sources properly (see the section that follows for more on this topic). In addition, there is no magic number of revisions. Some lucky ducks can get by with a rough draft and a few minor revisions. For most of us, however, writing is hard work, and it takes several attempts to get it right.

You assess. Now comes the really hard part—standing back from your work and reading it with a critical eye. Once you complete the revision process, again put the paper aside for a day or two. When you return to it for the final dusting off, put yourself in the place of your prof, who will be grading your work. Be brutally honest. What grade would Professor OfcourseI'mperfect give you? Another good way to assess your work is to see if you can coerce your roommate or a friend to read it and give you feedback.

ALWAYS GIVE CREDIT WHERE CREDIT IS DUE

To cite your sources, you need to find out which citation style is preferred by your prof and then be consistent in using it. This is fairly easy once you know the format (okay—we admit some of it seems arbitrary and convoluted, but you still need to use proper format in your papers). Two of the more common academic citation formats are MLA (Modern Language Association) and APA (American Psychological Association). Most campus libraries have a variety of resources, including excellent online tutorials, to help you with this.

The more difficult part of citing is knowing *when* you must cite (general rule: when in doubt, cite). It's straightforward when you use a direct quote in the body of your paper—lift a sentence or two, throw quotes around it, and mention the writer. Voila! Then you would give the full citation on either a reference page or in a footnote, depending on your style. The major problem students seem to have with direct quotes is that the lead-ins don't flow with the quotes and they feel awkward within the paper. In fact, some professors will tell you to avoid direct quotes. If they don't give you guidance on this, our advice is to use direct quotes sparingly.

The more pressing problem is that students don't cite sources when they summarize information, which is generally your professor's preferred way of reading the information. But it's very important to understand that any thoughts or conclusions that are not totally and exclusively yours must be cited, even if they aren't direct quotes, because if you do not cite, it counts as plagiarism.

The Confusing World of Plagiarism

Cheating, copying, using the ideas of others without giving them credit—this is the ugly world of plagiarism. But many students don't have a full understanding of what this term means. We think it's important, in fact, crucial, that you clearly and totally understand what your professors mean when they talk about plagiarism. Plagiarism is very serious business.

Most of you know you can't take someone else's exact words or work and pass it off as your own. (A soul-searching moment. . . . Did you ever copy someone's math homework in high school? Come on. Fess up.) That's been beat into your head since grade school. However, most cases of academic dishonesty are not because a student intentionally copied someone else's work. There are two other very common ways that students plagiarize, perhaps without consciously realizing it: "stealing" someone else's ideas and receiving inappropriate help.

PASSING OFF SOMEONE ELSE'S IDEAS AS YOUR OWN

If you don't remember anything else in this chapter, remember this: if you use someone else's ideas, you must give them credit. Professors want and expect you to consult other sources (this is what professors do in their own academic writing), but you need to tell them where you got that information. To put the complete citation on the reference page is not enough. You must also give credit within the body of your paper. It's also important to keep track of information you take off the Web. Some students have the habit of cutting and pasting directly from the Internet, assuming that "it's just off the Web," but Internet information must be cited just like any other resource you find. There is a ton of software out there to help professors determine if students have plagiarized, and some colleges purchase this software so it is available to all faculty. It's simple. All any teacher has to do is type in a sentence or two of what a student has written and see if there are matches. It doesn't even have to match exactly. Way too many students find themselves before an academic honesty judiciary and have no idea why they are there. We repeat once more for those who need it: cite!

 SAD BUT TRUE

Coreen enrolled in an elective course to help her learn how to be a more efficient and effective student. She was excited about learning some new skills that would help her throughout her college career. As part of this class, Coreen had to choose from a number of projects as part of the course requirements. Because she hardly ever read anything outside of what she absolutely had to, she decided to select the Pleasure Reading Project. At the time, it didn't seem like that much work—select a book to read, do a little pushed reading, and keep a weekly journal about how the project was going. But somewhere along the way, Coreen got overwhelmed and left her weekly journals low on her priority list. In fact, she got so far behind that she found a couple of reviews of her book choice online and just cut and pasted one of them and passed it off as her weekly journal. Because the professor thought the journal entry didn't sound like Coreen's voice, she googled the first sentence. Low and behold, her professor easily found the entry had been plagiarized. In addition to being totally embarrassed, Coreen was left with a zero on the assignment and an academic dishonesty comment on her transcript.

I GET BY WITH A "LITTLE" HELP FROM MY FRIENDS

The second common way for students to plagiarize is by receiving inappropriate assistance. This may come in the form of receiving too much help in reworking a paper or turning in a project where another person actually does the work (or a majority of the work) for you. Sometimes this can happen without your realizing it. For example, you may go to your campus writing center for help with a paper in English and get an inexperienced tutor. It's her first day on the job and she wants to be so helpful that she actually rewrites your paper while you sit there and doodle. You turn in the revised paper and your professor doesn't think it "sounds" like you, so she asks you if you wrote it. How do you respond? You sort of wrote it. Even if you got what you thought was appropriate help, you could still be brought up on academic dishonesty charges. Remember that it's up to you to know what is plagiarism and what isn't. Ignorance of the rules is no excuse.

Creating First-Rate Presentations

At some point in your college career, you will be called upon to do individual and group presentations and projects. With the emphasis in college classrooms being more focused on collaborative efforts as well as on oral communication, it becomes important to improve these skills. Working in groups is difficult for many students. You have those who are the worker bees—you know the type—they want to do everything so it's done "right." Then there are the queen bees. They want to tell everyone else what to do but don't do any part of the real work themselves. Finally, we have the slacker bees who do next to nothing but are willing to take lots of credit. The key thing about working in groups is trusting your fellow members—knowing you can count on everyone to do his or her part. The following guidelines can help you build that trust. (If you are doing an individual presentation, you will need to do all these tasks too—and be sure not to be a slacker to boot.)

- **Break it down.** Begin by outlining all the tasks that need to be done. It might help to make a time line of how the project will progress. What kind of presentation is this? Who is the target audience? How much time do you have? What

🎯 GET IT TOGETHER

Even if you tend to be a slacker, you can still shine in group work. Remember that when you work in a group you only have to do a small part of the entire project. So volunteer for the smallest role, and then do a r-e-a-l-l-y good job at it. Your fellow students won't remember that you didn't do much if what you did do was done well.

do you want the audience to learn from this talk? Once you understand what you need to do, it will be easier to get it done.

- **Set goals.** Everyone should write down project deadlines in their planners. We find it's a good idea to work backward as you make your time line; that is, start with the date the project is due and fill in what you need to get done. This approach allows you to build in plenty of time and gives you more flexibility. The group should meet regularly (even if it is only an IM meeting) to make sure they are reaching their goals.

- **Everyone has a job.** This may be the toughest part of group work because you have to think about the strengths and weaknesses of each group member. And group members need to be honest with themselves and other members. It's also good to establish some group ground rules. What happens if tasks are not getting done or if someone is not carrying her weight? Making accusatory remarks the day before the project is due is not the best way to go.

- **If at all possible, steer clear of conflict.** What will you do if someone slacks off and doesn't get the work done? What if someone does the work, but it is not done very well? What if someone holds different ideas about how to do the project that conflict with your own? Talk about these issues in your first meeting and set some rules for dealing with these situations.

- **Give it some zing.** It used to be that students simply created posters or overhead slides for their presentations. Now it is much more common to incorporate technology—PowerPoint, video clips, or other multimedia. Whatever you use, remember two key things. First, make sure the technology you use is compatible with the resources in the classroom. And second, be sure that students in the back of the room will be able to see your visual aids.

● **Practice makes perfect.** If your project includes an oral presentation, your group needs to plan to get together to practice. Know in advance who will say what, stay within your allotted time frame, and be sure you have any visual aids or technology needs in place. Think about the following issues as you listen to your group:

- Are you talking too fast or in a monotone that will bore your audience to death?

- Are you speaking loudly enough for those in the back of the room to hear you? Now is not the time to use your little voice.

- Do you really know your stuff and are you communicating what you know to the audience. Are you referring to notes or are you reading your paper (bor—ing!) Are you rambling?

- Can the audience follow your points easily?

- Have you pulled your ideas together at the end of your talk?

- Have you stayed within your time limits?

- Do you gesture and move appropriately or are you actually distracting your audience with your movements?

SAD BUT TRUE

As Shelton was preparing for his class presentation, he spent a lot of time making a video that he would incorporate into his talk. He went all over campus interviewing students about their thoughts on lowering the drinking age from twenty-one to eighteen, so it was a topic his fellow students were certainly interested in. However, although he brought his digital video camera to class, it was not compatible with the technology available in the classroom. After several fitful attempts to make it work, he was ultimately unable to show it to his classmates. A word to the wise: make sure you know what technology is available before you go to all that trouble for nothing.

If You Read Nothing, Else Read This

○ One of the most important things to remember when doing research is to get started early.

○ Whether you are looking for resources in the library or on the Internet, be sure to have a clear idea of the focus of your research.

○ To evaluate information you find on the Web, think about credibility and bias.

○ Know exactly what constitutes academic honesty on your campus. Plagiarism involves considerably more than copying someone's homework.

○ When doing group presentations, plan ahead and break up the tasks so that everyone shares in the work.

CHAPTER 21

IT'S MORE THAN MULTIPLE-GUESS: PREPPING FOR AND TAKING OBJECTIVE EXAMS

- Concerned that you don't know what exams will be like in college?
- Worried that if you do poorly on an exam you won't know how to get back on track?
- Think that studying five hours the night before a test is the same as studying five hours spread out over a period of several days?

If so, read on . . .

L et's face it. Preparing for exams is probably the least enjoyable part of being a college student. It takes a considerable amount of time and it's stressful. We guess the only thing less fun than prepping for tests is actually taking them. So why do professors continue to torture you by making you take exam after exam, year after year? Don't they remember what it was like when they were undergraduates? Probably. But why should they let you off the hook? They had to take tough tests, and so do you.

Actually, professors give you tests because it's important for them (and for you) to know what (and if) you're learning. Although it sounds as if it would be great to have a college career where you never had to take a test, write a paper, or give a speech, the fact is you probably wouldn't learn very much under those conditions. No matter what you do, knowing you'll be evaluated is an important part of learning, even beyond the classroom. It's often what drives you to learn. Once you get out in the world of work, you will be evaluated for promotions and raises—not necessarily through tests, but through some kind of measurement of your performance.

Exams come in all shapes and sizes. In this chapter we will give you a feel for the most common type of exams—objective exams. We realize you have probably taken all the types of tests that we'll discuss somewhere along the way in your schooling. What you may not have done, however, is adjust your studying according to the kind of test you will take. That's something you will most certainly have to do in college.

The most common types of objective exams are

- Multiple-choice

- True or false

- Matching

These test types are referred to as "objective" because there is only one correct answer (or there's only supposed to be one correct answer), and this answer can be clearly articulated. For a well-written multiple-choice question, for example, there should be one answer that is obviously correct—that is, if you studied.

As long as there are tests, there will be prayer in public schools.

—Bumper sticker

You have probably been taking objective tests in school, particularly multiple-choice tests, ever since you can remember. Maybe this is the way studying has gone for you in the past: the night before (or maybe even an hour before) the exam, you skim the chapters at lightning speed and look over your notes. In fact, many students tell us they think this is the only way to do it, because they believe they remember more of what they study at the last minute. (We think this is hogwash, by the way. In chapter 18 we discussed that you remember more when you reflect, rehearse, and review.)

Studying for objective exams in college can take a bit getting of used to, especially if your experiences in high school encouraged memorization. You may have the idea that objective exams have only straightforward questions that demand straightforward answers—you know, just the facts, ma'am. So preparing for them should be a matter of memorizing the material. But college professors often ask questions that require you to pull together lots of information in order to answer them. This makes preparing for objective exams a little more involved.

Studying for Objective Exams

If you have kept up in the course—you've done the reading, annotated your text, reviewed your lecture notes, and constructed appropriate rehearsal strategies (whew!)—getting ready for objective exams shouldn't cause much trauma. Preparing will be generally a matter of additional rehearsing and reviewing. However, two key factors will determine how you will do on objective tests: understanding the task and distributing your study time over several days before the test.

Think back to chapter 14, where we talked about tasks. Remember, it's important not only to know what kind of test you will have, but also the level of questions you will be asked. If you don't know the level of questions, you'll have a difficult time approaching studying in the most effective way. We know many students who memorized piles of facts only to discover that few of the test questions simply ask for the facts.

There are two basic kinds of questions asked on objective tests: memory-level questions and higher-level questions.

MEMORY-LEVEL QUESTIONS

Memory-level questions can usually be thought of as questions that focus on facts. That is, you don't have to put pieces of information together to come up with the answer. You can rely on basic rote learning or what is commonly called memorization. You may have encountered lots of tests like this in high school. Here are some examples of memory-level questions:

1. Short-term memory holds
    a. Unlimited information
    b. Just a little information
    c. 7 ± 2 pieces of information
    d. 9 ± 7 pieces of information
    (Answer is "c.")

2. True or false: chunking expands STM capacity by grouping pieces of information into units.
    (Answer is "true.")

Note that in both of these examples, if you memorized facts about memory, you would be able to answer these questions easily.

No more prizes for predicting rain. Prizes only for building arks.

—Anonymous

HIGHER-LEVEL QUESTIONS

However, most of the questions you will encounter will be more difficult, higher-level items. Higher-level questions go beyond facts and ask you for applications, examples, syntheses, analyses, and conclusions. Such questions are sometimes called "thinking" questions. Objective tests in college will most likely include more thinking than memorization questions. Here are some examples of higher-level questions:

1. All of the following would be considered examples of maintenance rehearsal except
   a. Repeating a phone number several times so you can call it again
   b. Learning a date for your history quiz by relating it to something in your own life
   c. Saying an address three times to yourself as you are on your way out the door to a party
   d. Memorizing key terms in your biology book by looking them over several times
   (Answer is "b.")

2. True or false: short-term memory differs from long-term memory in both duration and capacity.
   (Answer is "true.")

STUDY ACCORDING TO THE TASK

Once you figure out the task—the kinds of questions your professor expects you to answer—you can focus your studying efforts to match the task. If the task is memorization, study by asking yourself primarily "what" questions. Answer the questions precisely and thoroughly as you are rehearsing and reviewing. Questions such as "What is the purpose of short-term memory?" or "Define 'encoding' " will provide you with the information you need to recognize the correct answer if a test item is multiple-choice

GET IT TOGETHER

Many students struggle with exams in college because they don't realize the shift in the types of questions asked. So they prepare by memorizing terms or bold-faced words and then don't understand why they failed the exam. If you find you are not doing as well as you would like on your exams, consider the way you are learning . . . are you preparing for higher-level questions? If not, try to predict and answer some challenging questions as we discussed in chapter 18.

or to know whether an item is true or false. The key in memorization tasks is to be able to categorize the information so you don't get it mixed up. In the case of our examples, you want to be able to distinguish the characteristics of short-term memory from those of long-term memory.

For objective tests that ask higher-level questions, you'll have to take a different approach. You still want to ask yourself questions, but now you'll need to go a step further and ask yourself "how" and "why" questions, think of examples, and draw conclusions. If you ask yourself these kinds of questions, you'll be able to handle whatever your prof throws out on the exam.

STUDY WITH OTHERS

Students tell us that studying with others is a good way to prepare for objective exams. You can ask each other questions and get honest evaluations about how good an answer you have given. If you approach your questions and answers seriously, studying with others can also be a confidence builder. If you study with someone else, writing questions on index cards can help you target your studying. Or if you have already made other written items such as concept cards or charts, you can formulate

☹ SAD BUT TRUE

Mason and several of his friends were all in the same anthropology course. Because the tests consisted largely of objective-type questions, Mason thought it would be a good idea to form a study group so they could all help one another out. No one really liked the course very much, but Mason thought they might all survive it and maybe even pull out half-decent grades if they got together on a regular basis. The group decided to meet every Thursday evening and also the evening before each exam. Their intentions were good: everyone was supposed to keep up, take notes as best they could, and be prepared to talk through the information. They planned on quizzing each other before the tests. Unfortunately, things didn't go so well. After the first week, the so-called study sessions turned into discussions of the places in town where they could hear the best bands, talking about relationship problems, and general gripe sessions about this and other courses. Then someone always got hungry and it was off for pizza or wings. Most of the group fell behind. Mason's idea of forming a study group was good; his big mistake was involving friends who couldn't stay on task.

your questions directly from those. You can also use the questions you have posed in the margins of your lecture notes to test yourself.

It's important to remember that being part of a study group requires that each member contribute something. The purpose of a study group is to exchange ideas and discuss information. But many students feel that working in study groups is a waste of time. We believe that opinion is common because, most times, students meet in groups with their friends and goof off more than they study. To avoid this pitfall, have a plan of what you will do in your study group, and don't plan to meet until after each member has studied some on his or her own. For example, the night before an exam, members of the study group could ask each other questions to determine their readiness for the test—this assumes each member has already studied the material. So go to your study group prepared. Have questions ready about information that isn't clear to you. Be ready to ask (and be able to answer) challenging questions that match the task outlined by the professor.

STUDY OVER A PERIOD OF DAYS

Another key to being successful on objective tests is to distribute your studying and learning over a period of days. Although cramming can get you through occasionally, using cramming as your study method of choice can be stressful, unproductive, and in some cases downright foolish. Students who begin prepping a reasonable amount of time before the test are usually more relaxed and confident, and they do better. But what is a reasonable amount of time? It's different for everyone and depends on the amount of information covered on the test, how much you already know about the topic, how much you have kept up, and the type of test you will have. In general, however, think about these questions:

- **What are the big concepts covered in this test?** You should be able to jot down the big picture.

- **How familiar are you with the concepts?** You should be able to gauge the amount of test prep time you will need by the amount of information you already know. The trick is to be honest with yourself. How much information do you really know, and how much do you only sort of know? Don't be in denial.

● **What does your schedule look like for the few days before the exam?** You'll need additional time built into your study schedule for exam preparation. You don't want your test preparation for one class to cut down on your regular study time for another class. If you let it, preparing for a big exam can make you fall behind in your other courses.

● **How will you group concepts for study?** Many students make the mistake of preparing for tests in a very unfocused way. They "look through" their text or they "read over" their notes during each study session. Quite frankly, this is a very inefficient way to study. It's much more effective to organize your studying by concepts and to study so you know one concept very well before moving on to another. For example, if one of the major concepts that you'll be tested on in biology is meiosis, study all the information on that topic from both text and lecture in one study session. Then, in your next study session, review what you have learned about meiosis—talk yourself through the information and ask yourself questions—and move on to mitosis. Studying this way helps you keep the information straight and also helps you really know and understand each concept.

In general, begin your study process a few days in advance (we suggest at least three days for most courses). And don't confuse studying with reading. Before you begin your exam prep, you should have all your reading assignments finished. In addition, you'll probably need to add some time to your normal studying schedule to get ready to study for the exam. Before you start studying, organize all your notes and other study materials and then divide the material into concepts to be studied. Be sure to have a goal for each of your study sessions. Begin each new study session with a review of what you learned in the previous session.

🔊 LISTEN UP

Time ≠ learning (or, not necessarily). Students are fooled into thinking they know the information simply because they have put in some time (or even a lot of time). To really learn, you need to think deeply, and you need to monitor what you know as you go along.

The pacing of your study sessions before a test also depends on when the professor stops lecturing on material that will be covered on the exam. Some professors lecture on test material up to the class period before the exam. If that's the case, you'll have to be sure you spend some time studying the information presented late so you are prepared to answer questions. It helps, however, if you have done all your reading and have studied most of the test material so all you have to do is fill in the gaps with the lecture information.

Tips for Taking Objective Exams

All right—you have studied in a way that matches the task and you have distributed your studying over a period of days. You're confident that you know the information (at least most of it). You are seriously ready to kick some exam butt. However, there are some additional tips that may help you maximize your performance even more— tips for getting more questions right once you are actually taking the test.

Have you ever found yourself in this situation? You actually did study smart for a test. You knew the information and you had confidence in your ability to earn a good grade. But then you got into the testing situation and you forgot easy material, were distracted by minor noises, thought too deeply about questions, and got confused over ideas you were certain you knew very well. These things have probably happened to every student at some time or other, particularly in classes that are anxiety producing. But some of these events can be prevented if you know they can be stumbling blocks. The savvy student acknowledges they can happen and does her best to cope with them. In order to maximize your performance try the following:

- **Get to the classroom early.** Take your seat, get out your pen or pencil, close your eyes, put your feet flat on the floor, straighten your spine, put your shoulders back, and take several deep breaths through your nose—in and out, in and out. That's it, relax.

- **Don't talk with others about the course material right before the exam.** We've all been there. You

LISTEN UP

If a classmate tries to talk to you before an exam and you want to tell him to go away (but you don't want to appear rude), try telling him you are taking a few minutes to relax before the exam but you'd be happy to talk once the test has ended. Just try to take a few deep breaths and block out the distractions in the room. This simple relaxation technique can help you concentrate better on the test.

think you're prepared, and then your classmate says, "What about transforming the units to mass? What was that all about?" You hadn't even considered this in your studying and you begin to panic. But it may be that the information is trivial or that your classmate may have learned it incorrectly.

- **Speak positively to yourself.** Tell yourself that you know the information and that you expect to make a good grade on the test. (Note: this is not a replacement for actual studying; it helps only if you really do know the material.)

- **Read the directions carefully, especially on the first test.** The directions will give you information about how to think about the questions. For example, you may be instructed to select the best answer. In this case, more than one of the answer choices may be correct, but only one is the best answer.

SAD BUT TRUE

Lavon felt truly unprepared when he went in to take his psychology exam, but he figured, "What the heck. It's only multiple choice, so at least I have a chance of guessing and, with any luck, I'll pull at least a C." His day didn't start off well. He overslept (bad omen) and arrived in the classroom ten minutes late . . . and without a #2 pencil. The prof gave him "the look" when Lavon came to the front of the classroom to get a copy of the test and was clearly annoyed about having to lend him a pencil. Because fifteen minutes of class had already passed and he had one hundred questions to get through, Lavon didn't bother to read the directions, which to his mind seemed rather extensive for a multiple-choice test. He just dove in and started bubbling in answers on his sheet. When the five-minute warning came, he did some speed-reading and ended up at least having an answer for each question. He turned in his exam (and returned the pencil to the prof) and headed back to his dorm. On his way back, he caught up with Alexis, another student who had just taken the psychology test. She was fit to be tied, ranting about how the scoring of the test was so unfair. "What are you talking about?" asked Lavon. "Didn't you read the directions?" she said. "Professor Miller put a penalty on for guessing. If you weren't sure of the item and left it blank, you only had a half-point taken off, but if you guessed and got it wrong, you had a full point taken off. I just think it's so unfair. I've never taken a test where there was a penalty for guessing." Lavon was speechless. Not only did he not study enough, he got to class late and he didn't bother reading the directions. He learned several valuable lessons that day, perhaps the most important of which was to always read the directions.

- **Do the easy questions first.** What's easy will vary from one person to the next. If you're not sure of the answer to the first question, go on to the second. Continue until you have answered all the questions you know. Then go back and tackle those you're unsure of.

- **Consider all the alternatives.** Read each choice, even if you are sure the best answer is choice "a." Sometimes a minor change in wording makes one answer better than another. Or sometimes choice "d" reads "both a and c," which you'd miss if you only read choice "a."

- **Narrow your choices.** Turn each of the answer choices into a true or false question if a multiple-choice item confuses you. Sometimes this helps clarify which choice is correct. If you are unsure of an item, you can also use both what you know and other items that deal with similar information to eliminate implausible answer choices.

- **Watch for qualifiers.** On true or false tests, items that contain words such as "always" or "never" are usually false (things rarely happen always or never). Questions that contain words such as "seldom" or "frequently" are usually true.

- **Tackle the items you are least sure of last.** Don't waste too much time on one item, only to have to "Christmas tree" the remaining items because you have run out of time. If it stumps you, skip it and return to it. Then eliminate answer choices that you know are incorrect, make a choice between what is left, and move on.

- **Never leave an objective item blank, unless you are penalized for guessing.** Even if you are clueless as to the right answer, you have a 50 percent chance of getting true or false questions correct and a 20 to 25 percent chance of getting multiple-choice question correct (for five- and four-choice answers, respectively). Chances diminish on matching items, but it usually doesn't hurt to guess.

Be test wise. Putting these tips into action can gain you valuable points on all your objective tests.

Eenie, Meenie, Minie, Moe . . . If You Have to Guess

Of course we know this will never happen to you, but here are a few quick tips to help that friend of yours, who must guess, make the best possible choices.

- On multiple-choice exams, look for patterns in answer choices for the items you are sure of. Most professors have a favorite answer choice spot, and if you don't have a clue about the answer, their favorite is the best guess you can make.

- If you can't figure out your prof's favorite and have no other idea (you haven't been able to eliminate any of the choices), "b" or "c" is usually the best choice. Most professors don't like to use "a" very often—they would rather bury the answer than make it the first of the choices.

- It's better to select a longer answer choice than a shorter one when you're guessing, especially if one of the four or five choices is significantly longer than the others.

- For true or false questions, do all the questions you know first and then go back and mark either all true or all false for the remaining items. This approach works only when you've really studied and know most of the answers. If you have twenty true or false questions and you know the answers to only five of them, marking the other fifteen as all true or false may not buy many points—even with a 50/50 chance.

- Once you guess, move on. Go with your gut feeling and resist the temptation to go back and change your answers to the point where you have rubbed large holes in your paper. In fact, the only time you should change an answer on an objective test is when you have either thought of additional information that makes you change your mind or picked up additional information in another item.

Procrastination is suicide on the installment plan.

-Anonymous

An A+ for You: Evaluating Your Test Performance

For most students, the test is old news when it's returned and gone over in class. Our experience has been that when students do well, they yell something to this effect to someone across the room: "Hey, man what did you get? I got an A!" If, however, they did poorly, they cram the test in the back of their book and never look at it again. You know, there's that denial thing going on again—if I hide this it will just magically not exist. But you can learn a lot from your exams. Remember, all of college is a learning experience, even things you hate, such as tests. If you want to improve your performance (if you didn't do so well) or maintain high performance (if you did great), you should take a little time to examine the types of objective items you got right and wrong. There is usually a pattern to your errors. If you evaluate how you did, you'll also be able to figure out how to tweak your studying for the next exam.

If you did poorly on an exam, particularly if you thought you did well, it's important to figure out just what the problem is. If your prof doesn't go over the test in class, or if he simply posts grades and all you see is a score, you need to make an appointment to go over your test. Don't feel as though it's an imposition. Having office hours and meeting with students is part of every professor's job. Once you're there, make specific note of the kinds of items you got wrong. Look for patterns. For example, did you miss lots of items that came from the textbook or from the lectures? Did you miss items that were examples? Did you miss more true or false items than matching items? Did you miss higher-level questions but answer all the factual questions correctly? Once you have a better handle on the kinds of items you're missing, you can adjust your preparation for the next exam accordingly.

Evaluating your exam performance is important to do after every test, but it is particularly important to do after the first one. This is especially true if you didn't do so hot. The sooner you evaluate what you did right and wrong, the sooner you can get back on track and still pull a good grade in the course.

If You Read Nothing Else, Read This

○ Studying for objective exams usually requires more than just memorizing facts. In college, most professors will ask higher-level questions that require you to think critically about the materials.

○ Be test wise. There are lots of little tips that can help you increase your scores on objective tests.

○ When you have to guess, try to do it in an organized way. Never leave an item blank on an objective test unless you're penalized for guessing.

○ Always, always, always evaluate your performance so you don't make the same mistakes over and over.

CHAPTER 22

BLUEBOOK BLUES: PREPPING FOR AND TAKING ESSAY EXAMS

- Worried about taking essay exams in college?
- Concerned about what your professor will be looking for in essays?
- Think you can BS the professor on exams?

If so, read on . . .

The first question that is usually asked after a professor announces that she will be giving essay exams is, "How long should each answer be?" Usually this question is asked in all sincerity, but because professors are sometimes frustrated that length is their students' main concern, many answer in a deadpan manner, "As long as it needs to be to answer the question," and move on, hopefully to questions that focus more on intellectual or content issues.

There's no doubt about it. Most students would much rather have a root canal than take essay tests. If they have to take tests, they would rather take objective tests because they figure that on objective tests at least you can guess. It's almost impossible to guess on essay questions because you either know the information or you don't. Essay exams seem to stress students out because

1. They try to study for essay exams in the same way they study for multiple-choice exams.

2. They don't think of themselves as good writers who can organize their thoughts in a brief period of time.

3. They can memorize the facts but can't weave the information together, so they are not good at seeing the big picture.

4. They find it difficult to predict what the essays will be about and worry that they will study the wrong information.

If you are dreading taking essay exams in college, then this is the chapter for you. Using the strategies in this chapter should help you prepare for and succeed on your essay exams (and, actually, will help you with your academic paper assignments as well).

Studying for Essay Exams

Professors use essay questions to see if you can filter through the volumes of course information to find out what is important. Then they expect you to explain in your own words why it is important. Because you have to recall the information without any cues and because you have to put it into your own words, studying for essays is different than studying for multiple-choice exams. There are a few basic steps involved in preparing for essay exams.

> Writing is easy. All you do is stare at a blank sheet of paper until drops of blood form on your forehead.
>
> —Gene Fowler

Predict test questions. As you study, make up questions that could actually be asked on the test. That means every time you read, annotate, or review lecture notes and other material you should be thinking about what kinds of essay questions could be asked using that information. It is actually a good idea to write down some predicted test questions as you go. Think about what the professor has stressed in the syllabus and in class; often profs give away the essay questions by emphasizing the topics in lectures. Then once you have learned the information, you can evaluate your understanding of the concepts by answering the questions you predicted.

As you are reading, don't memorize material. For an essay exam, you really don't need to know the same level of picky detail that you need to know on objective exams. Instead, you will need to see how all the information relates to the big picture. Rather than focusing on just the facts, look for relationships between ideas, and use details as a

> **THE INSIDE SCOOP**
>
> When writing your answers to essay exams or short-answer exams, remember this tip: when in doubt, leave it out. If you're not sure if the information you are thinking about including in your essay is correct, don't include it. If you include wrong information (like an incorrect date or name), your professor has no choice but to take points off your score, but if you leave out a relatively unimportant piece of information and the rest of your answer is correct, you will probably lose fewer points.

way of supporting your points. This means noting themes, patterns, causes and effects, comparisons and contrasts, and other relationships as you see them. These are the things that essay exam questions are made of. Think about the examples in the text and how they relate to or explain the main ideas.

Elaborate on information as you learn it. This means you should expand on the information you are learning. One simple way to elaborate on information is to use examples from your own experience when you can (this can be tough to do in some courses, like history or entomology, but try it where it seems appropriate). You should also make an effort to connect what you are learning to what you already know about the topic, which helps make the information personal, and therefore, more memorable. Making maps, charts, or diagrams to help you reorganize the information can help you see interrelationships and connections between ideas.

Write out a practice essay. We realize this is a lot to ask, but if you know that you struggle with writing or that you often have trouble organizing your essays, this is an essential step. All you need to do is answer one or two of the questions you've predicted. If you suffer from writing anxiety, practicing at home is a great remedy—really.

Studying for essay exams begins when you first open your book to read, not the night before the exam. Once you use our approach, you'll probably find that you feel a lot better prepared.

It's All in the Way It's Worded

You are sitting in the classroom looking at your test paper, when suddenly you realize you are not sure what the professor means when she asks you to "illustrate the tenets of the feminist movement." How does "illustrate" differ from "define"? Many students lose points because they do not pay attention or respond to the language used in the question. To help you interpret these questions, we offer a handy guide to typical essay-question words. As noted in the last chapter, objective exam question words generally divide into two types—memory level and higher level. The words professors use to ask essay questions can be divided along these lines as well.

MEMORY-LEVEL QUESTION WORDS

These questions ask you to recall information from your text or lecture notes. Suppose you were learning the information in the memory passage from chapter 17. An example of a memory-level essay question on that material would be "Summarize the three types of memory storage."

Some common memory-level question words include

- **Define**. This is the most basic type of question. When you are asked to "define X" or you are asked, "What is X?" you need to give the meaning of the term or concept. (Note: if you discussed several different definitions in class, be prepared to give more than one definition in your response.) No matter what type of essay question you are given, it is always a good idea to define your terms.

- **Illustrate.** Generally, this type of question is asking you to describe the concept using specific examples. You need to make sure that in your response you explicitly state how the examples connect with the concept and how the ideas you are illustrating relate to one another.

- **Summarize.** Briefly explain the concept you've learned.

- **Trace.** This question word asks you discuss events or developments over time.

> **URBAN LEGEND**
>
> A philosophy professor gave an essay exam that asked students to define "courage." The highest grade was given to the student who turned in his paper minutes after the exam was handed out after writing "This is."

HIGHER-LEVEL QUESTION WORDS

These question words ask you to explain or apply information you have learned; you'll typically find higher-level questions on college-level essay exams. They are generally more difficult than memory-level questions because you will need to interpret the information to be able to answer the question. An example of a higher-level essay question on memory would be "Compare and contrast the characteristics and functions of short-term and long-term memory."

Some common higher-level question words include

- **Compare and contrast.** This phrase asks you to describe what two or more things have in common (compare) and how they differ (contrast). Remember, if the question asks you to compare and contrast you must do both (compare and contrast) in order to fully answer the essay.

- **Relate.** In this case you need to show relationships between ideas.

- **Cause and effect.** This type of question asks you to show how one event (or more) made something else happen and then to discuss the consequences of that event.

- **Prove (justify, support, defend).** To answer this type of question you need to provide evidence and/or examples to support your stand.

- **Evaluate.** This type of question asks you to assess information about the topic and then discuss its pros and cons.

- **Analyze.** To respond to this type of question, you need to examine a topic closely and discuss its importance or what it means.

- **Synthesize.** This type of question asks you to pull together two or more pieces of information. This is not the same as a compare and contrast question because you need to provide a reason for putting these two or more ideas together (not just discuss their similarities and differences).

- **Argue.** This type of question asks you to take a side and defend your point against the other side. In this type of question you will need to explain both your stance and a counterargument as well.

You can tell by comparing the two lists of question words that your chances of being asked higher-level questions is considerably greater than being asked memory-level questions. One of the keys to doing well on essays is to take the time to read and reflect on what the questions are asking you to do. Remember to think carefully about the question before you begin to write.

THE INSIDE SCOOP

Did you ever start to write an essay only to forget some of the points you wanted to make? Did a professor ever tell you that your essay would have been better if you'd only made a stronger argument? Making a jot list can help you with both of these issues. First, when you make your jot list, the act of writing down all the information helps you remember what you know about the topic. Then, once it is written down, you can reorganize the order of the points in a way that makes sense, which creates a stronger argument.

Elements of a Good Essay

Although every professor has her own criteria for grading essays (and you should find out what these are before your first exam), there are some common elements to a well-constructed essay.

A GOOD ESSAY IS ORGANIZED

Plan before you write. After you read the question, jot down all of the key points you want to cover in your essay. Then think through the best, most logical order for the points you will discuss.

A GOOD ESSAY IS FOCUSED

Be sure to answer each and every part of the essay fully, but don't try to BS the professor. In college, the person asking you the essay question is probably an

LISTEN UP

Be careful about using words such as "always" or "never" unless you are absolutely sure the word is justified (and not an exaggeration). It's also better to use generalizations when you can't remember an exact fact. For example, it is better to write "in the late 1960s" if you can't remember whether an event happened in 1968 or 1969. Usually, the more general term will be sufficient.

expert on the question's topic. So there's a good chance he knows way more than you (or even your textbook) about the matter. Your professor will know if you are trying to pad your answer with a bunch of nonsense. Instead, stay focused on the question and write what you know, but don't worry too much about how long your answer is (unless, of course, your professor tells you that you should). Of course, you may want to be concerned if you've only written two sentences and your classmates have each filled a bluebook . . .

A GOOD ESSAY "SINGS"

Whenever you make a point in an essay, be sure that it is well supported or documented. Use information from your texts, lectures, and any other sources referred to in class. If your essay reads as if you have just pulled the idea out of thin air, your professor will not buy it, and you will lose points on the exam. So use examples, specific details, names, and facts to substantiate your argument. At the very least, your answer should make sense.

A GOOD ESSAY IS GRAMMATICAL

When you are finished writing your essay, read it over looking for grammar and spelling errors. Although your professor may not take off points specifically for grammar issues (do find out your professor's policy on grammar and spelling errors before your first exam), your essay will certainly read better if it has few of these errors; this, in turn, will lead to a higher grade.

Put It in Writing

The professor has handed out the exam and you are ready to go. But wait. There are a few things you need to do before you start to write.

BEFORE YOU START WRITING

The first step in writing a good essay is to plan your time. Whenever you take an essay exam, spend the first few minutes budgeting the allotted time. Be sure to leave ample time for planning as well as for writing the essay and reviewing it when it's done. You also want to take the point value for each question into account when making your plan. Suppose you have three essay questions to respond to in a fifty-minute class—which is a lot to do in such a short amount of time but not at all uncommon. The first essay is worth fifty points and the other two are worth twenty-five points each. How would you budget your time? We'd suggest the following:

8 minutes	Planning and organizing
16 minutes	Essay 1 (worth 50 percent)
10 minutes	Essay 2 (worth 25 percent)
10 minutes	Essay 3 (worth 25 percent)
6 minutes	Review and proofread

☹ SAD BUT TRUE

Lynn was unable to finish her political science essay exam because she did not read the direction stating, "Choose and respond to any two questions." Instead, Lynn attempted to answer all six, ran out of time, and was unable to give the level of detail needed in any of her responses. Basically, she just had time to write a few main points for each question, but not to use examples or details to support her arguments. In addition, Lynn's essays were loaded with grammar and spelling errors because she did not have time to review them. Lynn's professor only read the first two answers and took off a lot of points for responses that were too vague and too general. Take-home message: read the directions. We have at least one student each year who makes this mistake—don't let it be you.

This is a pretty tight time frame, and you'd need to stick to your plan to make it through all three questions. Notice that this plan leaves a good deal of time for getting your essays together at the beginning of the exam; students who take the time to do this step find they write out their responses to the essay questions faster and more easily than those who do not.

If you are given a choice, the next step is to decide which question or questions you will answer. Then annotate the questions. Note key words in the margin and make a note of all the tasks asked in the essay. Notice the key words annotated in this sample history essay question.

> **Evaluate the factors leading to Johnson's decision to enter the Vietnamese Conflict. Discuss the importance of both domestic and foreign affairs in shaping Johnson's decision.**
>
> Evaluate factors in LBJ's decision—need to make judgment based on events
>
> Discuss imp. of—
> 1. domestic affairs
> 2. foreign affairs

Next, make a jot list of the information you want to cover. A jot list for the question above might look like this:

1. Domestic affairs
   Great Society
   Civil rights movement
   Hawks and doves
   JFK legacy

2. Foreign affairs
   "Domino effect"
   Cuba
   China
   Ho Chi Minh
   Cabinet advisors' advice

. GET IT TOGETHER

What should you do if you run out of time while still writing your essay? Don't just quit. That won't gain you any extra points. Rather, outline the points you would have made and point your instructor to your jot list of topics. You will probably at least get partial credit. And as anyone will tell you, something is better than nothing.

Notice how there are not a lot of words on the jot list, just enough to help you remember what you want to talk about. Your next step would be to organize the topics in order of importance.

> How can I tell what I think till I see what I say?
>
> —E. M. Forster

ESSAY AS ONE, TWO, THREE

You probably learned to write five-paragraph essays in high school to suit all your essay-writing needs. But in college you'll need to be more flexible in your writing (some essay questions may take up to twenty paragraphs to answer). So think about your essays as being composed of three main parts—the introduction, the body, and the conclusion—rather than five paragraphs.

1. **The introduction.** After you have annotated the question and made (and organized) your jot list, begin your essay with a good introduction. Your introduction can restate the question or pose a new one: "How did domestic and foreign affairs influence Johnson's decision to enter the Vietnamese Conflict?" The rest of your introductory paragraph should introduce all the key points you will make in your essay so the reader has a good idea of what you are about to discuss.

2. **The body of the essay.** The body of your paper is where you will develop your argument. Begin each paragraph with a topic sentence that expands upon one of the key points made in your introduction. Write in full sentences and complete paragraphs; use formal language (not slang or colloquialisms). Use transitions to get from point to point (or paragraph to paragraph). Words and phrases like "because," "therefore," "in contrast," "as a result," "first," "second," "third," and "finally" will help the reader follow your train of thought. And avoid "words" such as "sorta," "kinda," "ya know"—it is an essay, not an email.

THE INSIDE SCOOP

Students who write good, solid introductions receive scores that are almost one full grade letter higher than students who write just an average intro (even when the bodies of the papers were identical, researchers found that professors gave higher scores to the papers with the great intros). So your high school teacher was right when she told you to "write a snazzy introduction to grab the reader's attention."

Each paragraph in the body of your essay should contain only one major point and your support for it.

> A conclusion is the place where you got tired of thinking.
>
> –Arthur Bloch

3. **The conclusion.** The last paragraph of your essay should summarize the points you made and connect them to your central argument.

It should also emphasize the importance of your argument. And under no circumstances should you end your essay with a smiley face!

AFTER WRITING

Take a few minutes to review your responses. Be sure you answered all parts of the question and your response makes sense. Reading your responses can help you find and correct grammar and spelling errors. And, more importantly, sometimes when you review your answers, you think of points to add that will strengthen your response. You may even find entire paragraphs that are off topic and that you will end up crossing out to make your essay more coherent. Don't worry about making correction marks on your paper or using arrows to guide your professor to information you've added at the end. Trust us—you will be glad you set aside some time to do this.

URBAN LEGEND

(We both love this one!) Two students went to Florida for spring break. They had a history essay exam on the first day back from break, but they were having such a good time, they decided to stay on one more day. Both students were doing well in the history class and had made As on the previous exam and felt that the professor would cut them a break. When they returned to school, they went to their professor's office and told him they were sorry for missing the exam, but they had gotten a flat tire on the way home from spring break and couldn't get help for a long time, so they were late in getting back. The professor thought about this for a while, and the students were relieved when he said he would give them a make-up exam the next day. Both students arrived promptly the next morning, and the professor placed them in separate rooms, gave them the exam booklet, and wished them luck. Both students were completely caught off guard when they opened the exam booklet and read, "This item is worth one hundred points—which tire?"

Taking essay exams does not need to be an overwhelming task, especially if you keep the structure of a good essay in mind as you write. We suggest you revisit this chapter every time you need to take an essay test to remind yourself of the steps involved in good essay writing.

If You Read Nothing Else, Read This

○ **Prepare for the exam from day one.** Every time you read or study, think about possible test questions, note relationships between ideas (such as causes and effects), and look for the big picture.

○ **Decode your essay question.** Take a look at the question words used by the professor to determine what she is asking you to do. Then think about the level of thinking required by the question—this will be either memory-level or higher-level thinking.

○ **Organize your ideas by making a jot list and planning your time.**

○ **Think before you write, write well, then think about what you've written.**

CHAPTER 23

IS THAT YOUR FINAL ANSWER?

- Concerned that you won't study enough for your exams?
- Worried that it's next to impossible to prepare for cumulative midterms and finals?
- Think cramming will work just fine because it's always worked for you in the past?

If so, read on . . .

Exams. Tests. Quizzes. Whatever you call them, they have struck fear in the hearts of just about every college student we know. Although exams in college are a part of everyday life, most students probably would not view them as the fun part—challenging, maybe, but not their favorite part of the college experience. Most college students would acknowledge, however, that not only do you have to learn information, but you must also be able to document that you have learned something. That's what tests are all about.

Some students decide to wait until after the first test to really figure out what they need to do to prepare. But if you have only three exams and a final (and sometimes you'll face far fewer exams than that), you are putting yourself at a disadvantage if you wait. Instead, practice some of the general test prep and test-taking strategies we suggest to help you do well in almost any testing situation.

Smart Exam Prep

Although the last two chapters told you how preparing for essay exams differs from preparing for objective exams (multiple-choice, true or false, and so on), there are some general "good advice" tips that cut across all kinds of tests. You may have heard similar tips before, especially when you were getting ready to take high-pressure tests like the SAT or ACT, but it never hurts to hear them again as they relate to classroom tests.

Get a good night's sleep. It's plain and simple. You can't think straight or perform at your best when you are exhausted. You'll end up feeling muddled and won't be able to concentrate on your exam. So try to get a full night's sleep (or at least six hours) before your exams.

Make sure you have everything you need. Get all your materials together the night before so you don't have to rush around right before your exam. There is nothing worse than getting to your exam and realizing that you left your calculator (or pencil or bluebook or student ID) at home.

> Of course, it is very important to be sober when you take an exam. Many worthwhile careers in the street-cleaning, fruit-picking and subway-guitar-playing industries have been founded on a lack of understanding of this simple fact.
>
> —Terry Pratchett

Distribute your study time. Rather than cramming all your studying into one or two sessions, plan to study over several days. In general, the more times you interact with the material, the better you'll learn it.

Will, a junior engineering major, would forget his head if it wasn't attached to his body. We're not sure if Will ever went to an exam with everything he needed. For exams in his civil engineering class he was allowed to bring a calculator and a page of notes with him. He also needed his student ID to show for each test. Will used to call his roommates in a panic several times before every test saying things like, "Could you just look through my desk? There's a paper somewhere on it that has a bunch of formulas written in very small print. Could you please find it and drive it over to me in the next fifteen minutes?" The joke with Will's friends was that he was so forgetful that once he even forgot his shoes (honestly!). What Will needed to do was to pack up everything the night before his tests.

Monitor your learning. Know what you know and don't know. You can check your knowledge of the material on which you will be tested by asking yourself questions about the information as you review. This is really the most important part of studying. As we have heard from our students, there is no better feeling than walking into an exam knowing that you are ready for it.

Using these general strategies should help you no matter what the testing situation, but read on for strategies for dealing with special situations, such as the need to cram for exams, and studying for midterms and finals.

Taking Exams on a Computer

Taking computerized exams is stressful for many students, but it is becoming an increasingly widespread practice. In fact, if you plan to go on to graduate school, the Graduate Record Exam or GRE (which is like the SAT for grad school) is given only on computer. Many professors are switching to computerized testing in their classes as well (particularly in mathematics and the sciences). There are several things you can do to help you do well when you take an exam on a computer.

Don't abandon your normal test-taking strategies. If you always circle key words on an exam question to be sure you are addressing them correctly, keep a piece of scratch paper with you to jot down key words. If you leave questions blank to answer them later, find out if you will be able to go back on the computer test or if you will have to respond and then move on.

Become familiar with the technology. All too often, the computer is used in a course only for taking the exams, and students are wary about using the technology. Definitely do practice tests if the professor offers them. And if you know your exams will be given on a computer, make an effort to become comfortable using computers over the course of the semester.

Find out as much as you can about the exams. We know professors who give basic multiple-choice exams on computer, but we also know several who fully use the technology when making computerized exams. For example, one chemistry professor on our campus integrates three-dimensional models and videos of chemical reactions into his computerized exams. To answer the questions, students need to stop the video at a certain point in the chemical reaction.

THE INSIDE SCOOP

Research has indicated that students who can type fast tend to do better on computerized exams. So it is a good idea to learn how to use your computer and how to type, if necessary, before exam time.

Taking exams on computers does not have to be scary. If you learn as much as you can about both the technology and the exam before you take the test, who knows—you may even find you prefer computerized tests.

URBAN LEGEND

This one is almost believable. According to the story, a computer tech-support person once received the following phone call:

Caller: Hello, I'm calling because my computer cup holder is broken.

Tech guy: Did you say cup holder?

Caller: Yes; it is on the front of my computer. I put my drink in there and it just broke off.

Tech guy: Was the cup holder on your computer when you bought it or did you add it on later?

Caller: No it was there. It is called an "8X" holder.

At this point the tech guy begins to laugh as he realizes that the caller was using the CD-ROM drive as a cup holder.

A Word about Cramming

It's 7:00 P.M. on Thursday, you have been sick as a dog since Monday night, and you have a big exam Friday morning. You have been far too ill to study, but now it is down to the wire. At least you're able to drag your butt out of bed. But what will you do? In a word, cram. Cramming, as we have mentioned, is not the world's greatest way to prepare for exams. For some, cramming becomes a habit and a way of life (and we sincerely hope those students have learned some alternative study methods in *College Rules!*). But even for the most conscientious student, sometimes cramming simply cannot be avoided. So for those (hopefully) extremely rare occasions when you need to cram, here is some good advice on how to maximize your time and focus your effort.

Preview the material. Look at your syllabus, your text, and your notes to see what topics will be covered on the exam.

Be selective. Use the quick and dirty approach to reading. Read headings, subheadings, and bold-faced words to learn the main concepts in each chapter. Don't attempt to learn everything, because you just won't have enough time.

Target your lecture notes. Your professor generally emphasizes the most important points. Focus your attention on those key concepts and try to read about those topics in the textbook as well if you have time.

Spend time only on the material you don't know. If you had more time,

> Putting a computer in front of a child and expecting it to teach him is like putting a book under his pillow, only more expensive.
>
> —Anonymous

LISTEN UP

Some students think that caffeine or other substances will help them cram for exams (there is an alarming trend to take Adderall, a medicine for ADD), but these chemicals can actually make it harder to remember the information while you are taking the exams. Have some coffee if it helps you stay awake, but don't overdo it—taking an exam with a hangover from drugs (or even too much caffeine) can make you do much worse than you would have otherwise.

we'd suggest that you review the material you know and then try to connect it to the material you don't. But when you are cramming, just focus on the new stuff and learn it as best you can.

Repetition, repetition, repetition. The only way to learn a lot of material fast is to just repeat it over and over again until you have it memorized. Now, this is not a great way to learn information, as we have stated throughout *College Rules!*, but cramming is an occasion for emergency survival techniques.

Test yourself on the information. Better yet, midway through studying, have a friend or roommate ask you questions about the material. This can help you monitor your learning and determine where to focus your attention for the remainder of your studying. Even crammers need to monitor.

Get some sleep. Pulling an all-nighter to study will not help you if you are falling asleep while taking the test. You probably will not be able to get a full night's rest, but even a few hours' sleep can really make a difference in your ability to perform on the exam.

Stay calm during the exam. Because information studied in cramming sessions is not learned deeply, you are more likely to forget it under pressure. Take a few deep breaths, don't panic, and promise yourself that you won't put yourself in this situation again.

After the exam, take a few minutes to think about how you got into a situation where you needed to cram. Was it really a one-time emergency, or were there things you could have done differently to avoid the pressures of cramming? Think about the changes you'd need to make to steer clear of cramming for future exams.

Acing Exams

You've read and annotated the chapters and reviewed your notes, and now the professor is handing out the test. You didn't need to cram this time and are feeling pretty good about the material but a little nervous about taking the test. What should you do now?

Well, there are a few tips and tricks we've learned that will help you do the best you can.

Relax. Take a few minutes to relax before the exam is distributed. When you get to your seat, close your eyes, sit up straight and tall, and practice some deep breathing. If you are feeling anxious about the exam, breathing deeply is a great way to calm yourself.

Read the directions. We know far too many students who have lost points because they did not know what was expected of them. You may even want to circle the key words in the directions just to be sure you will remember them as you work through the test.

Preview the test. Look at the number of items and the exam format to be sure the test consists of the items you had expected. Also, consider the point distribution for the questions. If the questions in section one are worth five points each and those in section two only two points apiece, plan to spend more time on section one.

Answer what you know first. You don't have to start with question one. When you are taking your test, answer the questions you know first and skip over those you do not know. Come back to the skipped questions before the end of the exam.

Resist the urge to change answers. Don't change your answer unless you find information in a later question or remember something specific that tells you that your first hunch was incorrect.

Don't be in a hurry to leave. We know that when you are done taking a test you just want to get out of there, but you can often find careless errors or skipped items when you take the time to review your answers.

FOR ADULTS ONLY

Many of our nontraditional students have told us they get very nervous before exams. It may be because they haven't taken exams in a while or because they are worried about being compared to eighteen-year-olds and coming up short. Whatever the case, adult college students need to use good test-taking strategies so they do not psyche themselves out. Remember, you've studied, you are prepared, and you will do well (repeat this to yourself as necessary during the test).

Keep your mind on your own business. In other words, don't be distracted by what other students are doing. Sometimes students tell us they lose confidence when they see other students leaving before they are even close to being finished. But our advice is to not worry about others; maybe those students are leaving because they don't know any of the answers.

Some students have told us that there is a psychology to taking exams and that it is easy to make yourself overly stressed by reading too much into a question or worrying about what other students are doing. Try to remain calm as you enter the classroom, and congratulate yourself for a job well done (because hopefully you have aced the test) when you leave.

🕭 LISTEN UP

What should you do if you think the professor has made a mistake in grading your exam or if you think a question was really confusing? Most professors hate to talk to students about individual exam questions. This is most likely because they feel hounded for points. We think this is a shame, however, because students can learn a lot from reviewing exams (and professors can learn something about making better test questions). If you feel your professor should reexamine part of your exam, speak up. But you may want to email your professor rather than confronting him in class. Support your point with page numbers from the text or information from your notes or describe your thinking on a particular question. Ask your professor to meet with you to discuss the issue further. He just might throw out the question altogether.

Surviving Midterms and Finals

It is that time of year again. All classes stop, yet a strange buzz of activity is present all over campus. Sales of caffeinated beverages soar as students desperately try to remember all the material they've learned during the semester. And it is no small feat. If you are taking four courses, for each course you have had about 40 lectures and read 25 chapters, which means that by the time finals hit you will need to study 160 sets of lecture notes and 100 textbook chapters. Wow.

Our best advice is to plan for finals throughout your semester by using the reviewing strategies we have discussed. But despite your best efforts, finals do present a unique situation. Here are some time-tested survival strategies for getting through these tough weeks.

Consider finals week to be finals *weeks*. In other words, start early. Rather than waiting until the night before the beginning of finals week to begin studying, start a few weeks in advance by beginning to organize the information and review course content. Or better yet, plan to stay organized all along.

Set up study groups. A study group can be a real lifesaver when you're studying for big exams. After you have studied on your own, plan to meet with some classmates to quiz each other over the material. If it is a really tough subject and you are having trouble, you may want to have your group meet with a tutor.

Find your pace for studying. We don't think many students can study for ten hours a day and be particularly effective. Instead, figure out your studying threshold and take breaks before you burn out. In general, don't try to study for more than an hour or so without taking a short (five- or ten-minute) break.

Know what kind of exam you will have. Will your midterm or final cover all the material up to that point (is it cumulative)? Or will it cover only the material that has been presented since the last exam? You will prepare differently depending on how much material you need to review.

Study in reverse. Unless your professor tells you otherwise, focus your studying on the more current topics rather than the material you were already tested on.

Know when and where your final will be. In most colleges, finals are on their own schedule, so they will be at a different time and often in a different location than where you have met for class all term. You don't want to create further stress by realizing at the last minute that you don't know the building or room where you are supposed to take the test.

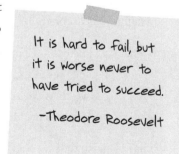

It is hard to fail, but it is worse never to have tried to succeed.

—Theodore Roosevelt

Sandy kept having nightmares that she would miss her 8:00 A.M. chemistry final exam. She set two alarm clocks and even had her mother call her to make sure she got up on time. Sandy got to the building with fifteen minutes to spare, only to find an empty classroom. Panicking, Sandy remembered the overhead the professor had put up on the last day of class regarding the exam. She had written down the time and date, but had not written down the room assignment for the final, assuming it would be in the same classroom. Now she had no idea where her exam was being held. When she finally found her class, she had missed thirty crucial minutes of exam time.

Plan your time strategically. Analyze your needs for each class when you plan out your study time. Now is the time to be realistic as well as strategic. If you are making a solid C in economics and would need an astronomical score on the final exam to pull a B, yet you're hanging between a B and an A in computer science, it may be better to spend more time on computer science. In other words, put your efforts into pulling for the A and let the other class stay at a C. You need to make these judgment calls before you make your studying plan. This is just one of the many choices you'll be making in college.

Plan several study sessions for each class. Your studying plan should include at least some time for each class. Remember, it is always better to spread out your studying for a class over several days than to cram it into one session.

Break up your studying. No one can concentrate for five hours on physics problems. Work on one subject for a while, then switch to another. It is best to switch to something that requires a different task, if possible. For example, switch from reading your history notes to working math problems.

Know what's at stake. Find out how much the midterm or final will count toward your final grade. In some classes, the final is worth the same as any exam; in others it can be worth as much as 50 percent of your total grade. Knowing this information can help you decide how to spend your studying time.

Don't burn out. Reward yourself, because studying for finals is hard work. At the end of each day, do something nice for yourself. Exercise to relieve tension, see a movie, hang out with friends, or eat a big bowl of ice cream. Basically, do something to take your mind off studying for a while. Taking a little time off every day can help you avoid finals burnout, wherein you become so exhausted you can't really focus on studying at all.

Relax and have some perspective. When it all comes down to it, you really won't remember the grade you made on your sociology final in years to come. Although a final seems like this monumental thing, in the long run it is just another test. So don't let yourself get into a panic. When you feel finals anxiety coming on, relax and take a deep

GET IT TOGETHER

We have seen students completely blow their GPA during finals week because they just couldn't seem to maintain their motivation for that last little bit. If you find you are having trouble refocusing, remind yourself that you can do anything for just one more week. So, we guess for this one we mean to say KEEP it together. You can do it.

breath (or a few deep breaths). If you put in the time, and put good study habits into practice, you will get through it just fine.

If you have been keeping up with the advice offered throughout *College Rules!*, preparing for finals may be easier for you than for some of your classmates. We wish you luck on your exams and in the rest of your college career.

URBAN LEGEND

A student was under a lot of pressure before final exams. He was worried that he wouldn't have enough time to study for the upcoming exams. He began to take amphetamines to be able to stay awake to study day and night. A week later he took the exam and left feeling confident that he had done well. The next day he received a call from the professor asking him to explain why he handed in an exam consisting of nothing but sheets of paper covered with his own name.

If You Read Nothing Else, Read This

○ There are some general guidelines for smart exam preparation: get some sleep, get together everything you need to take with you the night before the exam, and distribute your studying rather than cramming.

○ While taking your exams, try to relax and focus on the task at hand. Answer the items you know first to build your confidence and don't worry about what your classmates are doing.

○ Preparing for midterms and finals requires some extra planning. Study in reverse by focusing on the material you covered last. Meet with a study group, because misery loves company.

CHAPTER 24

JUST THE FAQS: FREQUENTLY ASKED QUESTIONS

ongratulations are in order. You may not have graduated yet, but you have made it to the last chapter of *College Rules!*—hooray and good for you. One step at a time and all that jazz. You might think that by now we must have answered every question any student might have about college success. But in this last chapter we want to wrap up some loose ends, to answer some questions that may not be important enough to merit a complete chapter but are still burning issues to some students. And some of these questions may, ahem, "remind" you of some of the good stuff we've talked about throughout *College Rules!*—the really good stuff, the stuff that will help you excel as a college student. In no particular order, here are some questions for you to think about.

Question: Although I know it's important to have lots of interests—it makes learning easier—I just don't. I wasn't interested in much in high school, and it hasn't changed in college. I do okay in my classes, but everything seems to be a struggle. Other students seem to get excited about learning. Not me. Any suggestions?

Answer: There are probably many ways to answer this question because it takes some students longer than others to develop interests, particularly in academic classes. It's even more difficult to develop interests if you can't figure out what you want to major in. More and more students are starting college with undeclared majors and use the first couple of years to see if they can find their niche. There's nothing wrong with that. If not knowing what you want to major in is keeping you from developing interests, talk with your advisor or seek out the office on your campus that can help you with career exploration. There are lots of assessment tools out there that can help you get a clearer picture of your strengths and weaknesses and then help you weed through possible majors that you might be suited for. On the other hand, if you are totally uninterested in college at this point in your life and you're going only because your parents want you to or because you have nothing better to do, you might want to reassess why you're in college at this point. A final suggestion is to join a couple of campus organizations. You never know—the people you meet, their motivation level, and the focus of the organization could help you develop interests. What starts as a social interaction can end up taking you down an academic path as well. And we have to say that using some of the strategies for reading your textbook (previewing the material, annotating the text, and so forth) can greatly increase your interest in both the reading and the lecture. Try it for one week—you just might be surprised.

Question: No matter what I do, I can't seem to get a handle on the time-management thing. It's not that I don't have the time. I do. And I have good intentions of following my schedule. (In fact, my planner looks great.) But in spite of my good intentions, I can't seem to get started. I'll get on the Internet, make phone calls, download music, go out with friends . . . anything to delay getting started. What can I do?

Answer: We have three key suggestions for you and a friendly reminder. First suggestion: take a first step rather than trying to change your study behaviors all at once. Time management is not an all-or-nothing proposition—even small changes can help greatly. Force yourself to get started. Make yourself stick to it for fifteen minutes, then a half hour. Sometimes just getting started is half the battle. Second suggestion: think about your internal body clock. Are you trying to get started at the time when you have the least energy? Are you waiting until the sun goes down to crack a book even though you're a morning person at heart? Use your down time to hang out with friends; study when your energy level is high. Third suggestion: take a look at where you are studying. Is it conducive to hitting the books, or are there so many distractions it would be impossible for any reasonable person to get much done in this environment? And while we're talking about distractions—turn off your cell phone! Now for the reminder: remember, all we're asking is that you commit 40 measly hours a week (give or take a few) to being a student, 40 . . . out of 168. That's only about 24 percent of the total hours in the week. You have another 128 hours to do everything else you want to do—party with friends, sleep, play video games, sleep, shop on the Web, sleep. Well, you get the picture. And if you put in a good forty hours of being a student, you'll not only earn good grades, but you'll also feel good about and gain confidence in yourself. If you take these suggestions to heart and try to change your habits and just can't, you might want to check out the office on campus that evaluates students for learning disabilities. It could be that you have ADD (Attention Deficit Disorder). It's more common than you might think.

Question: I have never run into this situation before. I am in a history class this semester and I have three different professors. Each of them teaches the course for about five weeks. Whose brainchild was this? The first prof was fine. I liked her lecture style, and she was very clear about what we could expect on the exam she gave. I did extremely well on her test. Now I'm two weeks into the second prof and I'm hatin' life. I don't even want to go to class. He talks in circles and even though I have asked questions in class, I don't have a clue about what he expects of us. Help! This isn't fair at all.

Answer: First off, go to class. Please. It's the one, most important thing you can do, even in this situation. It's especially important to attend class when you are struggling to figure out what to do. Before you go to class, read the book so you will have an idea what the prof will be lecturing about. And while you're in class, try to compensate for your professor's lack of lecture prowess by writing down as much as you can of what he says. Even in this age of technology, lots of professors continue to use the lecture as the centerpiece of their instruction. So take notes until your hand cramps. Don't read the campus newspaper. Don't work on the sudoku puzzle. And by all means don't nap. Using a pen or computer, take a good set of notes for the entire period. Get them as detailed as possible and try to organize as you go along. Profs who are in the lecture mode usually give tests that are primarily lecture based. If you don't have a complete and accurate set of notes, it will be

If you tell folks you're a college student, folks are so impressed. You can be a student in anything and not have to know anything. Just say "toxicology" or "marine biokinesis," and the person you're talking to will change the subject to himself. If this doesn't work, mention the neural synapses of embryonic pigeons.

—Chuck Palahniuk

tough noogies for you when test time rolls around. Then spend some time as soon as possible after the lecture to reorganize the information. That said, there are a couple of other things you might try. First, see if you can find someone who has had this prof in the past. Even if it wasn't under this particular circumstance where he cotaught the course, someone who has had him may be able to shed some light on the kind of tests he gives. Second, if the questions you asked in class didn't help you figure out the task, make an appointment to talk with him. You could tell him how you studied for the first professor's exam and mention how she tested. Ask him questions such as, "Am I on the right track? What else can I do?"

Question: I am in this class that students who have been around a while call a "weeder" class for science majors. The professor is very intimidating and seems to enjoy it when a student drops the class. Her response is, "Oh, good. Another piece of deadweight gone. Are there any more drop cards for me to sign?" Students have started calling her Dr. Drop. I'm holding my own, but the first exam is coming up fast, and I don't have a clue about how to study for it. I don't even have any idea what the test will be like and I'm scared to death to ask her. I can't drop the course because I need it so I can take the next course in the sequence. What should I do?

Answer: Your situation is a bit different from the last student's, but some of the same advice applies. The usual—go to class; talk with students who have had the prof before; do the normal things you would do in order to be successful in a difficult class. The bigger issue in this instance seems to be that she is intimidating, that you're scared to even approach her. If you don't feel comfortable about asking questions in class and you are afraid she'll bite your head off if you make an appointment to see her during office hours, try asking some questions via email. Most profs, even those who come off as intimidating, still want you to be successful and are usually willing to give you some guidance. Another suggestion is to take a look at the way you are studying for the class. Does that require some modification? Do you need to get a tutor? Would a study group help? Sometimes changing your approach to the material will help you understand it better. Also, go back and reread your syllabus and listen carefully in class. Both of those sources are good places to begin when you are trying to figure out your professor's expectations.

Question: High school was a breeze for me. I hardly ever studied and made great grades; I was a member of lots of clubs and was active in volunteer work in my community. I also had plenty of time to socialize with my friends because things seemed

to come easy to me. Now that I'm in college, I'm having a rough time. I didn't have to use strategies in high school and I'm finding that I'm overwhelmed now. I don't know where to begin. It's shaking my confidence. I'm beginning to think maybe I'm not cut out for college. Any pointers?

Answer: Remember what you read back in chapter 1—high school is different from college, and what worked for you then is probably not going to work for you now. Just as you have had to make adjustments in other ways, you have to face the fact that you will have more to do in a shorter period of time and that you will have to approach your schoolwork differently. More is expected of you too. One of the best suggestions we can give you is to try a bunch of different study strategies—don't be a one-trick pony—different tasks call for different strategies. Abraham Maslow, an expert in motivation theory, once said, "If the only tool you have is a hammer, you'll treat every problem as if it were a nail." What he meant was everyone needs more than one way to approach problem solving. The same holds true for studying. Let's face it. If you study for every subject and every course in the same way, you're destined to do poorly a good portion of the time. Rather, mix it up. Know lots of strategies and when to use them, and modify them to make them your own. Find out what works for you under what circumstances and then go for it. You will not only still have time to have an active social life, but you will also regain the confidence in yourself that you have lost.

Question: Although I think this studying-cycle thing sounds good, it seems to take up way too much time. How can I do all this stuff and still have a life? I want more out of college than keeping my nose stuck in a book all the time.

Answer: Getting on a study cycle will actually help you have more time to socialize and "have a life" if you do it right. Try to get yourself on a studying cycle for each class where you are either warming up, reading and annotating, rehearsing, or reviewing. Although you will be at a different place in the cycle for each of your classes—you may be annotating in philosophy and reviewing for an exam in physics—try to interact with each of your classes on most days. When you spend some time each day on each class, you are less likely to get behind and you will remember more of the information. And it's important to keep the "garbage in, garbage out" mentality. If you try to get away with cutting corners, your grades will suffer down the line. In addition, sometimes students believe they are investing a lot of time in studying just because they are spending more time than they spent in high school. If you studied only five hours a week in high school and now you are study-ing ten, you're probably still not investing enough time. But time ≠ learning; quality counts, but quantity does not.

Question: Everyone has to cram at some time, even good students. Once I got a bad case of the flu, and another time my grandfather died suddenly. In both instances, much of my normal study time was lost, and I had no alternative but to cram. In both cases, my grades suffered. How can I maximize my study efforts when time becomes a major factor?

Answer: This is a really hard question to answer, but we'll take a stab at it because you sound as if you are a good student who doesn't use cramming as a way of life. The way you cram effectively (is that an oxymoron or what?) depends on the task. If you have a test coming up, you might ask your professor to give you a few extra days because of your extenuating circumstances. Before doing this, however, check your syllabus to see if it says anything about making up exams or turning in late work. Some profs are sticklers for not giving any exceptions; others might be willing to cut you some slack. If the professor is going to be hard-nosed and make you take the test, do the best you can in the amount of time you have left to study. If you missed some classes, get the notes from a classmate. If the tests generally come primarily from the notes, spend most of your time studying them. Supplement this by reading the chap-ter summaries and concentrating on key terms or questions at the end of the chap-ters. If the tests generally come from the text, preview each chapter along with your notes to figure out the most important points. If the book has a website, look at that as well. Often textbook websites have study guides and other information that could help. Then spend the majority of your time learning those key ideas. Above all, put off any socializing and other nonacademic commitments until you get back on track.

We also humbly suggest that you plan to *always, always, always get off to a good start*. Getting off to a good start always matters, whether you're running a race, begin-ning a new relationship, or starting a new term. What you do at the start more often than not sets the pace for what will come. In your courses, it means that you do your early reading and assignments, follow a reasonable study schedule, get assistance if you need it. Students who start out strong usually finish strong. And even if they go into a slump due to illness or other unforeseen problems, they rebound faster.

Question: I'm sort of embarrassed to talk about this, but I went to a really small rural high school where the value of technology as a learning tool was nearly non-

existent. My family couldn't afford to purchase a computer for me to use at home, so my understanding of computers and technology is very weak, to say the least. I have been fortunate to get a full scholarship to college, but I'm afraid I'm going to have a hard time getting up to speed. What's the best way to get the knowledge I need—fast?

Answer: As you seem to be aware, technology is everywhere on college campuses, and professors expect you to at least be at their level. Of course, it's important to realize that some of your profs will stick to traditional teaching methods and never even utter the word "technology," while others will use every form available. Similarly, some campuses rely heavily on different technologies to teach—podcasts, online courses, WebCT, testing via computers, even evaluating your profs online—and others stick to delegating technology to more minor roles. However, most campuses have efficient email systems and access to online libraries that you will be expected to navigate pretty much on your own. The best thing you can do is see if your campus offers a course that can help you with the basics: email and attachments, finding and using information on the Internet, and course-support tools such as WebCT or Blackboard. Many campuses also have websites designed to help you become technologically savvy, so once you have the basics down, such websites can help you become a real pro. But our best advice is to get in there and try it out—experience will help you become more self-confident using the necessary technology.

Question: Well, like I told you, I didn't do well at all on the first history test, so I studied really hard for the second test and I still only made a D-. But I think if I just put in some additional time, I can pull an A on the next exam. Then if I get another A on the final, I should pull a B in the course. That's my goal. What do you think?

Answer: Being in denial about the grades you are earning or the amount and quality of time you are spending in student mode gets you nowhere. You have to figure things out and you have to be honest with yourself, what we often call the "get real" check. You have to ask yourself how you will change your approach to learning history in order to reach that goal. Is it really just about putting in more time? And, we hate to be a pessimist here, but if you have already earned an F and a D-, is it realistic to think you can earn a B in the course? The message here is be honest with yourself. If you don't have a realistic assessment of where you are, you can't make the necessary changes to get yourself where you need to be. Take honest stock of your situation frequently and make adjustments in your studying in order to meet your goals.

You might even want to consider withdrawing from this course and taking it again next semester.

Question: If you had only one piece of advice to give to new students, what would it be and why?

Answer: Understand your profs' demands, then select strategies that will meet those demands. We have called it "understanding the task" throughout *College Rules!* and it's extremely important to being a successful student. If you don't know where you need to end up, how can you have a plan to get there? Understanding course expectations involves more than knowing you will have three exams and a paper. You need to know what kind of exams (multiple choice or essay) and the level of thinking required (memorization or application or somewhere in between). If you can't figure things out after reading the syllabus and from listening to your prof's lectures, it would be a very good idea to meet with him or her. Classmates often don't have any more of a clue than you do, so it's best to go to the source. Once you know the task, you're not home free, but at least you have taken a big step forward in being able to select the right strategies and take the best approach to studying. And, one last time, loud and clear: in order to be successful in college, you'll have to go beyond rote memorization. Sure, most courses require some memorizing, but most college profs expect more. College is about being able to synthesize information and then apply it in new situations. It's about problem solving. It's about using writing as a way of indicating what you know. In fact, if you look up the words "learn" and "learning" in the dictionary, you'll see that the definitions go way beyond memorizing. You see descriptions like "gaining knowledge," "comprehension," "gaining wisdom," "acquired knowledge," and "mastery through experience and study." Remember, as you work through figuring out the tasks in your courses, think about more than memorizing stuff and then forgetting it. Think about real learning.

One Final, Unsolicited Piece of Advice

While in college, think about gaining the following skills—thinking critically, writing persuasively, problem solving effectively, and speaking convincingly. If you can develop these competencies over the next four (or five) years, you are ready to learn for a lifetime.

ABOUT THE AUTHORS

SHERRIE NIST-OLEJNIK received her Ph.D. from the University of Florida in 1982. Since that time, she has spent her career at the University of Georgia researching and writing about college student learning. Over the years, she developed a special interest in how students make the academic transition from learning in high school to learning in college. But it was her love of teaching that inspired *College Rules!*. Years of university teaching has led her to a firm belief that students can make a smooth transition from high school to college, and should be able to if they are given the tools.

Sherrie has published numerous research articles and book chapters that focus on studying and learning, and she has made over 125 presentations at professional meetings. In addition, she has written four textbooks focusing on reading, studying, and learning at the college level. These texts are used on college campuses nationwide.

Sherrie also has a keen sense of practicality. Because she has interacted with thousands of students over the course of her career, she knows firsthand the demands and stresses that are placed on them. She's heard all the excuses, learned all the lines, and listened to hundreds of students talk about their frustrations, mistakes, successes, and failures. These unique experiences, combined with her knowledge of research, enabled her to write a compelling, upbeat, and realistic guide for academic success in college.

Sherrie lives with her husband, Steve Olejnik (also a university professor), and her dog, Turley, in Athens, Georgia, home of the University of Georgia. She has one daughter, Kama, who lives in Los Angeles. After retiring from UGA in June, 2006, with professor emerita status, Sherrie has more time to pursue her love of cooking (someday she would love to go to cooking school) and traveling. She continues to be an active researcher and consultant.

JODI PATRICK HOLSCHUH is an associate professor in the Division of Academic Assistance at the University of Georgia. For the past fourteen years, Jodi has been involved in helping students make the transition from high school to college learning. An award-winning teacher, Jodi currently teaches courses that are geared toward teaching students effective and efficient study habits. In addition, she has served as an educational consultant in Texas and Georgia public schools, teaching teachers ways to prepare their students for college learning.

Jodi has made many conference papers and has written many articles and book chapters on the topic of helping students learn strategies for college success. She has also been involved in several projects with Sherrie Nist-Olejnik, including the *Transitions to Learning in College* video program and three college textbooks *Active*

Learning: Strategies for College Success, *College Success Strategies*, and *Effective College Learning*.

Jodi lives in Athens, GA with her husband, Doug, and her daughter, Maia and her son, Samuel. When she is not writing, teaching, or researching, Jodi loves rediscovering the world as her children learn new things. She also loves to read good books and travel to new places.

INDEX